THE
INNER MEANING
—— *of the* ——
HEBREW LETTERS

THE
INNER MEANING
— *of the* —
HEBREW LETTERS

Robert M. Haralick

JASON ARONSON INC.
Northvale, New Jersey
London

This book was prepared with LATEX and set in 11 pt. by Robert M. Haralick. The Hebrew font was designed by the author in postscript and converted to metafont by Visvanathan Ramesh.

10 9 8 7 6 5 4 3 2

Library of Congress Cataloging-in-Publication Data

Haralick, Robert M.

    The inner meaning of the Hebrew letters / Robert M. Haralick
        p. cm.
    Includes bibliographical references and index.
    ISBN 1-56821-356-5
      1. Hebrew language–Alphabet–Religious aspects–Judaism
2. Spiritual life–Judaism.   3. Judaism–Essence, genius, nature.
4. Gematria. I. Title.
PJ4589.H36 1995
296.3–dc20   94-44577

Manufactured in the United States of America. Jason Aronson Inc. offers books and cassettes. For information and catalog write to Jason Aronson Inc., 230 Livingston Street, Northvale, New Jersey 07647.

To
Rabbi Menachem M. Schneerson
and
Rabbi Aharon Goldstein

Contents

Introduction

The Basis

The world that God creates has many dimensions. There are the physical dimensions of space and time. The space dimensions permit us to reference *where* something is. The time dimension permits us to reference *when* something is. Also there are the dimensions of meaning. The meaning dimensions permit us to know *what* something is. And through the dimensions of meaning there arises the possibility of distinction: the distinction between the holy and the unholy.

There is an essential difference between knowing the *where* and *when* of something and knowing the *what* of something. Knowledge of the *where* and *when* is knowledge of the outside or garment. Knowledge of the *what* is knowledge of the inside or essence.

Knowledge of the garment or outside is outside. Knowledge of the essence or inside is inside. Knowledge of the outside can be obtained by non-participant observation. Knowledge of the inside is obtained only by consciously participating in the continual inside creation process. For therein are the dynamics of meaning. Such participation is where knowing, doing, and being are all the same. Inside is the place where knowledge of what something is is identical to being that something.

From this we learn that creation is the ongoing process by which we receive and complete the possibility of meaning always and continually given to us by the Holy One. This giving of the possibility of meaning is a giving that itself has an inner and outer aspect. The outer aspect is form and physicality. They are the carriers of meaning. But each specific physical form in and of itself does not constitute any meaning.

The inner aspect relates to our spirituality. It relates to how we use our will to take a stand either with the holy or, God forbid, with the unholy. For how we take a stand is how we complete the meaning possibility that is given to us.

The outer aspect and inner aspect are dual. The outer aspect functions by way of cause and effect. The inner aspect functions by way of self-cause or free will. This free will is not just free choice to do in a way uncompelled by outside forces. It is a free choice whether or not to understand and to interpret what we encounter in a way controlled by the the inner spark of Divinity within our soul. It is a free choice to do in accordance with the way we understand.

Our Relationships

We are involved in a variety of relationships with family, friends, work, community, country, world, and God. The understandings and interpretations we give to each of these situations all complete a meaning that we return to God. These understandings and interpretations are not necessitated by anything external. Nor are they fixed in some way so that our situation can have only one kind of interpretation. Each of our situations is inherently ambiguous, having meaning possibilities one way or another. And the choice of how to interpret, of which way to interpret, is ours.

By the meaning possibilities we complete, we establish what we have made ourselves. God tells us to choose life: choose to complete meaning possibilities that are holy. Do not choose death. Do not choose meaning possibilities that are unholy.

> See, I have set before thee this day life and good, and death and evil; in that I command thee this day to love the Lord thy God, to walk in His ways, and to keep His commandments and His statutes and His judgments: then thou shalt live and multiply. And the Lord thy God shall bless thee in the land into which thou goest to possess it.[1]

> I call heaven and earth to witness this day against you, that I have set before thee life and death, blessing and cursing. Therefore, choose life that both thou and thy seed may live, that thou mayest love the Lord thy God, and that thou mayest obey His voice, and that thou mayest cleave to him. For He is thy life and the length of thy days.[2]

By choosing meaning possibilities that are holy we serve God and we unite our will with the Divine will.

---

1. Deuteronomy 30:15-16.
2. Deuteronomy 30:19-20.

The meaning completions that we make return to the Divine, who then in perfect beneficence and justice creates for us new situations. In these new situations the Holy One, the Master of the Universe, creates for us enhancements and reflections of what we have returned and given to Him. He designs our successive encounters to give us new possibilities of completing and perfecting meanings in yet fuller and deeper and holier ways. By this means, the hand of God is wondrously in the world. This is the meaning of:

> All the earth shall be filled with the glory of the Lord.[3]

> Blessed is His glorious name forever; His glory fills the whole world.[4]

> Do I not fill heaven and earth, declares the Lord.[5]

> And one called to the other and said, "Holy, holy, holy is the Lord of Hosts; the whole earth is full of His glory."[6]

The Hebrew Letters

Now it is in the context of completing meanings and understanding that the Hebrew letters have much to teach us. For God creates the world through the Hebrew letters.[7]

> For when the world was created it was the supernal letters that brought into being all the works of the lower world, literally after their own pattern. Hence, whoever has a knowledge of them and is observant of them is beloved both on high and below.[8]

---

3. Numbers 14:21.
4. Psalms 72:19.
5. Jeremiah 23:24.
6. Isaiah 6:3.
7. Rashi, *Pentateuch and Rashi's Commentary, Genesis*, vol. 1, trans. Abraham ben Isaiah and Benjamin Sharfman (Brooklyn, NY: S.S. and R. Publishing, 1976), Genesis 2:23, p. 27.
8. *The Zohar*, vol. 2, trans. Harry Sperling and Maurice Simon (London: Soncino Press, 1978), p. 111.

Each Hebrew letter is, therefore, a spiritual channel through which the Godly light can ascend and descend.

Rabbi Chayim Tirer of Chernovitz, the Be'er Mayim Chayim teaches:

> Each letter in our holy Torah, small though it is, represents an entire world, an immense universe of Divine Light. I'd like to compare it to a builder's blueprint. On a small piece of paper the architect designs the layout of an entire building with its apartments, stairwells, roof, and hallways, drawing thin lines and circles, making little marks here and there. To the uninitiated, the blueprint appears like a small drawing of scribbles and lines. But the builder knows that each little square represents a magnificent vestibule with glorious arches and pillars, and each tiny circle symbolizes a corridor surrounded by a majestic colonnade. In the same way, each letter of the Torah signifies an indescribably awesome and exalted world, a heavenly universe that transcends our comprehension. And when the individual letters are linked to form a word, the worlds they represent combine, and a marvelous spiritual structure comes into being. Wonder of wonders.[9]

Rabbi Shneur Zalman of Liadi, the Baal HaTanya, the Alter Rebbe of Chabad, teaches:

> The name by which it is called in the Holy Tongue is a vessel for the life-force condensed into the letters of that name which has descended from the Ten Utterances in the Torah, that have power and vitality to create being *ex nihilo* and give it life forever. For the Torah and the Holy One, blessed be He, are one.[10]

To help us be a partner of God in creation[11] and to serve God, it is,

---

9. Avraham Yaakov Finkel, *The Great Chasidic Masters* (Northvale, NJ: Jason Aronson, 1992), p. 104.
10. Rabbi Shneur Zalman, *"Shaar Hayichud,"* in *Likkutei Amarim – Tanya*, bilingual edition (Brooklyn, NY: Kehot Publication Society, 1993), p. 289.
11. *The Babylonian Talmud, Seder Moed*, vol. 1, *Shabbat* (10a), trans. H. Freedman (London: Soncino Press, 1938), p. 35.

therefore, worthwhile to study the inner meaning of the Hebrew letters, since it is they that make up the vessels of the creative life force. And this creation is a continual creation as suggested by Isaiah:

> For as the new heavens and the new earth, which I am making shall endure before me declares the Lord, so will your name and descendants endure.[12]

The Zohar says:

> It is not written: "I have made," but "I am making," signifying continual creation out of the new ideas discovered in the Torah.[13]

Finally, Rabbi Simchah Bunam of Pshis'cha, the Rebbe Reb Bunam, teaches that Genesis 1:1, "In the beginning, God created heaven and earth," should be rendered

> "When God began to create heaven and earth." For the world is continually being created – every day, every hour, even this very instant the world is being sustained by the same primordial creative force with which it came into existence, the force of בְּרֵאשִׁית, *bereishit*, "In the beginning." If this creative force would depart for even a split second, the world would return to nothingness.[14]

There are twenty-two letters and five final forms, making a total of twenty-seven. The group of twenty-seven letters can be divided into three groups of nine. The first group of nine letters א, ב, ג, ד, ה, ו, ז, ח, and ט embodies the nine basic spiritual channels of the creative process. They are: pulsating unbridled force, container, nourishment, physical existence, power of being, connection, movement, life, and goodness. The second group י, כ, ל, מ, נ, ס, ע, פ, and צ have respective numerical values that are ten times the first group of nine.

---

12. Isaiah 66:22.
13. *The Zohar*, vol. 1, p. 19.
14. Finkel, *The Great Chasidic Masters*, p. 107.

> Ten generally represents the state of completion of any cre-
> ation . . . a decade represents the completion of a period
> of time. . . . the number ten represents the level of com-
> pletion in the natural world.[15]

Thus this second group of nine embody the nine basic spiritual channels projected into time and conditioned physical existence. They are: spirituality; the crowning achievement; learning, teaching, and purpose; perfection and completion; emergence; support; insight and consciousness; speech and freedom; righteousness and humility. And the third group ק, ר, שׁ, ת, ך, ם, ן, ף, and ץ embody the nine spiritual channels projected into cosmic existence.

By understanding how the Hebrew letters function as spiritual channels we can help ourselves in understanding the holy meaning possibilities inherent in our own situations and thereby better do our part as God's partners. The inner meaning of the Hebrew letters gives us the abstract reference frames in which this understanding dwells.

The Nature of the Explanations

The explanations of the inner meanings of the Hebrew letters that we offer is not what our technologically trained minds might expect. It is not so much an explanation of cause and effect mechanisms as it is an explanation of symbols. The symbols are explained by putting the symbols in interrelationships. The full meaning of the interrelationships is left unexplained, for the explanation is on a nonverbal level, on a sephirotic level of חָכְמָה, wisdom.

Nevertheless, it is possible to say that the energy and intelligence of the Hebrew letters are aspects of the one living dynamic light energy that God is always and forever bathing us in and providing for us. As we learn the meanings associated with these different aspects of the Godly light, we learn more about the Oneness of which we are all part.[16]

---

15. Menachem Schneerson, *Sichos in English*, vol. 6 (Brooklyn, NY: Sichos in English, 1980), p. 118.
16. Job 31:2.

We learn and become more able to put into practice real morality and more full and complete loving, as we more and more align our will with God's will. We learn that we become what we identify with and what we think we are. Therefore, we must be identifying with our essence, our Godly soul, and not with physical appearance. We must bring into our consciousness and have before our consciousness the purity and the holiness within. We must understand that everyone's circumstances are opportunities for manifesting who we are, regardless of the apparent difficulties and challenges of the circumstances.

When we choose to realize and put before our consciousness that our essence is our Godly soul, we become able to manifest the best possible actions without having to personally judge *for me* or *against me*, for we discover that whatever is, is always *for me*, for all comes from the goodness that God is always bestowing. Nothing is bestowed except the goodness of God.

The more we can so utilize the energy intelligences of the Hebrew letters the better our service to God becomes. We become better and more consistent revealers of the Godly light.

The Methodology of the Explanation

Each letter has an associated gematria value. Although the meaning of a Hebrew letter is alluded to by associating words beginning with the letter, or words having the same gematria value, there is a systematic disciplined methodology for doing this. First, the letters in each letter's spelled-out name, when vocalized with a possibly different set of vowels, form one or more words that give the revealed meaning of the letter. The letter's residue, its spelling with the first letter removed, will, with an appropriate vocalization, often constitute a second word. This second word gives the concealed meaning of the letter. When the letter's residue cannot constitute a word, we explore words that begin with some letter and whose remainder is the residue.

Each letter's name has associated with it the sum of the gematria values of its letters. Biblical words with the same gematria sum, especially words in the Pentateuch, will support the revealed meaning of the letter. Those that do support it are discussed and the Bible passages in which they are located are quoted.

The total or full gematria of a letter is obtained by spelling out each letter in the letter's name and summing up the value of all the resulting letters.[17] Again, biblical words with the same gematria sum, especially words in the Pentateuch, will provide additional support for the revealed meaning of the letter. Those that do support it are discussed and the Bible passages in which they are located are quoted.

Finally, some of the words formed by combining each letter with other letters provide additional support for the meaning of the given letter.

---

17. Matityahu Glazerson, *Repentance in Words and Letters* (Jerusalem: Yerid HaSefarim, 1992), pp. 16-17.

THE
INNER MEANING
of the
HEBREW LETTERS

When a Jew learns Torah, it must be openly evident that "My words are as fire."

– Menachem Schneerson, *Sichos in English*

The Creating of the World[1,2]

When the Holy One, the Ancient of Ancients, decided to make the world, all the letters of the alphabet were in their potential spiritual form. When this spiritual energy intelligence of the letters would become manifest, they would constitute the dimensions of life. For time eternal the Holy One joyously held these dimensions within Himself, contemplating how and why He would make them manifest.

In time eternal the Holy One organized the letter energy intelligences, activating their spirit. Just before the beginning, just before the creation of the universe, each of the letters presented itself before the Holy One. In reverse order they presented themselves, beginning with ת. The letter ת advanced to the front and said:

> May it please Thee, O Lord of the universe, to use me first in the creation of the universe. I am the concluding letter of אֱמֶת, truth. I am the **true law**, תּוֹרָה. Thou art called by these very names, אֱמֶת and תּוֹרָה. Surely it is most appropriate for the creation of the world to begin with ת.

The Holy One, blessed be He, said to her:

> Though thou art worthy and deserving, thou formest the realm of מָוֶת, deadly sickness, pestilence, destruction, and death. Therefore, it is not appropriate to initiate the creation of the world with thee.

So ת returned to her place.

Then the letter שׁ came forward and said:

> O God, may it please Thee to begin the world with me. I am the initial letter of Thy name שַׁדַּי, the Almighty, and it is most fitting to create the world through that Holy Name, for by this Name the cosmos will have **nourishment**.

---

1. This section is patterned after a section in the prologue of the Zohar. *The Zohar*, vol. 1, trans. Harry Sperling and Maurice Simon (London: Soncino Press, 1978), pp. 9-13.

2. From our point of view the creating of the world is a "process leading from God to man, a process of materializing the spiritual." Yosef Wineberg *Lessons in Tanya*, vol. 1 (Brooklyn, NY: Kehot Publication Society, 1988), p. xxvii.

1

The Holy One, blessed be He, said to her:

> Thou art indeed worthy. Thou art good and true. But I certainly cannot begin the creation of the world with thee since thou formest the realm of שֶׁקֶר, falsehood: false thought, false speech, false action. Existing in your realm are the liars and the slanderers, who work toward destroying truth and good names. Existing in your realm is שָׁפָל, the hollow, the base, the depressed, the indolent, and the negligent.

Having heard this, שׁ departed.

Seeing that ת and שׁ were turned away, ר and ק decided that they would come, teaming together, before the Holy One, for ר is the **cosmic container** and ק is **growth and holiness**. But as they approached, the Holy One said to them:

> ר, thou art the realm of רֶשַׁע, the realm of godlessness, wickedness, unrighteousness, lawlessness, injustice, and unlawful gain. ק, thou art the realm of קֶרֶס, collapse. I know how thou attachest thyselves to שׁ and formest the realm of קֶשֶׁר, conspiracy. Thou art conspirators together. Thy realm is of binding, tying, plotting, conspiring, and knotting. Thou makest it seem good to the man that I will create that he should desire things to be bound and limited, staying the same. With such a desire, he will not want to aspire to the loftier spiritual heights and grow beyond and transcend wherever he has been. He will become godless and cause collapse. There is no need for thee to say anything. I will not create the world with thee.

So ר and ק quietly turned around and went back to their places. Then צ stepped forward and said:

> May it please Thee to begin the creation of the world with me, as I am the realm of צַדִּיק, the realm of **righteousness** and **humility**.

But the Holy One would not begin the creation of the world with צ. He said:

Thy realm is indeed the realm of righteousness and humility. And thou art truly worthy. But I cannot begin the creation of the world with thee, for righteousness and humility must be concealed and not come out in the open, lest thou givest the world a cause for offense.

Hearing this, צ immediately understood and returned to her place. Then פ presented herself, saying:

May it please Thee to begin the creation of the world with me as my realm is the realm of **speech** and **freedom**. It is by speech that your Holiness is communicated and it is by appropriate acts of free choice that פְּרְקוֹן, redemption, and פְּדוּת, deliverance, can come about.

But the Holy One replied:

Thy realm of speech and freedom is indeed a worthy realm. But the very freedom inherent in thy realm permits transgression, פֶּשַׁע, and blemish, flaw, and loss of value, פְּגַם.

So פ returned to her place.
Then came ע, who pleaded, saying:

May it please Thee to begin the creation of the world with me, as my realm is the realm of **insight** and **consciousness**, the hidden meaning of עַיִן.

But the Holy One reminded ע, saying:

Only thy hidden realm is insight and consciousness. Thy revealed realm is the realm of עָווֹן, the realm of perverseness, sin, guilt, crime, and iniquity.

At this, ע departed.
Then ס appeared and said:

O Lord, may it please Thee to begin the creation of the world through me. My realm is the realm of **support**, סָמֶךְ. I uphold the fallen.

The Holy One immediately replied, saying:

> Thou art indeed worthy and playest a crucial role in up-holding the fallen. But if thou art involved in the beginning creation of the world, how can thy energy be devoted to upholding the fallen? What will be the fate of the fallen? Thou must remain in thy place.

At this, פ returned to her place.

Then נ entered, saying:

> May it please the Lord to begin the creation of the world with me, as my realm is the realm of נִיצָן, **emergence**, sprouting, spreading, propagating, shining, and **flourishing**. My realm is the realm of נִפְלָא, the wonderful.

But the Holy One said to her:

> Dear נ. Thou art worthy and good. Thy realm is indeed the wonderful realm of emergence. But in thy realm is also the untimely emergence, the untimely birth, נֶפֶל: abortion. As well thy realm has the action of נוֹפֵל, falling down, falling out, falling away, and sinking. In thy realm are the נוֹפְלִים, the fallen. And these are the ones for whom פ just returned to her place. Go return to thy place so that thy fallen can remain under her support.

נ immediately returned to her place.

Then ם came forward, saying:

> O Lord, may it please Thee to begin the creation of the world through me, for my realm is the realm of מַשְׁלִים, **perfecting** and **completing**. This is the realm of the מֶלֶךְ, the King, which is Thy title.

The Holy One replied:

> It is assuredly so, but I cannot begin the creation of the world through thee, for the world needs a manifest king. The world needs thee, the ל, and the כ, for the world cannot exist without a king. Return, therefore, to thy place along with ל and כ.

At this מ understood and returned to her place.

ל, following very carefully what had been happening, debated what she should do. She knew that her realm was the realm of לְמַד, **learning**, לְמֵד, **teaching**, and therefore, **purpose**. If the world required a manifest king, then it would certainly require purpose, learning, and teaching. So ל did not even venture forward.

Seeing that ל stayed in her place, כ left her place, descending from her throne of glory, saying:

> O Lord, may it please Thee to begin the creation of the world through me. My realm is the realm of כָּבוֹד, your honor, esteem, majesty, abundance, and glory. This is the realm of **crowning achievement**.

As כ left her place the thousands of the uncreated worlds began to shake. The throne trembled and quivered. The creation process was about to fall into ruins. The Holy One replied:

> כ! Why hast thou left thy place? What doest thou here? Nothing can exist without my abundance and glory. This is what needs your attention. Besides, within your realm is כָּלָה, extermination, extinction, annihilation, and destruction. Also within your realm is כָּלָה, the transitory, the temporal, and the ephemeral. Return to thy place and remain there.

So כ immediately departed and returned to her place.

Then the letter י presented herself, saying:

> May it please Thee, O Lord, to begin the creation of the world through me, since my realm is the realm of יְצִירָה, the realm of creating and forming. Therefore, I, **spirituality**, stand first in your sacred name יְ־ה־וָ־ה, your transcendence.

However, the Holy One turned down י, replying:

> It is sufficient for thee that thou art engraved and marked in my transcendence. Thou art a channel of My Will. Thou cannot be removed from My Name.

Hearing this, י returned to her station, letting ט make her plea.
Then ט came up, saying:

> May it please Thee to begin the creation of the world through
> me, since my realm is the realm of טוֹב, the realm of **good-
> ness**. Through me Thou art called good and upright.

But the Holy One said to her:

> I cannot begin the creation of the world through thee, since
> the goodness that thou representest is hidden and con-
> cealed within thyself. It is in concealment that thou runnest
> around with thy partner ח. Joined together thou formest
> חֵטְא, the word for sin, transgression, and fault.

So ט returned to her place.

ח had heard the reply and understood that there was no point in
pleading her case, even though hers was the realm of חַיִּים, the realm
of **life**.

Then ז walked forward, saying:

> May it please Thee to begin the creation of the world with
> me, as my realm is the realm of זִיעָה, **movement**. As well,
> since I am the seventh letter, in my realm is rest and the
> observance of the Sabbath.

But the Holy One replied immediately:

> In the realm of movement is also זַיִן, arms or weapons.
> With arms or weapons I cannot begin the creation.

Then ו stepped foward, saying:

> May it please Thee to begin the creation of the world with
> me, as my realm is the realm of וָו, **connection**. Thy holi-
> ness cannot be revealed without connection.

The Holy One replied, saying:

Thou and ה are letters of my Name, part of the mystery of My name, engraved and impressed in My name. Connection in thy realm and **power of being** in the realm of ה are necessary for the manifestation of my transcendence. I cannot begin the creation of the world with thou or ה.

Then ד appeared, saying:

May it please Thee to begin the creation of the world with me, as my realm is the realm of **physicality**. My realm is the realm of דֶלֶת, the **doorway** to the manifestation of your transcendence.

But the Holy One replied, saying:

Thy realm is indeed the doorway for the manifestation of My transcendence. But in the realm of physicality is דַּלּוּת, poverty and leanness. This is the poor and deficient aspect of thy realm. Only when physical existence is coupled with the recompense and nourishment of גְמָל is physical existence balanced. Thou and ג must maintain and balance each other. Return to your place.

Upon hearing this ד returned to her place and ג realized that there was no point in pleading her case.

Then ב entered, saying:

May it please Thee to begin the creation of the world through me, as my realm is the realm of בְּרָכָה, the realm of blessing. My realm is the **container** for blessing. The blessings pouring forth from the man Thou wilt create will be of lasting comfort to creation.

Now the Holy One replied differently. The Holy One said:

Assuredly, with thee I will begin the creation of the world, for it is with blessings that creation can be appreciated and be meaningful. It is with blessings that the holy is acknowledged.

The letter ℵ heard what was just said and just remained in her place. But the Holy One called her forth, asking her:

> Wherefore comest thou not before Me like the rest of the letters?

And ℵ answered:

> But Thou hast already bestowed on ב the gift of beginning the creation of the world. Wouldst Thou want me to try to take this gift away from ב?

The Holy One replied:

> Although I will begin the creation of the world with ב, thou wilt remain the first of the letters. My oneness shall not be expressed except through thee, for in thy realm is אֶחָד, oneness. Further in thy realm is אַלּוּף, the master, head, prince, and chief ruler of the unbridled force. It is by this dimension of existence, the dimension of אֱלֹהִים, the external dimension of Godliness, that the **pulsating unbridled force** of my being becomes known.

Then, the Holy One patterned all the letters, uniting the upper and lower worlds with them. Thereby the creation, the creating process, which always is, which always is beginning, and which always will be beginning, was begun with בְּרֵאשִׁית.

אֶלֶף

Aleph א: The Pulsating Unbridled Force

The leader and master letter of the Hebrew alphabet is the first letter
א, which is spelled אָלֶף, and has the numerical value of one. אָלֶף is
cognate to the word אֶלֶף, which means *thousand*.[1]

> To Sarah he said: "I have given your brother a *thousand*
> shekels of silver. This is to cover the offense against you
> before all who are with you; you are completely vindicted."[2]

> The Israelites journeyed from Rameses to Succoth. There
> were about six hundred *thousand* men on foot, besides women
> and children.[3]

> One beka per person, that is, half a shekel, according to the
> sanctuary shekel, for everyone that went to be numbered
> from twenty years old and upward for a total of six hundred
> and three *thousand* and five hundred and fifty.[4]

But אֶלֶף can also mean thousand in the sense of an *indefinitely
large number* or a quantity that is *innumerable*, especially when the
reference is God related.[5]

> May the Lord, the God of your fathers, increase you a
> *thousand* times and bless you as he has promised.[6]

---

1. The most frequent form of אלף in the Pentateuch is in grammatical forms
relating to אֶלֶף meaning thousand. Genesis 20:16, 24:60; Exodus 12:37, 18:21,
18:25, 32:28, 34:7, 38:25-26, 38:28-29. Numerous times in Numbers chapters 1, 2, 3,
4, 7, 10, 11, 16, 25, 26, 31, and 35. Deuteronomy 1:11, 1:15, 5:10, 7:9, 7:13, 28:4,
28:18, 28:51, 32:30, 33:17.
2. Genesis 20:16.
3. Exodus 12:37.
4. Exodus 38:26.
5. R. Laird Harris, Gleason Archer, and Bruce Waltke, eds., *Theological Wordbook
of the Old Testament*, vol. 1 (Chicago: Moody Press, 1980), p. 48.
6. Deuteronomy 1:11.

> How could one man chase a *thousand* or two put ten thousand to flight, unless their Rock had sold them, unless the Lord had given them up?[7]

> I have no need of a bull from your stall or of goats from your pens, for every animal of the forest is mine, and the cattle on a *thousand* hills.[8]

The gematria of אֶלֶף is 111. There are a number of other words used in the Pentateuch also having the gematria of 111. Many of them relate to making a physical change of position that in some sense initiates a process of spiritual ascent.

Just before Joseph's brothers sell him, the Pentateuch uses the word הוֹלְכִים, which has the gematria of 111 and which is the Kal present masculine plural form of the root הלך, meaning to *go, walk, step, wander, travel, go away,* or *depart.*

> And they sat down to eat bread; and they lifted up their eyes and looked, and, behold, a caravan of Ishmaelites came from Gilead, with their camels bearing spicery and balm and ladanum, *going* to carry it down to Egypt.[9]

When Moses is recounting the Exodus, he uses the word הָלַכְנוּ, which has the gematria of 111 and that is the Kal perfect first person plural of the root הלך.

> And the days in which we *came* from Kadesh Barnea until we were come over the Zered Valley were thirty-eight years; until all the generation of the men of war were wasted out from among the host, as the Lord swore to them.[10]

When Jacob, after leaving Laban, meets Esau he uses the word וְנֵלְכָה, which is the Kal imperfect first person plural cohortative form of the root הלך and has the gematria of 111.

---

7. Deuteronomy 32:30.
8. Psalms 50:10-11.
9. Genesis 37:25.
10. Deuteronomy 2:14.

And he said: "Let us take our journey and *let us go*, And I will go before thee."[11]

And when Judah convinces Jacob to allow them to return to Egypt with Benjamin to get more food, he uses the word וְנֵלְכָה.

> And Judah said to Israel, his father: "Send the lad with me and let us arise and *let us go*, that we may live and not die, both we, and thou, and also our little ones."[12]

When Korah and his conspirators rise up against Moses and Aaron, God speaks to Moses using the word הֵעָלוּ, which has the gematria of 111 and which is the Niphal imperative second person masculine plural of the root עלה, meaning to *go up, ascend, climb, mount, grow, flourish, be lifted up, surpass, transcend, excel, be greater than,* or *be superior to.*

> Speak to the congregation, saying: "Go up from about the dwelling of Korah, Dathan, and Abiram."[13]

After Jacob dies and a new king arises in Egypt, a king who does not know Joseph, the new king uses the word וְעָלָה, which has the gematria of 111 and which is the Kal perfect third person masculine singular form of the root עלה prefixed by the conjunction ו.

> Come, let us deal shrewdly with them or they will become even more numerous and if war breaks out, they will also join with our enemies and fight against us and *go up* from the land.[14]

When Moses is recounting how he came down the mountain with the first two tablets and saw that the people had made the golden calf and admonished them and pleaded for them before God, Moses then uses the word וַעֲלֵה, which has the gematria of 111 and which is the Kal imperative second person masculine singular form of the root עלה prefixed by the conjunction ו.

---

11. Genesis 33:12.
12. Genesis 43:8.
13. Numbers 16:24.
14. Exodus 1:10.

> At that time the Lord said to me: "Hew for thyself two
> tablets of stone like the first, and *come up* to me into the
> mountain, and make for thyself an ark of wood."[15]

In addition to words that indicate a change of position to mark
the beginning of a spiritual ascent, the word מַסְוֶה has a gematria of
111 and means *veil* or *face covering*. The Pentateuch uses this word
in telling how just after Moses spoke to the Israelites, giving them the
commandments that God had just given to him, Moses put a veil on
his face.

> And when Moses had done speaking with them, he put a
> *veil* on his face.[16]

Rashi explains that out of respect for the rays of majesty, Moses put a
veil on his face so that when he was not engaged in listening to God or
speaking to the Israelites, the people would not see the rays of majesty
and derive pleasure from them.[17] In the context of the letter א we can
understand the veil as meaning that א has a veil and is hidden when it
is not in action.

Relative to this veil of א, the first word in Leviticus is וַיִּקְרָא, which
is the Kal third person masculine singular imperfect with the conversive
ו, thereby making it the perfect tense of the root קָרָא, to *call out*,
proclaim, or *call by name*. And the א of this word appears as a small
א. The reason it is small is that it is God who lovingly calls Moses
by name.[18] And it is a small א because God above is calling the א
of Moses below. Rabbi Schneerson teaches that we too have a spark
of Moses in us. This spark of Moses in us is the small א. Therefore,
since Moses' power to spiritually advance is in his humility, alluded to
by the small א, and we too have a spark of Moses in us, the small א,
then by making a place for learning Torah, we can draw into ourselves

---

15. Deuteronomy 10:1.
16. Exodus 34:33.
17. Rashi, *Pentateuch and Rashi's Commentary, Exodus*, vol. 2, trans. Abraham
ben Isaiah and Benjamin Sharfman (Brooklyn, NY: S.S. and R. Publishing, 1976),
Exodus 34:33, p. 438.
18. Zalman Sorotzkin, *Insights in the Torah*, trans. Raphael Blumberg (Brooklyn,
NY: Mesorah Publications, 1993), p. 2.

that power of spiritual advancement, of spiritual service beyond what we have yet done.[19]

God, א above, is calling to the א of Moses below. God is telling Moses to unveil his א. God says:

> Speak to the children of Israel and say to them: When a man among you brings an offering to the Lord: from animals, from the cattle, or from the flock shall you bring your offering. If the offering is a burnt [elevation] offering from the cattle, he is to offer a male without defect. He must present it at the entrance to the Tent of Meeting, voluntarily, before the Lord. He is to lay his hand on the head of the burnt offering and it will be accepted on his behalf to make atonement for him.[20]

Here we are told to unveil our א and put our א into action. How? By voluntarily making an *offering*, קָרְבָּן. Now the word קָרְבָּן is related to the root קרב, which means to *draw near, come near, advance*, or *approach*. The related noun is קָרְבָה, which means *proximity, nearness, closeness, affinity*, or *relation*.[21] From this we learn that to unveil our א we must draw near to God by offering of ourselves. The offering is from the cattle or from the flock in us. By means of this offering we unite and knit together what had been separated by our incorrect action, our incorrect thought, our sin.

> The essence of the offering is that it is analogous to the sin, and that a man should offer to God his desires and passions, for this is more acceptable than all.[22]

Here desires and passions constitute our cattle and our flock. And the desires and passions offered are precisely those that are not directed toward our Divine service.

Supporting this, Rabbi Schneerson says:

---

19. Rabbi Menachem Schneerson, *Sichos in English*, vol. 41 (Brooklyn, NY: Sichos in English, 1989), p. 58.
20. Leviticus 1:2-3.
21. *The Zohar*, vol. 3, trans. Harry Sperling, Maurice Simon, and Paul Levertoff (London, Soncino Press, 1978), p. 333.
22. Ibid., p. 345.

אָדָם כִּי יַקְרִיב [23] if a man desires to draw close to Divinity (for the word קָרְבָּן implies a drawing close of one's faculties and senses) then מִכֶּם קָרְבָּן לַ־יְ־ה־וָ־ה,[24] you must offer of yourself.[25]

Offering of ourselves means refining the animals within us. It means refining the cattle and the flock, raising their level. And by raising their level we unite above and below, thereby drawing near to God and activating the א within us.

The first two words of Leviticus are וַיִּקְרָא אֶל. The small א of וַיִּקְרָא also indicates that we must search for a rearrangement of the letters of וַיִּקְרָא אֶל. One way they can be rearranged is קָרָא אֵילוֹ. אֵילוֹ means *his power, his strength, his might, his potency, his fortitude,* or *his valor.* קָרָא means *called.* So קָרָא אֵילוֹ can be rendered *He (God) called to his (Moses') strength.* For it takes strength to engage in the elevation and refinement process.

Now the animal desires and passions within us resist their own refinement. They resist because it is they who resist recognizing the line of Godly light. Therefore, it is these animal desires and passions that are the source of our insatiableness, anger, pride, lust, envy, sloth, and avarice. These represent the inflated א within us. Therefore, when God calls to us, he lovingly calls to the small א in us. He calls to our kind-heartedness, fortitude, humility, devoutness, rationality, thoroughness, and industriousness. When our humbleness is unveiled, we can respond to the call. And this is the reason it is explained that the small א in וַיִּקְרָא represents the humility of Moses.[26]

The full gematria of א is obtained by spelling out each letter in אָלֶף and adding up the total. We obtain אָלֶף לָמֶד פֶּא, which totals 266. When Moses sees the burning bush he uses the word אָסֻרָה, which has the gematria of 266 and is the Kal imperfect first person singular of the root סוּר, meaning *turn aside, go away, deviate, depart from, turn in,* or *leave off.*

---

23. Leviticus 1:2.
24. Leviticus 1:2.
25. Rabbi Menachem Schneerson, *Likkutei Sichot*, vol. 3, *Vayikra* (Brooklyn, NY: Kehot Publication Society, 1987), p. 3.
26. *Insights in the Torah*, p. 2.

And Moses said: "I will now *turn aside*, and see this great sight, why the bush is not burnt."[27]

In the passage that describes how any king of Israel shall write his own Torah and read it, the word סור is used in the Kal infinitive construct form.

That his heart be not lifted up above his brethren and that he not *turn aside* from the commandment, to the right hand, or to the left: to the end that he may prolong his days in his kingdom, he and his children, in the midst of Israel.[28]

When Pharaoh says to Moses, "I will let you go," Moses uses the word וְסָר, which is the Kal perfect third person masculine singular form of the root סור with the conjunctive prefix.

And Moses said: "Behold, I go out from thee, and I will entreat unto the Lord that the mixture of noxious animals may *depart* from Pharaoh, from his servants, and from his people tomorrow."[29]

The same word is used again in discussing when a garment is clean.

And the garment, either warp or woof, or whatever thing of skin it be, which thou shalt wash if the plague be *departed* from them, then it shall be washed the second time, and shall be clean.[30]

So from these passages we learn that for the energy intelligence of א to be active we must depart from uncleanliness, depart from plague, not turn aside from the commandments, and turn in toward God, toward the burning bush, regardless of what we may have been doing.

---

27. Exodus 3:3.
28. Deuteronomy 17:20.
29. Exodus 8:25.
30. Leviticus 13:58.

אֶלֶף is related to אַלּוּף, which can mean *master, champion, head, prince, chief ruler, tribal chief,* or *brigadier general.*[31]

> These were the chiefs of the sons of Esau: the sons of Elifaz the firstborn son of Esau: the *chief* Teman, the *chief* Omar, the *chief* Zefo, the *chief* Qenaz, the *chief* Qorah, the *chief* Gatam, the *chief* Amalek: these are the chiefs of Elifaz in the land of Edom.[32]

What does a chief or master do? He does אַלּוּף, he *teaches, trains, guides,* and *domesticates* the untamed א.[33]

> Just now you called to Me, "Father! You are the *guide* of my youth."[34]

The word אַלּוּף means *domesticated animal* such as *sheep, cow,* and *ox.*[35]

> But I was like a *gentle lamb* brought to the slaughter and I knew not that they had devised schemes against me saying: "Let us destroy the tree with its fruit and let us cut him off from the land of the living, that his name may be no more remembered."[36]

---

31. אַלּוּף occurs in Genesis: four times in 36:15, three times in 36:16, four times in 36:17, three times in 36:18, four times in 36:29, three times each in 36:30 and 36:40 and 36:41 and 36:42, twice in 36:43. This amounts to 32 times and they correspond to the 32 wondrous paths on the Tree of Life: the 10 Sephirot and 22 letters. In addition, there are related forms such as לְאַלֻּפֵיהֶם, which occurs in Genesis 36:30 and carries the meaning "according to their chiefs." We do not list these related forms.

32. Genesis 36:15-16.

33. See Proverbs 22:25 and Job 35:11 and 33:33 for related forms for teaching and learning.

34. Jeremiah 3:4.

35. Jeremiah 11:19 has the phrase כְּכֶבֶשׂ אַלּוּף, which means "gentle lamb or domesticated lamb." The word כֶּבֶשׂ means "young sheep or lamb" and the word אַלּוּף carries the meaning of gentle or domesticated. Psalms 144:14 has the form אַלּוּפֵינוּ which means "our oxen."

36. Jeremiah 11:19.

What kind of animal is an ox? The ox is a pure powerhouse that when domesticated is a beast of burden. The ox provides the *strength* and *fortitude*, אֹמֶץ, to do and accomplish useful and important physical tasks that man would find very difficult if not impossible to do with his strength alone. What kind of animal are the sheep and cow? The sheep provides wool that when made into clothes keeps man warm. The cow provides milk, one of nature's most perfect foods. Both the sheep and the cow can sustain and nurture man. Thus א pulsates. It is both the tamer and that which is tamed.

There is something very deep about א being tamed, for the א is the agency of the Divine Source. How is it possible for us to tame it?

Taming the א does not mean what it would mean on the surface; namely, that we develop the requisite skill to subjugate א according to our desire. Rather, it means that by learning the nature of א and then living our lives in accordance with that nature, the untamed aspect of א, that aspect that we would interpret as "upsetting our applecart" we no longer interpret as manifest in our lives.

The reality is that the untamedness of א is just as extensive in our lives whether we live in accordance with א's nature or not. The difference is not so much in the energy intelligence of the א as it is in how we handle those circumstances in which א brings us its untamed pulsating unbridled nature. For by living in an appropriate way, by appropriately choosing our motivation and responses, the potential untamed unbridled aspect of א is revealed as Godly light and returned to the source. The applecart gets upset only when we do not reveal that aspect of א as Godly light. In that case its concealment becomes our darkness. And when we reveal the Godly light, we are not even aware that the applecart had the possibility of getting upset.

אַלּוּף also can mean *intimate friend, companion of one's youth, intimate companion,* or *confidant.* The sense is one who is always in the company of another.[37]

> Who forsakes the *companion* of her youth and disregards the covenant of her God.[38]

---

37. Harris, Archer, and Waltke, *Theological Wordbook*, vol. 1, p. 47.
38. Proverbs 2:17.

A shifty man stirs up strife, and a querulous one alienates his *friend*.[39]

He who seeks love overlooks faults, but he who harps on a matter alienates his *friend*.[40]

From this we learn that the energy intelligence of א always accompanies us. This is its revealed meaning.

The concealed meaning of א is obtained from לֹף, related to the root לפף, which means to *bind* and *wrap* a cloth around as to swaddle a cloth or blanket around a baby. We must embrace, bind, and wrap ourselves around the unbridled force that א is. For that is the way both it and we become tamed.

The letter energy intelligence א is the *unifying force* of God as creator of the universe. On the Tree of Life, it encompasses the first three Sephirot כֶּתֶר, חָכְמָה, and בִּינָה, especially the first Sephirah כֶּתֶר, the concealed Sephirah, the hidden utterance of Bereshit.[41] This is reinforced by the fact that אֶלֶף spelled backwards is פֶּלֶא, which means *wonder* or *marvel*, so wondrous and so marvelous that it is beyond our strength and rational comprehension and, therefore, hidden from us.

The Talmud says:

Seek not things that are too hard for thee (that are above thy strength) and search not out things that are *hidden* from thee [too *wondrous* for thee].[42]

What is too *wondrous* for you, do not inquire into.[43]

In the song that Moses sings after the Israelites crossed the Red Sea and the Egyptians drowned as the parted sea came together again, he uses the word פֶּלֶא.

Who is like unto Thee among the mighty, O Lord? Who is

---

39. Proverbs 16:28.
40. Proverbs 17:9.
41. Rabbi Nachman, *Ayeh?* (Jerusalem: Breslov Research Institute, 1985), p. 40.
42. *The Babylonian Talmud, Seder Moed*, vol. 4, *Hagigah* (13a), trans. I. Abrahams (London: Soncino Press, 1938), p. 73.
43. Rabbi Nachman, *Ayeh?*, p. 40.

like unto Thee, glorious in holiness, fearful in praises, doing *wonders*?[44]

The root פלא means "to be wonderful." In the Hiphil form it means "to cause a wonderful thing to happen." And in the Piel form it means "to fulfull a vow." In biblical usage, it refers to that which is unusual and beyond comprehension and it is therefore something that awakens astonishment in us.[45]

Rabbi Schneerson teaches that wonder or marvel represents a level of Godliness that is completely beyond comparison with the world.[46] א is the true infinite reality, the אוֹר, the Light of Wisdom. This is where consciousness itself is the state of *truth*, אֱמֶת. It is both the *father*, אַבָּא and the *mother*, אִמָּא.

The numerical value of א is *one*. So א represents אֶחָד, the *oneness*, *uniqueness*, *changelessness*, and *indivisibility* of the eternal omnipotent God.

> א is numerically equal to 1, ח to 8, and ד to 4, alluding to the fact that a Jew's service is to draw done the One – God – into the seven heavens and earth, and into the four corners of the world.[47]

The word אֶחָד has the gematria of 13. The word *love*, אַהֲבָה, also has the gematria of 13. Rabbi Menachem Mendel of Kossov teaches that this numerical correspondence has particular meaning relating to this verse:

> You shall love your neighbor as [you love] yourself. I am the Lord.[48]

For in perfect neighborly love, unity is achieved. When we love our fellow man and he loves us, there are two loves, two אַהֲבָהs. Now 2

---

44. Exodus 15:11.
45. Harris, Archer, Waltke, *Theological Wordbook*, vol. 2, p. 723.
46. Rabbi Menachem Schneerson, *Sichos in English*, vol. 48 (Brooklyn, NY: Sichos in English, 1991), p. 153.
47. Rabbi Menachem Schneerson, *Sichos in English*, vol. 23 (Brooklyn, NY: Sichos in English, 1985), p. 9.
48. Leviticus 19:18.

times 13 is 26, which is the gematria of יְהֹוָ־ה. This means that in the unity of reciprocal love God is manifest.[49]

The word אֶחָד, one, is itself א prefixed to the word חַד. חַד means *one* or *single*. It also is the prefix meaning *mono-*, *uni-*, or *one-*. But coming from the root חדד, which means to *be sharp*, to *be sharpened*, or to *be fierce*, חַד is the adjective (masculine form) meaning *sharp*, *shrill*, or *acute*. And coming from the root חדה, which means to *rejoice*, *be glad*, חַד is the adjective (masculine form) meaning *glad*. Finally, חָד is the third person masculine singular of the root חוד, meaning to *riddle*, propound riddles, or speak enigmatically. From this we learn that the unbridled force is one, it is sharp, fierce, and *enigmatic*, carrying within it a *joyousness* and *gladness*. The nature of this joy can be seen from common expressions such as חֶדְוַת חַיִּים, which means *joy of life*, חֶדְוַת יְצִירָה, which means *joy of creation*, חֶדְוַת עוֹלָמִים, which means *eternal joy*, and חֶדְוַת רוּחַ, which means *spiritual happiness*.

א is the infinite, the endless, the illimitable, אֵין סוֹף. The א is the beginning and ending of all grades. It is called One because although the manifested attributes of God are many, God is still only one. The top points of the א allude to its upper hidden supernal aspect. The bottom points of the א allude to its extension to what is below.

The letter א can be understood by seeing that it is composed of three parts: a י, the tenth letter of the Hebrew alphabet, for its lower left foot having ten toes, and another י for its upper right hand having ten fingers. Sandwiched between these is a ו, the sixth letter of the Hebrew alphabet, which corresponds to the six directions of man. Thus א is shaped like a man. Together its three parts total 26, which is the numerical value of יְהֹוָ־ה, the four-letter name of God.[50] This tells us that the א acts as a witness to the name of the Holy One.[51] Also, the upper and lower י can be likened to wings on the ו, which is likened to one. The Arizal teaches that the upper and lower יs represent the higher and the lower waters and the ו represents the firmament between

---

49. Avraham Yaakov Finkel, *The Great Chasidic Masters* (Northvale, NJ: Jason Aronson Inc., 1992), p. 112.

50. Compare with *The Bahir*, trans. and comm. Rabbi Aryeh Kaplan (Northvale, NJ: Jason Aronson, 1995), p. 135.

51. Rabbi Jacob Ben Jacob Ha-Kohen, "Explanation of the Letters," in *The Early Kabbalah*, trans. Ronald Kiener (New York: Paulist Press, 1986), pp. 155-156.

them.[52] The higher water is the experience of nearness to God. The lower water is the experience of farness from God. The firmament is what we cross to go from far to near. It connects the higher water with the lower water. The light of the firmament is Torah. The light's transcendent aspect is the upper י. Its immanent aspect is the lower י.[53]

The divinity of א is related to words like אֵל, the God name that is associated with *loving-kindness* and *mercy*, the Sephirah חֶסֶד; אֶהְיֶה, the God name associated with the *eternal*, the Sephirah כֶּתֶר, crown; אֱלֹהִים, the God name associated with *judgment* and the Sephirah גְבוּרָה, strength; אֲדֹנָי, which means *my Lord* or *my Master* and is the God name associated with מַלְכוּת, kingdom. There are related words such as אָדוֹן, which means *master, sir, commander, ruler, proprietor*, or *owner*; אָבִיר, which means *mighty one*[54]; and אַדִיר, which means the *great* or *powerful*.

The God name אֱלֹהִים can be understood as God's immanence in the world. Reading the letters in reversed order, we read מיהלא, which is יה within מלא. יה is the God name associated with the Sephirahחָכְמָה, wisdom, and מלא is the root meaning to *fill*, and to *be full*. The word מְלֹא means *multitude, fullness*, or *filling matter*. So אֱלֹהִים can be understood as that aspect of יה, God, that fills matter.

Also revealing is when we read the letters אֱלֹהִים in regular order. We have יה within אלם. Now הֵי is the the interjection *hey*, which is used as an exclamation to call attention to or to express surprise, exultation, or bewilderment. הֵי also means *here is* and it is one of the spellings of the letter ה. In Aramaic, הֵי means *who*. אֵלֶם means *dumbness* or *silence* and אִלֵם means *mute* or *dumb*. Also אַלָם means *powerful person*. אָלַם is the Niphal form meaning to *be made dumb*. It has a second meaning of to *grow* or *be strong*. From this reading אֱלֹהִים can be understood as: Hey! Here is material reality. It is that which has been made silent. But do not let its silence fool you, for it is filled with the strength of who, the strength of God.

---

52. Rabbi Yitzchak Ginsburgh, *The Hebrew Letters* (Jerusalem: Gal Einai Publications, 1992), p. 24.
53. Ibid., p. 30.
54. Genesis 49:24.

אֵ is related to the word אֲנִי, *I*, and to the word אַיִן, which means *nothing* or *nothingness*. Since the letters of אֲנִי and אַיִן are identical we learn that nothing – that is, humility – is the foundation of what is needed to build the self, which is the אֲנִי.[55] There is the related word אָנוּ, *we*, and the word אָדִיב, which means *polite*, *obliging*, or *well-mannered*.

The word אָמֵן, *Amen*, means *it is true*, *so be it*, or *may it become true*. It is a biblical word serving as the people's response affirming an oath.[56] The person who responds "Amen" after an oath uttered by someone else is accounted as if he had uttered the oath himself. Amen is associated with agreement to fulfill a request and it is also a prayer for fulfillment: may it become true.[57]

At the time of the second Temple, אָמֵן was the congregation's response to prayers and blessings. Rabbi Schneerson teaches that

> our Amen approves, sustains, and draws the blessing into reality, to the point that it will overcome any obstacles.[58]

Amen, אָמֵן, does have, however, a deeper meaning. The Talmud[59] explains that אָמֵן is made up of the initial letters of the phrase אֵל מֶלֶךְ נֶאֱמָן, which means "God is a faithful King." Here the God name אֵל is the source of all Divine Influence. This influence extends all the way from the Heavenly Abode of the Sephirah כֶּתֶר, Keter, to the level of King, מֶלֶךְ, which in the Tree of Life is the Sephirah מַלְכוּת, Malchut. And this influence that extends from Keter to Malchut always extends in a faithful, אָמֵן, manner.

This interpretation is reinforced by the fact that the gematria of אָמֵן is 91. And 91 is the combined gematria of יְהֹוָה and אֲדֹנָי. The God name יְהֹוָה is related to the *pulsating unbridled force* above

---

55. Rabbi Matityahu Glazerson, *Repentance in Words and Letters* (Jerusalem: Yerid HaSefarim, 1992), p. 84.

56. Numbers 4:5, Deuteronomy 27:15-26.

57. *The Babylonian Talmud, Seder Nezikin*, vol. 4, *Shebuoth* (36a), trans. A. Silverstone (London: Soncino Press, 1938), p. 162.

58. Rabbi Menachem Schneerson, *Sichos in English* (Brooklyn, NY: Sichos in English, 1985), p. 248.

59. *The Babylonian Talmud, Seder Moed*, vol. 1, *Shabbat* (119b), trans. H. Freedman (London: Soncino Press, 1938), p. 589.

nature and the God name אֲדֹנָי is related to the *pulsating unbridled force* that permeates the world. The two God names together mean that essential Godliness (יְ־הֹ־וָ־הֹ) pervades all throughout the world (אֲדֹנָי).[60]

אמן is the root that in the Kal form means to *bring up*, to *nurture*, to *nurse*, or to *foster*. In the Niphal form it means to *be true*, to *be found true, trustworthy, firm*, or to *be faithful*. In the Piel form it means to *train* or to *educate*. In the Pual form it means to *be educated* or *be skilled*. In the Hiphil form it means to *believe* or to *entrust*. In the Huphal form it means to *be believed*. And in the Hitpael form it means to *train oneself* or to *practice*. Reinforcing this is the related noun אָמָּן, which means *artist, expert*, or *master craftsman* and the noun אֻמָּן, which means *craftsman* or *skilled worker*.

The close relationship of man to divinity can be seen immediately since אָדָם means *man*. And what can man do from the אִין, the *nothing* of א? Man can accomplish great tasks because a simple vowel change transforms אֶלֶף, *one*, to אֶלֶף, a *thousand*.

How does man, אָדָם, accomplish great tasks? By causing change in accordance with his will, which has become united with God's will. By becoming אַשָּׁף, a *magician, wizard*, and *enchanter*.[61] For it is by man's thoughts that knowledge and understanding can become the manifested energy of א.[62] It is by his *love*, אַהֲבָה, that *man* embraces and becomes *betrothed* or *engaged*, אָרַס, to the *infinite spirituality*, אֵינסוֹף, that always is. It is by his intentions, his *words* and *utterances*, אָמַר, that this energy of א takes form in man's *responsible actions*, מַעֲשֶׂה אַחֲרַאי. Indeed, the א of אָדָם stands for אֱנוֹשׁ, *human being*, mortal; the ד stands for דִּבּוּר, his *power of speech*; and the ם stands for מַעֲשֶׂה, his *power of action*.[63] It is in this manner that man is אָדוֹן, *commander*, *ruler* and *proprietor* of the energy intelligence of א. Rabbi Glazerson

---

60. Rabbi Schneerson, *Sichos in English*, vol. 44, p. 13.

61. As used here, *magician* does not mean one who works magic separate from or in a separate existence from God. Rather, it means one who understands that the process of serving God, of uniting one's will with God is itself a wonderful, magical, miraculous process. As the initiator of this process man can be called a magician.

62. *Shabbat* 104a says that א ב means אַלּוּף בִּינָה, learn understanding.

63. Compare with Rabbi Yosef Schneersohn and Rabbi Menachem Schneerson, *Basi LeGani* (Brooklyn, NY: Kehot Publication Society, 1990), p. 40.

tells us that the א of אָדָם corresponds to the mind because the mind is the אוּלְפָּן, which means *studio* or *intensive teaching center*. The mind is the headquarters of wisdom. The ד corresponds to דִבּוּר, which means *speech*, and the ם corresponds to the מַעֲשֶׂה, which means *action* or *deed*.[64]

Man's close relation to the soil comes about because אָדָם is cognate to אָדֹם which is the Hebrew word for the color *red*, and it also means a *gold coin* like a *ducat*, *florin*, or *gulder*. אָדָם with the addition of the letter energy intelligence of the power of being ה becomes אֲדָמָה which means *earth*, *soil*, or *ground*. And from the root דמה meaning to *resemble*, to *be like*, אֶדְמֶה means "I shall resemble or I will resemble."

I will resemble the most High.[65]

This can be interpreted to mean that אָדָם, man, resembles the earth and that man resembles God. Man resembles the earth in that man is the receiver of the Godly *pulsating unbridled force*, א. Man resembles God in that just as God is unbounded and above limitation, so also man has unbounded potential.[66]

Man is called אָדָם when he unites himself with א, or the source. Otherwise, he is merely דָם, a maker of blood.[67]

When the ם of אָדָם changes to ן, there results אֶדֶן, which means base or *foundation*. Man, through his connection with the red soil, serves as the base for the manifestion of the energy intelligence of א.

The Koretzer Rabbi teaches that

א means the "Source, the Leader." The word אִישׁ, *man*, is composed of the א and the word יֵשׁ, *there is*. This signifies that there is in Man the Source, that Divinity abides in man.[68]

---

64. Rabbi Matityahu Glazerson, *From Hinduism to Judaism* (Jerusalem: Himelsein Glazerson, 1984), p. 33.
65. Isaiah 14:14.
66. Rabbi Schneerson, *Sichos in English*, vol. 7, p. 117.
67. Louis Newman, *Hasidic Anthology* (New York: Charles Scribner's Sons, 1938), p. 91.
68. Ibid., p. 83.

The energy intelligence force of א is the abstract principle of all that is and is not. It is the intrinsic thought intelligence of *air*, which in Hebrew is אֲוִיר. It is אֵשׁ, *fire*. It is אֶרֶץ, *earth*. It is ethereal and imperceptible by itself. It is timeless, beyond measure, and beyond understanding, for it is creative transcendent immanence, the imperishable perennial, אֵיתָן, pulsation and thrusting of life. It creates, but it is not created. It has no existence, but it is everywhere. It disappears when it is found. To seek it is to lose it. It is in a realm beyond thought and consciousness.

The energy intelligence force of א by itself cannot manifest. But with a suitable living *container* or *vessel*, the *light* that it is can be revealed. A vessel that desires to receive for itself alone will conceal the light. Only a vessel that loves, אוֹהֵב, that desires to receive for the sake of imparting, can keep the א in motion and thereby reveal the light.

בֵּית

Bet ב: Container

The second letter of the Hebrew alphabet is Bet, ב, spelled בֵּית. It represents two, the concept of *duality*. *Midrash Rabbah* states:

> Why was it [the world] created with a ב? To teach you that there are two worlds.[1]

Thus the letter ב represents two things joined together, one capable of being revealed and one forever shrouded in mystery.[2] The energy intelligence of the ב can be understood relative to the energy intelligence of the א. The Zohar teaches:

> The א is the image of the male principle as against the ב which is the image of the female principle.[3]

The revealed meaning of ב is בַּיִת, which means *dwelling place*, *house*, or *home*. The house is a place in which we are. It is the place where our essence becomes manifest.[4] There are over 2,000 instances of some form of the word בַּיִת in all of the biblical Scripture; Genesis alone has some forty-five instances of בַּיִת.[5]

> And Jacob journeyed to Sukkot and built him a *house*, and made booths for his cattle; therefore, the name of the place is called Sukkot.[6]

> And it came to pass from the time that he had made him overseer in his house, and over all that he had, that the Lord blessed the Egyptian's *house* for Joseph's sake: and

1. *Midrash Rabbah, Genesis*, vol. 1 (1:10) (London: Soncino Press, 1983), p. 9.
2. *The Zohar*, vol. 1, trans. Harry Sperling and Maurice Simon (London: Soncino Press, 1978), p. 32.
3. Ibid., vol. 2, p. 260.
4. Rabbi Menachem Schneerson, *In the Garden of the Torah* (Brooklyn, NY: Sichos in English, 1994), p. 2.
5. Genesis 12:8,15; twice in 13:3; 17:12,23,27; 19:2; 24:23,27,38; 28:17,19,21,22; 31:13; 33:17; 34:19; 35:1,3,6,7,15,19; twice in 38:11; 39:5,20,21,22,23; twice in 40:3; 40:7; 41:10,51; 43:18,19; 45:2,16; 46:31; 47:12; 48:7; 50:4,8.
6. Genesis 33:17.

the blessing of the Lord was upon all that he had in the house and in the field.[7]

But *house* can also refer to house of God, as in the place בֵּית אֵל, Bet-el.

And God said to Jacob: "Arise, go up to *Bet-el*, and dwell there. And make there an altar to God, who appeared to thee when thou didst flee from the face of Esau thy brother.[8]

Or it can be a house of God, as in temple.

The first of the first-fruits of thy land thou shalt bring to the *house* of the Lord thy God.[9]

Or it can be house of prison.

And Joseph's master took him and put him into the *house* of prison, a place where the king's prisoners were bound: and he was there in the house of prison.[10]

Or it can be house as in *household*, meaning ancestors, descendants, and kindred.

These are the heads of their father's *houses*: the sons of Reuben, the firstborn of Israel, Hanoch and Pallu, Hezron and Carmi: these are the clans of Reuben.[11]

And the children of Israel did according to all that the Lord commanded Moses: so they pitched by their standards, and so they set forward, everyone after their families, according to the *houses* of their fathers.[12]

Or it can be the house of Israel.

---

7. Genesis 39:5.
8. Genesis 35:1.
9. Exodus 23:19, 34:26.
10. Genesis 39:10.
11. Exodus 6:14.
12. Numbers 2:34.

For the cloud of the Lord was upon the tabernacle by day, and fire was on it by night, in the sight of all the *house* of Israel, throughout all their journeys.[13]

Or house can mean anything in a house.

Thou shalt not covet thy neighbor's *house*: thou shalt not covet thy neighbor's wife, nor his manservant, nor his maidservant, nor his ox, nor his ass, nor anything that is thy neighbor's.[14]

The prefix meaning *in, at, by, among, with, by means of,* or *through* is בּ. We are in the house so that the house can be a means of doing something; through it we can exercise our capabilities. The Hebrew word for *in it* or *in her* is בָּהּ. And in the house is our capability of אָהֵב, loving, and בִּינָה, reasoning and *understanding*.[15] And this loving and understanding shall be our prayer.

My house shall be called a house of prayer for all peoples.[16]

By this we understand that God's house is the house in our physical world in which God dwells. And this house is our house. It is our house in which God dwells.

Reinforcing this is the verse that precedes the description of the Tabernacle.

And let them make a sanctuary, that I may dwell within them.[17]

Rashi comments that "make me a sanctuary" means "make for my name a sanctuary, house of holiness."[18] Notice that the ending phrase is "dwell within them" and not "dwell in it." This can be interpreted to mean that God dwells in each and every one of us.

---

13. Exodus 40:38.
14. Exodus 20:14.
15. *Shabbat* 104a.
16. Isaiah 56:7.
17. Exodus 25:8.
18. Rashi, Exodus 25:8.

The gematria of בֵּית is 412. The word הָאוֹת, meaning *the token* or *the sign* has the gematria of 412 and is used when God is telling Moses to lead the people out of Egypt.

> And He said: "Certainly I will be with thee; and this shall be *the sign* to thee, that it is I who have sent thee: when thou hast brought the people out of Egypt, ye shall serve God upon this mountain."[19]

The word הָאוֹת is used again in the warning about false prophets.

> If there arise among you a prophet, or a dreamer of dreams, and he give thee a sign or a wonder, and *the sign* or the wonder come to pass, of which he spoke to thee, saying: "Let us go after other gods, which thou hast not known, and let us serve them," thou shalt not hearken to the words of that prophet, or that dreamer of dreams: for the Lord your God puts you to the proof, to know whether you love the Lord your God with all your heart and with all your soul.[20]

The word תַּאֲוָה has the gematria of 412 and means *desire, longing, lust, craving, delight*, or *desirable thing*. It is first used to describe how Eve felt about the tree of knowledge.

> And when the woman saw that the tree was good for food and that it was a *delight* to the eyes, and a tree to be desired to make one wise, she took of its fruit, and did eat, and gave also to her husband with her, and he did eat.[21]

תַּאֲוָה is used to describe the craving of the mixed multitude for the kind of food they ate in Egypt.

> And the mixed multitude that was among them fell a *lusting*: and the children of Israel also wept again and said: "Who shall give us meat to eat? We remember the fish,

19. Exodus 3:12.
20. Deuteronomy 13:2-3.
21. Genesis 3:6.

which we did eat in Egypt for nothing: the cucumbers, and the melons, and the leeks, and the onions, and the garlic. But now our soul is dried away. There is nothing at all beside this manna before our eyes."[22]

And again it is used when God gives the Israelites permission to eat meat.

When the Lord thy God shall enlarge thy border, as He hath promised thee, and thou shalt say: "I will eat flesh," because thy soul *desireth* to eat flesh; thou mayest eat flesh after the desire of thy soul.[23]

תְאַוֶּה is used in the discussion about the tithe of corn, wine, oil, and the firstlings of the herd and flock and the eating of the tithing before God.

And thou shalt bestow that money on all the *desires* of thy heart: on oxen, or sheep, or wine, or strong drink, or whatever thy soul requires; and thou shalt eat there before the Lord thy God, and thou shalt rejoice, thou and thy household.[24]

From this we draw the interesting lesson that it is the nature of the vessel to crave, to lust for the light to fill it. And the fulfillment of this lusting is not necessarily guaranteed to bring the light, for the lusting may be only an attachment to an appearance without essence. The fulfillment of such lusting does not reveal any light. It only increases the desire. Therefore, we have to be particularly careful to cleave to God, that our desire be always for the essence, for the holiness, and not for an empty surface appearance. And when our desire is for holiness, then we find:

Desire fulfilled is a tree of life.[25]

---

22. Numbers 11:4-6.
23. Deuteronomy 12:20.
24. Deuteronomy 14:26.
25. Psalms 11:23.

The full gematria of ב is obtained from בֵּית יוֹד תָּו, which has the value of 838. The word וְכָתַבְתִּי has the gematria of 838 and is the Kal perfect first person singular with the conjunction prefix ו of the root כתב, which means to *write, register,* or *record.* God uses the word וְכָתַבְתִּי in telling Moses to come up Mount Sinai a second time so that God will write the commandments on the second pair of stone tablets.

> And the Lord said to Moses: "Hew for thyself two tablets
> of stone like the first and I will write upon these tablets
> the words that were on the first tablets, which thou didst
> break."[26]

From this we learn that the vessel ב is that on which God writes. The light revealed by the vessel is God's writing. This is the light. This is reinforced by the fact that the second word in the Pentateuch is בָּרָא, which means *created.* The root ברא can be broken up into רא and ב. The ב stands for בַּיִת, *house.* The רא stands for אור, which means *light.*[27] To be created therefore means to be housed in light. From this point of view, all of reality is a house in relation to God.[28]

Our task is to think, say, and do that which will reveal the light that already is. And what the vessel does in receiving the light is with respect to the vessel the same relation as what the light is with respect to God. For the word מִשְׁפַּחְתִּי, which also has the gematria of 838, means *my kindred* and kindred means relation.

> But thou shalt go to my father's house, and to *my kindred,*
> and take a wife for my son.[29]

> Then shalt thou be clear from this my oath when thou
> comest to *my kindred.* And if they grant it not to thee,
> thou shalt be clear of my oath.[30]

---

26. Exodus 34:1.
27. Rabbi Matityahu Glazerson, *Hebrew: The Source of Languages* (Jerusalem: Yerid HaSefarim, 1988), p. 31.
28. Rabbi Yitzchak Ginsburgh, *The Hebrew Letters* (Jerusalem: Gal Einai Publications, 1992), p. 44.
29. Genesis 24:38.
30. Genesis 24:41.

The form of the letter בּ is closed on three sides and open on the left.

It is closed on one side as symbolic of that which is written:

And thou shalt see my back.[31]

and open on the other side so as to illumine the higher worlds. (It is also open on one side in order to receive from the higher worlds, like a hall in which guests gather.) For that reason it is placed at the beginning of the Torah, and was later on filled in.[32]

Being closed on three sides and open on the left

teaches us that it is the house of the world. God is the place of the world and the world is not His place.[33,34]

The house is where we belong. It is a place in which our personality develops, a place in which we define ourselves physically, mentally, emotionally, and spiritually. The house has the energy intelligence force of the archetype of all *containers* or *vessels*, the *physical support*, the *building* or *structure*, בְּנְיָן, without which nothing is. And what does the vessel contain? The vessel contains the *light*, אוֹר, and the *fire*, אֵשׁ, which always is. It contains it by *burning*, בְּעֵרָה, it. In fact, only through the vessel can the light be revealed. By aligning our will with God's will, we can reveal the light through our body which is the vessel. The unity thereby created is the revealment of the light. Any act that falls short of making our will be God's will is not an act of Divine service. Any act that is not an act of love is one that conceals the light. When we reveal the light, we transform our body, our vessel, our container to a sanctuary, which is a container of holiness.

---

31. Exodus 33:23.
32. *The Zohar*, vol. 3, trans. Harry Sperling, Maurice Simon, and Paul Levertoff (London: Soncino Press, 1978), p. 67.
33. *The Bahir*, trans. and comm. Rabbi Aryeh Kaplan (Northvale NJ: Jason Aronson, 1995), p. 6.
34. *Midrash Rabbah, Genesis*, vol. 2 (58:9), trans. H. Freedman (London: Soncino Press, 1983), p. 620.

The letter בּ is also the energy intelligence force of בְּרָכָה, *blessing*[35] and בְּרִיאָה, creation. The duality of the letter energy intelligence בּ is our blessing and creation.[36] More than once we read in Scripture that God created male and female and God blessed them.[37] Our creation, which is what we receive from God, is our blessing. For as stated in Scripture:

> I have set before you this day a blessing[38]

And to fulfill this blessing we must understand for what purpose we have been created. Scripture tells us:

> I have created him [man] for my glory.[39]

From this we learn that when we create by our thoughts, speech, and action that which reveals the glory of God, we fulfill our blessing.

There are many prayers that begin with *blessed,* בָּרוּךְ. Rabbi Nachman teaches that as the word is said, the letter בּ comes forth and pleads with the soul not to part from it, not to let the experience of blessing depart from our heart.[40]

Blessing, בְּרָכָה, with different vowels is בְּרֵכָה, which means *pool, pond,* or *wellspring.*

> And be thou a blessing,[41] בְּרָכָה: this means, be thou a pool, בְּרֵכָה: just as a pool purifies the unclean, so do thou bring near [to Me] those who are afar.[42]

Our physical world is our pond and wellspring for it is only through the physical world that Godliness can manifest. And it is in our physical

---

35. *Midrash Rabbah, Genesis,* vol. 1 (1:10) (London: Soncino Press, 1983), p. 9.

36. Ben Zion Bokser, *From the World of the Cabbalah* (New York: Philosophical Library, 1954), p. 130.

37. Genesis 1:27, 5:2.

38. Deuteronomy 11:26.

39. Isaiah 43:7.

40. Rabbi Nachman, *Garden of the Souls* (Monsey, NY: The Breslov Research Institute, 1988), p. 42.

41. Genesis 12:2.

42. *Midrash Rabbah, Genesis,* vol. 1 (39:11), p. 322.

world that we ourselves can make blessings. And by our blessings we create wellsprings of holiness.

How is it that plurality, diversity,[43] and duality of the letter בּ, which stands for two, can be associated with creation and blessing? True blessing manifests when we work with *opposites*, bringing them together to achieve a common beneficial purpose. Indeed the very notion of harmony in creation must involve opposites such as heaven and earth, concealment and revealment, light and vessel, expansive and constrictive, love and strength, and so on. By acting with cooperation and alliances, our created reality becomes a blessing for us and mankind. We can see this even from the form of the letter בּ. For בּ resembles a house with one side open that is always welcoming new guests.

The concealed meaning of the letter energy intelligence of בּ can be uncovered by an examination of יִת, which by itself is an abbreviation for יִתְבָּרֵך, which means *may He be blessed* and is the first word in the Kaddish prayer. When combined with ד, יִת becomes יָתֵד, which means a *peg* or *hook*. This reminds us that by blessing we fasten ourselves (with a peg or a hook) to the Divine. When combined with ם, יִת becomes יָתֹם, which means to *be an orphan*. This reminds us that when our blessing is so narrow that it encompasses only the ם of מַיִם, *water* (emotion), the blessing will orphan us. When combined with ר, ית becomes יִתֵּר, which means to *add* or *overdo*. It can be used as a prefix to make compound words where it then carries the meaning of *over*, *super*, or *hyper*. We can then understand its meaning as abundance, surplus, or excess, for when we can contain the light and reveal it by our blessing, we put ourselves in a state of abundance, a state in which there is not just fullness, but such a surplus or excess of fullness that the abundance is infinite.

It is significant that the first word of Torah begins with a large בּ. Whenever a word in Torah has a letter of a different size, it signifies that another important interpretation must be looked for. The first word of Torah is בְּרֵאשִׁית, which is usually translated as *in the beginning*.

> Said R. Yudai: "What is the meaning of בְּרֵאשִׁית? It means 'with Wisdom,' the Wisdom on which the world is based,

---

43. Psalms 104:24.

and through this it introduces us to deep and recondite mysteries. In it, too, is the inscription of six chief supernal directions, out of which there issues the totality of existence. From the same there go forth six sources of rivers which flow into the Great Sea. This is implied in the word רֵאשִׁית ב, which can be analyzed into בָּרָא שִׁית (He created six). And who created them? The Mysterious Unknown." R. Hiya and R. Jose were walking along the road. When they reached the open country, R. Hiya said to R. Jose, "What you said about בְּרֵאשִׁית signifying בָּרָא שִׁית (created six) is certainly correct, since the Torah speaks of six primordial days and not more."[44]

In *Midrash Rabbah* we read:

R. Berekiah said: The Heaven and earth were created only for the sake of Israel, for it is written,[45]

Because of רֵאשִׁית God created the heaven and the earth.[46]

and רֵאשִׁית cannot but signify Israel, as is proved by the text,

Israel is the Lord's hallowed portion, His רֵאשִׁית of the increase.[47]

Rabbi Nachman continues the interpretation of *Midrash Rabbah* by linking it to the verse:

Israel, I take pride in you.[48]

which he interprets to mean that it is for the sake of the pride and joy that God would receive from Israel that God created the entire world.[49]

---

44. *The Zohar*, vol. 1, p. 13.
45. *Midrash Rabbah, Leviticus*, vol. 4 (36:4), p. 461.
46. Genesis 1:1.
47. Jeremiah 2:3
48. Isaiah 49:3.
49. Rabbi Nachman, *Likutey Moharan*, vol. 3, trans. Moshe Mykoff (Jerusalem: Breslov Research Institute, 1990), p. 9.

בְּרֵאשִׁית can be understood as the word רֹאשׁ, which means head, contained within the word בֵּית, which means house. So בְּרֵאשִׁית can be understood as head enclosed by *house*.[50]

As the *head* is the א and the house is בּ, we have א within בּ or א enclosed by בּ. Now, רֹאשׁ has the meaning not only of head, but also top, *leader, chief, start,* or *beginning.* So from this we discern that the בּ containing the א means that within בּ is א, the inner principal, that which is most fundamental and most causative. Also, the א being enclosed by the בּ means that it is the expression of the א which is the *container* בּ of the א. And since the expression בּ is the only way the א can be known, the א will never be found without its container בּ. And from the point of view of the container בּ, it is the intention of the container that constitutes the א inside. From this we learn that the secret, most hidden, place of the spiritual is the physical.

The upper left corner of בּ points upward to heaven. Thereby we as a living vessel, a living container, understand that God exists and always is, that nothing happens by chance. All has a purpose and that purpose is to help us to grow and reveal the Oneness of God. The base of בּ points back to א. This means that אֱלֹהִים can be understood only by creation itself. It means that א and בּ must be in a partnership אָב, which means *father.* When we create a healthy partnership between א and בּ, the א relates to בּ as a father to a *son,* בֵּן. Father and son is אָב וּבֵן. Rabbi Nachman says that father means Jacob and son means his children. Father relates to wisdom and intellect and son relates to body.[51] When אָב וּבֵן is contracted the result is the word אֶבֶן, which means *stone,* a symbol of *permanency.*[52] There is permanency when we reveal the light and create a blessing. Any other act has a transitory illusionary existence, for it is only the energy intelligence of blessing that is capable of removing illusion and revealing a cosmos that is one. Another way of saying this is that when we desire to receive in order

---

50. Although this is not said outright, it is hinted at in *The Zohar,* vol. 1 (London: Soncino Press, 1978), p. 64.

51. Rabbi Nachman, *Likutey Moharan,* vol. 3, p. 75.

52. Genesis 49:24 has the phrase אֶבֶן יִשְׂרָאֵל. Rashi, using the exegetical principle of Notrikon, says that אֶבֶן denotes אָב (father) and בֵּן (son).

to impart,[53] we reveal the *light* through our vessel. In this manner, we connect to the infinite reality, we experience fullness and certainty and become blessed. When we desire to receive for ourself alone, we connect to fragmentation and illusion, for the desire to receive for oneself alone is always deficient, having elements of frustration, or resentment, or anger, or uncertainty. These cannot be a blessing.

Indeed, when our desire is to receive for ourself alone, we become more determined by our uncertain fragmented world. But when our desire is to receive for the sake of imparting, we become free. In this world of freedom and completion, we are certain and in our certainty, we can nourish the light.

---

53. Phillip Berg, *Kabbalah for the Layman* (Jerusalem: Research Centre of Kabbalah, 1981), p. 20.

נָמֵל

Gimmel ג : Nourishment

The third letter of the Hebrew alphabet is Gimmel, ג, spelled גּמֶל.
The number three signifies the combining of the two energy intelligences
of א and בּ into a perfect third energy intelligence ג. Hence, ג is the
organic *nourishing* activity of בּ animated by א. The Maharal explains
that

> the ג signifies the capacity to neutralize the dissimilarity
> of two contrasting forces and unite them into a lasting and
> more wholesome unit.[1]

How does it do this? It does it by openly attaching itself to the א within
the energy intelligence of the בּ, thereby forming the word גַּמְלָא, which
means a *bridge uniting two areas*.[2]

The revealed meaning of ג can be understood by its cognates. There
is the verb root גמל (גָּמַל), which means to *ripen* or to *nourish until
completely ripe*.[3]

> And it came to pass on the morrow, that Moses went in to
> the Tent of the Testimony; and, behold, there was budded
> the rod of Aaron, for the house of Levi, and it put forth
> buds and bloomed blossoms and bore *ripe* almonds.[4]

גמל is also the verb root meaning to *recompense, remunerate, requite,
repay, reimburse* make *retribution*, or *reward*,[5] and is also the verb root
meaning to *deal with*,[6] to *load on*, or to *do good to*.[7]

In the Niphal form it is the verb root meaning to *be weaned*.[8]

---

1. Rabbi Michael Munk, *The Wisdom in the Hebrew Alphabet* (Brooklyn, NY: Mesorah, 1988), p. 75.
2. *The Babylonian Talmud, Seder Moed*, vol. 4, *Moed Katan* (6b), trans. Dayan Lazarus (London: Soncino Press, 1938), p. 33.
3. Numbers 17:23.
4. Numbers 17:23.
5. Deuteronomy 32:6, Joel 4:4, 1 Samuel 24:17.
6. Genesis 50:15,17.
7. *The Babylonian Talmud, Seder Moed*, vol. 1, *Shabbat* (104a), trans. H. Freedman (London: Soncino Press, 1938), p. 500.
8. Genesis 21:8, 1 Samuel 1:22.

And the child grew and *was weaned*: and Abraham made a
great feast on the same day that Yitzhak *was weaned*.[9]

Here weaned means not only weaned from his mother's milk, but also
it means weaned from temptation.[10] As a noun, גָּמָל means *remu-*
neration and גָּמֻל means *mature*. There is the verb root גמל (גָּמַל),
meaning to *drive a camel*. The associated noun גָּמָל means *camel*[11] and
גַּמָּל means *camel driver*. But there is more than this, for the camel
received its Hebrew name גָּמָל not only because its long neck resembles
a ג, but because it can go for a long time without drinking just as a
weaned child can go for a long time without drinking.[12]

The energy intelligence of ג is then able to bring the desires of the
conscious mind into being by nourishing until completely ripe, weaning
it from the realm of desire or thought until it is in the realm of complete
manifestation. It is thereby able to manifest the wealth of the conscious
mind even if that means driving a camel through the desert or through
the wilderness of the abyss.

The shape of ג is that of a ו that represents the erect man with a
י for its feet in motion.[13] Why are the feet in motion? They are in
motion to enable the man to run and find those poorer than he is so
that he may give them *nourishment*.

Because it is fitting for the benevolent to run after [seek
out] the poor.[14]

And this is the meaning of גְּמִילוּת חֲסָדִים, the *practice of loving-*
kindness or the *practice of loving deeds*.

And thou shalt shew them – this refers to their house of
life; the way – that means the practice of *loving deeds*; they

---

9. Genesis 21:8.

10. *Midrash Rabbah, Genesis*, vol. 1 (53:10), trans. H. Freedman (London: Soncino
Press, 1983), p. 468.

11. Genesis 12:16; 24:10,11,14,19,20,22,30,31,32,35,44,46,61,63,64, 30:43; 31:17,34;
32:7,15; 37:25; Exodus 9:3; Leviticus 11:4; Deuteronomy 4:7.

12. Rabbi Munk, *The Wisdom in the Hebrew Alphabet*, p. 71.

13. Rabbi Yitzchak Ginsburgh, *The Hebrew Letters* (Jerusalem: Gal Einai Publications, 1992), p. 54.

14. *The Babylonian Talmud, Seder Moed*, vol. 1, *Shabbat* (104a), p. 500.

must walk – to sick visiting; *therein* – to burial; *and the work* – to strict law; *that they shall do* – to [acts] beyond the requirements of the law.[15]

Our Rabbis taught: In three respects is the practice of loving deeds superior to charity: charity can be done only with one's money, but the practice of loving-kindness can be done with one's person and one's money; charity can be given only to the poor, but the practice of loving-kindness can be done both to the rich and to the poor; charity can be given to the living only, but the practice of loving-kindness can be done both to the living and to the dead.[16]

And it is the meaning of גְּמוֹל דַּלִּים, being generous to the needy. Rabbi Schneerson teaches:

Being generous to the needy is related to the concepts of *mashpia* ("source of influence") and *mekabel* ("recipient"). The entire order of spiritual worlds is based on a flow of influence from a giver (a higher realm of existence) to a recipient (a lower realm of existence). Thus through uniting a *mashpia* with a *mekabel*, one brings about unity and a state of completeness in the entire spiritual cosmos, transforming our world, the lowest of all worlds and redeeming it entirely from a state of need.[17]

The *Bahir* explains why ג is the third letter.

It has three parts, teaching us that it bestows kindness.

But did Rabbi Akiba not say that ג has three parts because it bestows, grows, and sustains. It is thus written:

The lad grew and was bestowed.[18]

---

15. *The Babylonian Talmud, Seder Nezikin*, vol. 1, *Baba Metzia* (30b), trans. Salis Daiches and H. Freedman (London: Soncino Press, 1938), p. 188.
16. *The Babylonian Talmud, Seder Moed*, vol. 3, *Sukkah* (49b), trans. Israel Slotki (London: Soncino Press, 1938), p. 233.
17. Rabbi Menachem Schneerson, *Sichos in English*, vol. 43 (Brooklyn, NY: Sichos in English, 1991), pp. 80-81.
18. Genesis 21:8.

He said: He says the same as I do. He grew and bestowed
kindness to his neighbors and to those entrusted to him.

And why is there a tail at the bottom of the ‍נ? He said: the
נ has a head on top, and is like a pipe. Just like a pipe, the
נ draws from above through its head, and disperses through
its tail. This is the נ.[19]

Rabbi Kaplan interprets this to mean that נ draws wisdom from above
and dispenses wisdom through its tail.

The word נְמֵל has the gematria of 73. Also with the gematria of
73 is the word בְּלוּלָה, which means *mixed*.[20] It is used most often
in stating how a temple offering is to have fine flour mixed with oil.
Exactly so does the proper combining and mixing of the two spiritual
energy intelligences of א and ב produce a *nourishing* activity. This is
reinforced by the fact that the word וַיֹּאכְלוּ, which means *and did eat*,
also has the gematria of 73.

And he took butter, and milk, and the calf which he had
dressed, and set it before them; and he stood by them under
the tree, *and they did eat.*[21]

And he pressed upon them greatly; and they turned in to
him and entered into his house; and he made them a feast,
and did bake unleavened bread, *and they did eat.*[22]

And the servants brought out jewels of silver, and jewels of
gold, and garments, and gave them to Rivka: he gave also
to her brother and to her mother precious things. *And they
did eat* and drink, he and the men that were with him, and
tarried all night.[23]

And he made them a feast, *and they did eat* and drink.[24]

---

19. *The Bahir*, trans. and comm. Rabbi Aryeh Kaplan (Northvale, NJ: Jason
Aronson, 1995), pp. 8-9.
20. Leviticus 2:5; 7:10; 9:4; 14:10; 23:13; Numbers 7:13,19,25,31,37,43,49,55,61, 67,
73,79; 8:8; 15:6; 28:5,9,12,13,20,28; 29:3,9,14.
21. Genesis 18:8.
22. Genesis 19:3.
23. Genesis 24:54.
24. Genesis 26:30.

And they took stones, and made a heap; *and they did eat* there upon the heap.[25]

And they did eat bread, and tarried all night on the mountain.[26]

And they beheld God, *and did eat* and drink.[27]

We can tell from these contexts that the nourishment spoken of is not just physical nourishment. It is also *spiritual nourishment*. But yet it is more than spiritual nourishment, for the word חָכְמָה, which means *wisdom* and is the name of the second Sephirah on the tree of life, also has the gematria of 73.

And thou shalt speak to all that are wise hearted, whom I have filled with the spirit of *wisdom*, that they may make Aharon's garments to consecrate him that he may minister to me in the priest's office.[28]

In the hearts of all that are wise hearted, I have put *wisdom*, that they may make all that I have commanded thee: the Tent of Meeting, and the ark of the Testimony, and the covering that is on it and all the furniture of the Tent, and the table and its furniture, and the pure candlestick with all its furniture, and the altar of incense, and the altar of burnt offering with all its furniture, and the laver and its pedestal, and the uniforms and the holy garments for Aharon the priest and the garments of his sons.[29]

Then Bezal'el and Aholi'av and every wisehearted man, in whom the Lord put *wisdom* and understanding to know how to work all manner of work for the service of the sanctuary, did according to all that the Lord had commanded. And Moses called Bezal'el and Aholi'av, and every wisehearted man, in whose heart the Lord had put *wisdom*, everyone whose heart stirred him up to come to the work to do it.[30]

---

25. Genesis 31:46.
26. Genesis 31:54.
27. Exodus 24:11.
28. Exodus 28:3.
29. Exodus 30:6-10.
30. Exodus 36:1-2.

And Joshua the son of Nun was full of the spirit of *wisdom*.[31]

Furthermore, when גִּמֶל is spelled out as גִּמֶל מֵם לָמֶד, its total gematria is 227, which is the gematria of יְאִיר, meaning *light* and the gematria of בְּרָכָה, meaning *blessing*. From this we learn that it is the organic *nourishing activity* of ג that shall give light, יְאִיר.

> When thou lightest the lamps, the seven candlesticks *shall give light* toward the front of the candlestick.[32]

And it is this activity that is a blessing, בְּרָכָה.

> I will bless thee, and make thy name great; and thou shalt be a *blessing*.[33]
>
> That He may bestow on you a *blessing* this day.[34]
>
> Behold, I set before you this day a *blessing*.[35]

The concealed meaning of ג can be revealed by understanding מל, which when written as מָל is an alternate to מוּל, which is the root meaning to *circumcise*, to *cut off*. What to cut off is apparent from the spiritual meaning of circumcise, which is to *purify one's heart*.

> *Circumcise* therefore the foreskin of your heart, and be stiffnecked no more.[36]
>
> And the Lord thy God will *circumcise* thy heart, and the heart of thy seed, to love the Lord thy God with all thy heart, and with all thy soul, that thou mayest live.[37]
>
> *Circumcise* yourselves to the Lord, and take away the foreskins of your heart.[38]

---

31. Deuteronomy 34:9.
32. Numbers 8:2.
33. Genesis 12:2.
34. Exodus 32:29.
35. Deuteronomy 11:26.
36. Deuteronomy 10:16.
37. Deuteronomy 30:6.
38. Jeremiah 4:4.

How does one *purify* one's heart? By restricting the desire to receive for oneself alone, thereby transforming it to the desire to receive in order to impart. In this case, מַל becomes combined with the energy intelligence of א to form מָלָא, which means *full, complete,* and *overflowing.*

> The glory of the Lord (יְ־הֹ־וָ־ה) *filled* the tabernacle.[39]

> The glory of the Lord (יְ־הֹ־וָ־ה) *filled* the house.[40]

> And Joshua the son of Nun was *full* of the spirit of wisdom.[41]

> The glory of the Lord (יְ־הֹ־וָ־ה) *filled* the house of the Lord (יְ־הֹ־וָ־ה).[42]

> The glory of the Lord (יְ־הֹ־וָ־ה) had *filled* the house of God (אֱלֹהִים)[43]

So מָלָא means the infinite abundance of the revealed light. Related forms are מָלֵא, which means *filled, stuffed, satisfied, completed,* and מִלֵּא, which means *fulfilled* and to *set with jewels.* When מל is combined with the energy intelligence of ב, there results מְלַבֵּב, which means *enticing, endearing, inviting, heartwarming.* When מל is combined with the energy intelligence of ג there results מֵלַג, which means *boiling water* and is the verb to *benefit.*

How is the desire to receive for oneself alone restricted? By boiling the water, rising up over the negative emotions. And what does this create? It creates a benefit. Combining with the energy intelligence force of ה results in מִלָּה, which means *word.* Combining with the energy intelligence force of ל forms the biblical verb מָלַל, which means to *say, speak, talk, utter,* or *articulate.* Combining with ץ forms מֶלַץ, which means *eloquent speech.* For it is by words and speech that we communicate our conscious desire to the cosmic subconscious mind for its manifestation. Combining with the energy intelligence of ח results in מֶלַח, which means *salt.* And what is salt used for? It is used for seasoning and preserving food, the food of the conscious mind. That

---

39. Exodus 40:34.
40. Ezekiel 43:5, 2 Chronicles 7:1.
41. Deuteronomy 34:9.
42. 1 Kings 8:11, Ezekiel 44:4, 2 Chronicles 7:2.
43. 2 Chronicles 5:14.

is exactly what the manifested structure, order, and form is, a time-preservation of the conscious mind.

When combined with the energy intelligence of ט it forms מֶלֶט, which means to *escape, run away,* and *be saved.* Thus when combined with ט, which itself represents goodness, we desire to receive in order to impart and thereby escape from the desire to receive for oneself alone. Also formed is מֶלֶט, which means *cement,* and the root מלט, which means "to cement." For the communication of our conscious desires to the cosmic subconscious mind cements our reality to the consequences that these desires have. From this binding, there is no escape.

When combined with ך, there forms the root מלך, which means to be a *king,* to *reign,* or *rule.* There forms מֶלֶךְ which means king, *sovereign ruler,* or *monarch.* The conscious mind is the ruler. Also formed is מֶלֶךְ, which means *trifle, something of no value.*

The structure and form brought into reality and manifested by the desires of the conscious mind in and of themselves form a kingdom having no intrinsic value. They are a trifle. The real value lies in what they symbolize. And this is related to the desires and intentions of the conscious mind. The structure and form only serve the mechanism through which the light is revealed. That which is of value is the light, for that is the Godliness in us. It is the Divine spark within, the Godliness that is our true identity. And when we identify with Godliness, we realize that it is only through physical existence that Godliness can manifest. And in physical existence it is the *nourishment* given to our bodies that permits us to act in ways in which Godliness can manifest.

Substance or *matter* in Hebrew is גֶשֶׁם. Body in Aramaic is גִשְׁמָה[44] and also the word גּוּף.[45] Furthermore, when the nourishment of ג advances to *cosmic nourishment,* ש, the word גֶשֶׁם changes to שֶׁמֶשׁ, which means *sun.* Now the sun is partially responsible for nourishing our physical existence. Rain is also partially responsible for nourishing our physical existence. And the word for *rain* in Hebrew is גֶשֶׁם.[46] Scripture says:

---

44. Daniel 3:28, 4:30, 5:21, 7:11.
45. Nehemiah 7:3, 1 Chronicles 10:12.
46. Leviticus 26:4.

If in My statutes you walk and My commandments you keep
and you do them, then I will give you *rains* in their season
and the land shall yield her produce, and the trees of the
field shall yield their fruit. And your threshing shall reach
unto the vintage, and the vintage shall reach unto sowing
time; and you shall eat your bread with satiety, and dwell
in safety in your land. And I will give peace in the land.[47]

Also, note that the root to *carry out*, to *realize*, to *effect*, or to
execute is נשם.

All this reinforces that it is only through physical existence that
the Divine light can be revealed and it is the *nourishment* we are given
that makes for the possibility that we can reveal the Divine light, a
revealment that happens when we make use of this nourishment by
properly carrying out our thoughts, speech, and action.

---

47. Leviticus 26:3-6.

דָלֶת

Dalet ד: Physicality

The fourth letter of the Hebrew alphabet is ד, which is spelled דָלֶת.
The word דָלֶת is cognate with the word דֶלֶת, which means *door, gate,
portal,* or *entrance.*

> And Lot went out at the *door* to them and shut the door
> after him.[1]

> And they strongly urged the man, Lot, and came near to
> break the *door*. But the men put out their hand and pulled
> Lot into the house to them and shut the *door*.[2]

> Then his master shall bring him to the judges; he shall also
> bring him to the *door*, or to the *door* post; and his master
> shall bore his ear through with an awl; and he shall serve
> him for ever.[3]

> And it shall be, if he say to thee, I will not go away from
> thee: because he loves thee and thy house, because he is
> happy with thee; then thou shalt take an awl, and thrust it
> through his ear to the *door*, and he shall be thy servant for
> ever.[4]

The gematria of דָלֶת is 434. This is the gematria of the word
בְּבֵיתֶךָ which means *into your house.*[5]

> And thou shalt teach them diligently to thy children, and
> shalt talk of them when thou sittest *in thy house*, and when
> thou walkest by the way, and when thou liest down, and
> when thou risest up.[6]

---

1. Genesis 19:6.
2. Genesis 19:9,10.
3. Exodus 21:6.
4. Deuteronomy 15:17.
5. Genesis 31:41, Exodus 7:28, Numbers 18:11, 18:13, Deuteronomy 6:7, 11:19,
21:13, 22:8, 25:14.
6. Deuteronomy 6:7.

> And thou shalt teach them to thy children, speaking of them when thou doest sit *in thy house* and when thou doest walk by the way, when thou liest down, and when thou risest up.[7]

> Thou shalt not have in thy bag diverse weights, a great and a small. Thou shalt not have *in thy house* diverse measures, a great and a small. But thou shalt have a perfect and just weight, a perfect and just measure shalt thou have: that thy days may be lengthened in the land which the Lord thy God gives thee.[8]

Through the door, we welcome guests into our house. That which is in our house we uplift and make sacred; we *sanctify* it and we *hallow* it. The word for *to sanctify* or *to hallow* is לְקַדֵּשׁ, a word whose gematria is also 434.

> And this is the thing that thou shalt do to them *to hallow* them, to minister to me in the priest's office.[9]

> And they shall eat those things with which atonement was made to consecrate and *to sanctify* them.[10]

The biblical word תֵּלֵד is the third person feminine future of the root ילד and it also has the gematria of 434 and means *shall bear* or *shall give birth to* a child. It is that which we bear or give birth to that is the guest whom we let into our house.

> Then Abraham fell upon his face, and laughed, and said in his heart: "Shall a child be born to him that is a hundred years old? and shall Sara, who is ninety years old, *give birth*?[11]

> By my covenant will I establish with Isaac whom Sara *shall bear* to thee at this time next year.[12]

---

7. Deuteronomy 11:19.
8. Deuteronomy 25:13-14.
9. Exodus 29:1.
10. Exodus 29:33.
11. Genesis 17:17.
12. Genesis 17:21.

And it shall be, that the firstborn which she *gives birth* to shall succeed in the name of his brother who is dead, that his name be not wiped out in Israel.[13]

When the word דֶלֶת is spelled out as דָלֶת לָמֶד תָו the total has the gematria of 914. This is the gematria of the biblical word וּמִמִּשְׁפַּחֹתָם, which means *and of their families.*[14] From this we learn that ד, *physical existence*, is the spiritual door through which each of us individually enters to give birth and bear, the child by which we extend our spirituality in the family of the Divine of which we are a part. It is, therefore, the door to the four-letter Tetragrammaton יְ־הֹ־וָ־הֹ. For physical existence is the door for the transcendent יְ־הֹ־וָ־הֹ to project into time and conditioned physical existence. It is we who open that door.

The mechanism of the door is a response to the organic activity of ג. Thus the ד *draws out,* דלה, as water is drawn out from a well. ד is a door that draws and takes into itself that which it draws out of the ג.

Now a priest of Midian had seven daughters, and they would come to *draw* water and fill the troughs to water their father's flock. When the girls returned to Reuel their father, he asked them, "Why have you returned so early today?" They answered, "An Egyptian rescued us from the shepherds. He even *drew* water for us and watered the flock."[15]

The purposes of a man's heart are deep waters, but a man of understanding *draws* them out.[16]

The interpretation of ד drawing out is supported by the Talmud.

And why is the roof of the ד stretched out toward the ג? Because he [the poor] must make himself available to him.[17]

---

13. Deuteronomy 25:6.
14. Leviticus 25:45.
15. Exodus 2:19.
16. Proverbs 20:5.
17. *The Babylonian Talmud, Seder Moed,* vol. 1, *Shabbat* (104a), trans. H. Freedman (London: Soncino Press, 1938), p. 500.

The ד is composed of the vowel פַּתָח, which can be interpreted as meaning *opening*, פֶּתַח, for its roof, and the vowel סֶגוֹל, which can be interpreted to mean *treasure, property, possession*, or *remedy*, סְגֻלָּה, or *adaptation* or *adjustment*, סִגּוּל, for its side. And that is the reason that the side of the ד is thicker in the middle and not just a straight line.

The *Bahir* interprets the word פְּתָחֵי as *openings* rather than doors in the verse

> O gates, lift up your heads! Up high, you everlasting doors, so the King of glory may come in.[18]

We read:

> It is thus written: "The openings of the World." There He placed a Patach above and a Segol below. It is for this reason that it is thick.

> What is the Patach? It is an opening. What is meant by an opening? This is the direction of north, which is open to all the world. It is the gate from which good and evil emerge.[19]

Rabbi Kaplan explains:

> The letter ד consists of two lines, one from right to left on top, and the other straight down on the right side. The first line connects חָכְמָה, wisdom, to בִּינָה, understanding, while the second line connects חָכְמָה, wisdom, to חֶסֶד, love. The vowel associated with חָכְמָה, wisdom, is Patach, while Segol is associated with חֶסֶד, love.

> The word דֶלֶת means door, while the word פֶּתַח means opening. Since חָכְמָה, wisdom, represents our highest perception of the Divine, it is God's opening to reveal Himself.

---

18. Psalms 24:7.
19. *The Bahir*, trans. and comm. Rabbi Aryeh Kaplan (Northvale, NJ: Jason Aronson, 1995), pp. 13-14.

Segol is related to the word Segulah, a remedy that works for no apparent reason. Segol thus parallels the Sefirah of חֶסֶד, love, which gives freely, even without reason.[20]

From this we realize the spiritual distinction between entranceway or opening and door. The door is that which is in the entranceway and moves to allow what is on one side of the entranceway to pass through and get to the other side. The door stands in the entranceway to our house, בּ. Rabbi Ginsburgh explains that

> the full meaning of the ד is the door through which the humble enter into the realization of God's dwelling place below.[21]

The numerical value of ד is 4. The *physical* world is composed of four elements: fire, air, water, and earth. These four correspond to the four basic chemical elements of life: carbon, which is fire, since the basis of organic matter is carbon and what is alive has within it the fire of life; oxygen, which is air, since it is the component of air that is the breath of life; hydrogen, which is water, since it is the dominant element in water; and nitrogen, which is earth, since it forms the basis of what nourishes the earth. And interestingly enough, the atomic numbers of these chemical elements are 6,8,1, and 7, respectively. So they sum to the 22 letters of the Hebrew alphabet.[22]

The inner side of ד is hollow and empty[23] just like physicality, which, in and of itself, is hollow and empty. *Physical existence* is only דָּבָר, a *thing*, an *affair*. As physicality, ד resists its own *destruction*, דֶּבֶר. It acts as a door remaining open to energies that would nurture it and staying shut to energies that would destroy it. But the outer side of the ד is complete.[24] This tells us that ד is a door to spirituality. For the *physical* is the secret hiding place of the *spiritual*.

20. Ibid., p. 113.
21. Rabbi Yitzchak Ginsburgh, *The Hebrew Letters* (Jerusalem: Gal Einai Publications, 1992), p. 67.
22. Ibid., p. 75.
23. Rabbi Jacob Ben Jacob Ha-Kohen, "Explanation of the Letters," in *The Early Kabbalah*, trans. Ronald Kiener (New York: Paulist Press, 1986), p. 157.
24. Ibid.

This is its revealed meaning.

The word דֶלֶת is related to the word דַלּוּת, which means *poverty* or *leanness.*[25,26] Pure physicality is poor and deficient, for it can receive but it cannot give. Therefore, in and of itself, physical existence cannot resemble God. Only when *physical existence* is coupled with the organic beneficent energy of ג can the door open and the connection to the Divine be made through the י, which is on the tip of the ד. This is the דִבֵּר, the *commandment.* This is the דֶרֶך, the *way,* the *road,* or *path* in which the energy intelligence of ד is to be used.

> For I have chosen him, so that he will direct his children
> and his household after him to keep the *way* of the Lord
> by doing what is right and just, so that the Lord will bring
> about for Abraham what He has promised him.[27]
>
> Teach them the decrees and laws, and show them the *way*
> to live and the duties they are to perform.[28]
>
> Walk in all the *ways* that the Lord your God has com-
> manded you, so that you may live and prosper and prolong
> your days in the land that you will possess.[29]
>
> Observe the commands of the Lord your God, walking in his
> *ways* and revering Him. For the Lord your God is bringing
> you into a good land – a land with streams and pools of
> water, with springs flowing in the valleys and hills; a land
> with wheat and barley, vines and fig trees, pomegranates,
> olive oil and honey; a land where bread will not be scarce
> and you will lack nothing.[30]
>
> And now, O Israel, what does the Lord your God ask of you
> but to revere the Lord your God, to walk in all his *ways,*
> to love him, to serve the Lord your God with all your heart

---

25. *Shabbat* 104a says that ד ג means גְּמוֹל דַּלִּים, be generous to the poor.
26. *The Zohar,* vol. 1, trans. Harry Sperling and Maurice Simon (London: Soncino Press, 1978), p. 12.
27. Genesis 18:19.
28. Exodus 18:20.
29. Deuteronomy 5:33.
30. Deuteronomy 8:6-9.

and with all your soul, and to observe the Lord's commands and decrees that I am giving you today for your own good.[31]

Rabbi Yosef Schneersohn of Lubavitch teaches:

All material things are an analogy for the understanding of Godliness. In truth, of course, everything is Godliness and Godliness is everything. But in order to make this comprehensible the Almighty created a *physical* world comprising many components, each of which is an analogy for the understanding of Godliness.[32]

From this we can conclude that it is our own understanding that is the door that stands in the entranceway that always is. It is our degree of consciousness that determines whether our door is open or whether our door is closed. It is our own degree of consciousness that determines whether we relate and act in physical reality in a manner consistent with its analogy for the understanding of Godliness.

The concealed meaning of ד is לת. This is cognate to לָדַת[33] which is the infinitive construct form of the verb root ילד, which means to *bring forth*, to *bear*, to *beget*. *Physicality* is what is brought forth by the inner essence. And when we convert physicality itself to serve as the inner essence, then it becomes the garment of our giving. Thus it should come as no surprise that לָתֵת, to *be giving*, is the gerund form of the root נתן, meaning "to give." Therefore, physicality is the inner *sanctuary*, דְּבִיר.

And the priests brought in the ark of the covenant of the Lord to its place, into the *sanctuary* of the house to the most holy place under the wings of the keruvim.[34]

And for the entering of the inner *sanctuary* he made doors of olive wood: the lintel and side posts forming five sides.[35]

---

31. Deuteronomy 10:12-13.
32. Rabbi Yosef Yitzchak Schneersohn, *Likkutei Dibburim*, vol. 1, trans. Uri Kaploun (Brooklyn, NY: Kehot Publication Society, 1987), p. 150.
33. 1 Samuel 4:19.
34. 1 Kings 8:6, 2 Chronicles 5:7.
35. 1 Kings 6:31.

Hear the voice of my supplications, when I cry to Thee,
when I lift up my hands towards Thy holy *sanctuary*.[36]

לת is an abbreviation of לֹא תַעֲשֶׂה, which means a negative precept,
a "don't." Don't think that physical existence, materiality, is all there
is. Don't treat physical existence only with the hardness of physical
existence. Indeed, an aspect of the concealed meaning is given by the
root לתת, which means to *malt* and לֶתֶת, which means malt. Malt is
a grain softened by being steeped in water and allowed to germinate.
It is used in brewing and distilling liquor. Liquor contains one kind of
essence of the grain. As it is with the grain, so must it be with physical
existence. We must soften it and permit it to germinate by holding
open the door. We must allow our spirituality to germinate and give
birth into a life with materiality.

Further understanding of ד can be obtained by observing how it
combines with other letter energy intelligences. ה is the energy intelligence of the power of being and ח is the energy intelligence of life.
When ד combines with ה and ח it forms the root דחה, which in biblical
Hebrew means to *push away* or *thrust*.

Let them be as chaff before the wind: the angel of the Lord
thrusting them.[37]

Thou didst *push* me hard and I nearly fell: but the Lord
helped me.[38]

The wicked is *thrust* down in his calamity: but the righteous
has hope in his death.[39]

Physical existence is *possessive* and *acquisitive*. And it is this possessiveness and acquisitiveness that we must thrust away. But just as we
thrust away this possessiveness we can understand that we thrust out
or express *physical existence* through being and living. That is, the
power of being and life express themselves through physical existence

---

36. Psalms 28:2.
37. Psalms 35:5.
38. Psalms 118:13.
39. Proverbs 14:32.

and nourish physical existence, which itself is the containment of or the vessel for the unbridled pulsating force.

The root for the verb to love is אהבה. This says that love can be understood as a packaging with the container archetype ב, of the infinite energy pulsation of א, and with the being of ה. But if we precede this with a ד, we become more concerned with the container than with the life, and we produce דְּאָבָה, which is the word for *sorrow, anxiety, grief, sadness, anguish, distress, regret.*

> Therefore they shall come and sing in the height of Zion, and shall flow to the bounty of the Lord, for wheat, and for wine, and for oil, and for the young of the flock and of the herd: and their soul shall be like a watered garden; and they shall not languish in *sorrow* any more. Then shall the virgin rejoice in the dance, both young men and old together: for I will turn their mourning to joy, and will comfort them, and make them rejoice from their *sorrow*. And I will satiate the soul of the priests with fatness, and my people shall be satisfied with my goodness, says the Lord.[40]

What is the cosmic meaning of sorrow? The Hebrew code tells us that sorrow is something expressed in physical existence, ד, which is energized by the undifferentiated pulsations of א, maintained in the archetype container ב, and given a power of being by ה. And over what is the sorrow expressed? It is expressed over ד, over something the ego perceives to be wrong in the illusion of its materiality. But since everything that happens to us happens by the hand of God, and God is all beneficent, whatever happens must be for our ultimate good. We wallow in sorrow only when we forget this. But when we get to the deep meaning our sorrow changes to joy.

What happens when the ב of דְּאָבָה is exchanged with a ג? The word דְּאָבָה changes to דְּאָגָה, which means *worry, anxiety, uneasiness, fear,* and *concern for.*

> The people will eat rationed food in *anxiety* and drink rationed water in despair.[41]

---

40. Jeremiah 31:11-13.
41. Ezekiel 4:16.

Tremble as you eat your food, and shudder in *fear* as you drink your water.[42]

They will eat their food in *anxiety* and drink their water in despair, for their land will be stripped of everything in it because of the violence of all who live there.[43]

Here we have replaced the archetype ⊐, container, by the archetype ג, organic beneficence and wealth. When beneficence and wealth are expressed and formed into *physical existence* without wrapping them with the Divine, we are left with only ego, which feels an uncertainty and the ego worries about, feels uneasy about, is anxious about, and fears what might happen to its material existence that our beneficence and wealth have helped form.

When duality, ⊐, is maintained in the archetype container ⊐ and permitted a physical existence ר, there results the word דְבַב, which means *hatred*. We can hate only that which is not truly part of ourselves, something that we perceive to be really not of our essence. And what is our true essence? It is the Godliness and Divine spark within. This Godliness is not dual. It is one.

The word for *saying, talking, word, speech, talk,* or *utterance* is דִבּוּר. This is quite revealing, since it is telling us that utterance has cosmic implications. By an utterance we bring into physical existence, ר, contain it, ⊐, and connect it, ו, to the cosmic container ר. When this happens, the connection ו changes to a י indicating that the Divine source א has projected into *physical existence*. The change produced by the action generates the word דְבִיר, which is the western part of the temple, the inner sanctuary, the Holy of Holies.

The word to *stick together, cling, adhere, paste, glue* or *join* together is דָבַק. That which is growing ק, maintained in the archetype container ⊐, and formed in the world of manifestation must stay where it is. It must be attached. And the attachments limit the being of the energy intelligence of ר. Only by setting our desires to receive in order to share do we free the letter energy intelligence of ר from its physical attachments and give it the freedom to cleave to the Divine.

---

42. Ezekiel 12:18.
43. Ezekiel 12:19.

Now choose life, so that you and your children may live and that you may love the Lord your God, listen to His voice, and *cleave* to Him. For the Lord is your life and He will give you many years in the land He swore to give to your fathers, Abraham, Isaac and Jacob.[44]

---

44. Deuteronomy 31:19-20.

Hey ה: Power of Being

The fifth letter of the Hebrew alphabet is Hey, ה, which can be spelled either as הֵא or הֵי. As a prefix ה functions as the definite article "the." As a suffix, ה is the indicator for the feminine gender of a noun. As a word, הֵא means *lo*, or *behold*, or *here is*. Joseph uses the word הֵא in speaking to the Egyptian people, giving them seed to sow their next crop and declaring that one fifth of what they harvest must be returned to Pharaoh.

> Behold, this day I have bought you and your land for Pharaoh.
> *Here is* seed for you, so you can plant the land.[1]

Joseph who speaks this verse is the patriarch associated with the Sephirah Foundation, יְסוֹד. This Sephirah is the agency through which our feelings of moving toward or away and the balance of these feelings come together with our commitment to do something about these feelings. In יְסוֹד we make a plan for how these feelings and commitments will be manifested.

Manifesting these feelings is our *power of being*, the power of self-expression. And with this power of self-expression we plant the land. Planting the land means expressing ourselves. And for what purpose do we express ourselves? We express ourselves to live, to give the gift of the seed. We express ourselves to give the gift of self.[2]

Furthermore,

> The gift itself is the relation and expression of self drawing
> the receiver into the essence of the giver.[3]

The garments of our expression are thoughts, words, and actions. That which is not manifest we bring into our awareness and our consciousness by our thoughts. By words and actions we can bring what is in our thoughts to the awareness and consciousness of others.

---

1. Genesis 47:23.
2. Rabbi Yitzchak Ginsburgh, *The Hebrew Letters* (Jerusalem: Gal Einai Publications, 1992), p. 80.
3. Ibid.

Ezekiel uses the word הָא in telling the Israelites how they did not remember to serve the Lord and because they did not remember and because of the abominations they did do, terrible things will happen.

> Because thou hast not remembered the days of thy youth, but thou hast enraged me in all these things, *behold*, I also will recompense thy ways upon thy head, says the Lord God.[4]

Daniel uses the word הָא in telling what King Nebuchadnezzar exclaimed when, because they would not serve his golden idols, he ordered the three men Shadrach, Meshach and Abednego into the seven times hotter furnace. After the men were put into the furnace the king said:

> *Lo!* I see four men walking around in the fire, unbound and unharmed, and the fourth looks like a son of the gods.[5]

These verses tell us that in this land of Egypt, we are given seed to plant the land. But we must not act in a way that exasperates God. For that carries terrible consequences. And when we serve God by the gift of our expressions, we will, in effect, walk in the furnace of Egypt unharmed.

In Aramaic, הָא means *this* or *that*. Since הא has the numerical value of 6, ה is related to the letter energy intelligence of ו, whose numerical value is also 6. ו has the meaning of *connection* and *unification*. From this we learn that in every this or that we must make connection and unification by drawing down the Godliness into the this or that.

The letter ה is alternately spelled הֵי. The word יה does not occur in Scripture, with any vocalization. But with the letters reversed, יָה is the name of God associated with the Sephirah חָכְמָה, Wisdom.

Because יָה is my strength and protection [וְזִמְרָת].[6] He

---

4. Ezekiel 16:43.

5. Daniel 3:25.

6. Most translations render "my strength and my song." Some render, consistent with Rashi, "my might and vengeance." See, for example, Zalman Sorotzkin, *Insights in the Torah*, vol. 2, *Shemos* (Brooklyn, NY: Mesorah Publications, 1993), p. 161.

became to me my salvation [deliverance].[7] This is my God [אֵל] and I will enshrine Him, my father's God [אֱלֹהֵי], I will exalt Him.[8]

The usual translation of וְזִמְרָת is *song*. But the root זמר has other meanings than song. It has a second meaning of *praise* or *object of praise*. It has a third meaning of *choice things* as in Genesis 43:11. It has a fourth meaning of to *prune*, to *cut off*, or to *pinch off*. And it has a fifth meaning as *strength, power,* or *protection*.[9] Cassuto understands זִמְרָת as זִמְרָתִי, which means my *help* in the sense of *power to help*.[10] Indeed the verse that precedes the phrase "God is my strength and protection" of Psalms 118:14, is

Thou pushed me hard and I nearly fell; but the Lord *helped* me.[11]

El connects Psalms 118, verses 13 and 14, the following way.

In order to illustrate how good it is to trust in the Lord, and that there is no other savior, David tells his people to consider his own example. He turns to his evil urge, i.e. yetzer hara, and says "though you have repeatedly pushed me, trying to make me fall (referring to the temptation to kill Nabal and Saul who both had wanted him dead) God has assisted me and I have not given in to this urge. (compare 1 Samuel 25:31, and chapter 26, 10-13) In all these instances it was the 2 lettered name of God who has become my salvation. The same God who has been my salvation has at the same time been zimur, zimra, i.e. the cutting down,

---

7. See also Psalms 118:14 and Isaiah 12:2 for the identical construction עָזִּי וְזִמְרָת יָהּ וַיְהִי לִי לִישׁוּעָה.
8. Exodus 15:2.
9. R. Laird Harris, Gleason Archer, and Bruce Waltke, eds., *Theological Wordbook of the Old Testament*, vol. 4 (Chicago: Moody Press, 1990), p. 91.
10. U. Cassuto, *A Commentary on the Book of Exodus* (Jerusalem: Magnes Press, The Hebrew University, 1987), p. 174.
11. Psalms 118:13.

pruning of my enemies. I merited this because I battled my
evil urges.[12]

So here we can understand that our help comes from the agency of
God called חָכְמָה, Wisdom. And with wisdom we exclaim: This is my
אֵל, my God. Thus with wisdom we exclaim that God is the eternal
and everlasting force causing the continuing flow of ongoing existence
to all that is transitory.[13] Thereby we open a path to bring the Godly
light to חֶסֶד, loving-kindness, since אֵל is the name of God associated
with the Sephirah חֶסֶד. We bring the Godly light to חֶסֶד by וְאַנְוֵהוּ,
I will enshrine Him. I will build a habitation or dwelling for Him.[14]
This means that in me I will build a temple and I will manifest loving-
kindness. By so doing, God will dwell in me. The God Who will dwell
in me shall be my father's God, אֱלֹהֵי. The Sephirah called father is
חָכְמָה, Wisdom. And my father's God will I exalt. This means that
by acting with loving-kindness I will upraise (exalt) the Godly light in
חֶסֶד.

Related to this there is an interesting interpretation for the word
בְּהִבָּרְאָם, which appears in the Pentateuch with a smaller ה in the
phrase:

אֵלֶּה תוֹלְדוֹת הַשָּׁמַיִם וְהָאָרֶץ בְּהִבָּרְאָם

These are the generations of the heaven and the earth *in
having created them* [when they were created].[15]

The letters בְּהִבָּרְאָם can be rearranged forming the word בְּאַבְרָהָם,
which means *for Abraham* or *for the sake of Abraham*. Abraham is the
patriarch associated with the Sephirah Loving-kindness, חֶסֶד.[16]

---

12. *The Book of Psalms with Romemot El*, vol. 2, trans. Eliyahu Munk (Jerusalem:
Eliyahu Munk, Shalom Aleichem 4), p. 878.
13. *Sforno Commentary on the Torah*, trans. Raphael Pelcovitz (Brooklyn, NY:
Mesorah Publications, 1987), p. 315.
14. Ibid.
15. Genesis 2:4.
16. *Midrash Rabbah, Genesis*, vol. 1 (12:9) (London: Soncino Press, 1983), pp.
94-95.

When King Hezekiah was deathly ill and recovered after praying and weeping before God, he wrote a psalm using the God name יָהּ. He begins by describing the meaning of his sickness. He said:

> In the desolation of my days will I go into the gates of the grave. I am deprived of the rest of my years. I will not see יָהּ, the Eternal. יָהּ, the Eternal is in the land of the living. I will no longer look upon men, [but I will be] with those who dwell in withdrawal.[17]

So here we see that Hezekiah says that if he should die he will no longer be able to raise the Godly light of loving-kindness, חֶסֶד. Therefore, he will no longer be in the land of the living.

After the Israelites quarreled with Moses because they thirsted for water, they wondered whether the Lord was present among them. Rabbi Tzvi Elimelech of Dinov teaches that their question was: Is or is not God with us? indicating that they were questioning the existence of God.[18] Then Moses struck the rock to make water issue from the rock so that the people could drink. Immediately after, in Refidim, Amalek came and fought with the Israelites. When the people of Amalek were overwhelmed, the Lord said to Moses to inscribe in a document: "I will utterly blot out the memory of Amalek from under heaven." So when Moses built an altar, he said the altar means:

> Because [God's] hand is on the throne of יָהּ, the Lord will make war with Amalek from generation to generation.[19]

So from this we learn that Amalek is the root of evil in the world. Amalek tries to hide God by making us doubt God. When we doubt that God is present among us, Amalek, who has waited for us,[20] springs on us and we have to fight a crisis.

This interpretation associating Amalek with doubt is reinforced by its gematria. Amalek, עֲמָלֵק, has the gematria of 240. The root ספק,

---

17. Isaiah 38:11.
18. Avraham Yaakov Finkel, *The Great Chasidic Masters* (Northvale, NJ: Jason Aronson, 1992), p. 131.
19. Exodus 17:16.
20. See Deuteronomy 25:17-18.

which means to *doubt*, also has the gematria of 240.[21] When we doubt God, we inevitably will not do good. So Amalek symbolizes evil.[22]

The phrase אֵל אַחֵר, which means *other god* also has the gematria of 240.[23] Literally the phrase means the hinder or the back part of god. The root אחר means to *be behind, delay, tarry, detain,* or *procrastinate.* From this we learn that it is heresy (other god) to delay our faith in God. For delay of faith is the seed of doubt. The place, Refidim, where Amalek first fought with the Israelites is also relevant to understanding the effect of doubt. For Refidim, רְפִידִם, can be understood as the combination of two words: רפה, the root meaning *to be weakened,* and יָדַיִם, the plural of the noun יָד, meaning *hand, power,* or *strength.*[24]

Three common expressions involving these two words are: רְפוֹת יָדַיִם, which means *weakness, feebleness,* or *slackness;* רְפֵה יָדַיִם, which means *weak* or *powerless;* and רָפוּ יָדָיו, which means to be *weakened, disheartened,* or *discouraged.* And this is related to יָד since it is by the fullness of wisdom, חָכְמָה, the Sephirah whose associated God name is יָהּ, that doubt, and its consequence weakness, has no room to exist in us.

יָהּ has the gematria of 15. The word וּבֹאוּ also has the gematria of 15, and is the Kal second person masculine plural imperative form with conjunctive prefix for the root בוא, which means to *come.* Pharaoh, in talking to Joseph about getting Joseph's family to come to Egypt, uses the word וּבֹאוּ.

> Take your father and your households *and come* to me; I
> will give you the best of the land of Egypt and you shall
> live off the fat of the land.[25]

When God speaks to Moses about what to tell Pharaoh relative to the

21. Rabbi Matityahu Glazerson, *Hebrew: The Source of Languages* (Jerusalem: Yerid HaSefarim, 1990), p. 77.
22. Rabbi Elijah Judah Schochet, *Amalek: The Enemy Within* (Los Angeles: Mimetav Press, 1991), p. 17.
23. Rabbi Nachman, *Likutey Moharan,* vol. 1B, trans. Moshe Mykoff (Jerusalem: Breslov Research Institute, 1989), p. 136.
24. *Pesikta de-Rab Kahana,* trans. William G. Braude and Israel J. Kapstein (Philadelphia: Jewish Publication Society of America, 1975), p. 39.
25. Genesis 45:18.

next plague of frogs, God uses the word וּבָאוּ, which is the Kal third person plural perfect with conjunctive prefix of the root בוא.

> The Nile shall swarm with frogs *and they shall come* up and enter your palace, your bedchamber and your bed, the houses of your courtiers and your people, and your ovens and your kneading bowls.[26]

The word וּבָאוּ is used by Moses and the elders of Israel when they tell the Israelites the Godly blessings that will come to the Israelites when they heed the word of God and the curses that will come to the Israelites when they do not heed the word of God.

> *And shall come* upon you and take effect all these blessings if you will but heed the word of the Lord your God.[27]

> But, if you do not heed the word of the Lord your God to observe faithfully all His commandments and laws which I enjoin upon you this day, *then shall come* upon you and take effect all these curses.[28]

From this we learn that we ourselves come to Egypt, the land the limitation. Pharaoh gives us the best of this land. And when the Pharaoh within us has a hard heart, God brings the plagues upon us, individual by individual. When we heed God's words and faithfully observe His commandments, then God will bring blessings upon us. And if we do not heed God's words and do not obey His commandments, then God brings curses upon us. And all this happens through the agency of the letter energy intelligence of ה.

The letter energy intelligence ה is intimately connected with the *power of being* for the root to *be* is היה. From this we learn that it is the mechanism of the ה by which the Divine, which is associated with the letter י, does manifest in our existence. For from the letter intelligence of ה, the Divine expresses and we experience this expression as a *Divine manifestation*.

Associated with this is the way the Talmud explains the verse

---

26. Exodus 7:28.
27. Deuteronomy 28:2.
28. Deuteronomy 28:15.

These are the generations of the heaven and the earth in having created them [בְּהִבָּרְאָם].[29]

in terms of another verse.

Trust ye in the Lord for ever; for in יָהּ the Lord is an everlasting rock.[30]

The Talmud interprets בְּהִבָּרְאָם, in having created them, as בְּהֵי בְּרָאָם, which means: with the letter ה, an abbreviation for יְ־הֹ־וָ־הֹ, did God create them.[31]

> It implies that if one puts his trust in the Holy One, blessed be He, behold He is unto him as a refuge in this world and in the world to come. . . . [Since] He created them with the ה; hence I may say that this world was created with the ה and the future world with the י.[32]

Thus, God brings the creation into being through the agency of the letter ה. This is the revealed meaning of the letter energy intelligence ה.

The shape of the letter ה is composed of three lines, one separated from the other two. The three lines are the three garments, the means of expression, of the soul. The garments are thought, speech, and action. The line separated from the other two is the line that stands for action. This is because action has a more separate existence from thought and speech.

The letter intelligence of ה can be understood as being formed with a י for its left leg and a ר for the remainder. The ר is the letter energy intelligence of *materiality*, while י is the letter energy intelligence of spirituality. When materiality and spirituality are married, there results ה. This teaches us to always combine the physical with the spiritual to sanctify and make our life holy. But if we do not combine the material with the spiritual, then we depart from holiness. Rabbi Nachman teaches that the letter ה

---

29. Genesis 2:4.
30. Isaiah 26:4.
31. *Midrash Rabbah, Genesis*, vol. 1 (12:10), p. 96.
32. *The Babylonian Talmud, Seder Kodashim*, vol. 1, *Menahot* (29b), trans. Eli Cashdan (London: Soncino Press, 1938), p. 191.

resembles a porch {Rashi: open on the bottom}. Anyone who wants to depart, let him depart! {Rashi: Whoever wants to depart from it for evil ways, departs.}[33]

There is a small space between the ' and the ד of the ה. This small gap is important for it is the space through which the light of the Divine is always able to reach us, no matter how dark or bad things may seem. Rabbi Nachman teaches:

> Why is its [left] leg suspended? It is because if the sinner returns to God, he is brought up. {Rashi: He is brought up through the upper opening, between the leg within [the ה] and its roof.} Why not bring him up through the other one? It will not help {Rashi: Why not bring him up through the lower opening, the one through which he went out? It will not help because when someone comes to purify himself, he needs help in overcoming the evil inclination. He is therefore aided with an additional opening}.[34]

This same gap is the window of repentance.[35] It is the space through which we carry out our repentance and reenter the world of the living.[36] The gap is also the shape of the opening in the eye of man.[37] It enables us to see how to do according to the Will of the Holy One.

The letter intelligence ה can also be understood as being formed with a ו for the left leg and a ד for the remainder. The ו is the letter energy intelligence of connection and the ד is the letter energy intelligence of physical existence and materiality. Hence the letter intelligence ה links *physicality* to *spirituality*, to the Divine. The ד occurring in the

---

33. Rabbi Nachman, *Likutey Moharan*, vol. 10, trans. Moshe Mykoff (Jerusalem: Breslov Research Institute, 1993), p. 37.

34. Ibid., pp. 37-39.

35. Rabbi Matityahu Glazerson, *Repentance in Words and Letters* (Jerusalem: Yerid HaSefarim, 1992), p. 34.

36. Rabbi Matityahu Glazerson, *Letters of Fire*, trans. S. Fuchs (Jerusalem: Feldheim, 1991), p. 33.

37. Rabbi Jacob Ben Jacob Ha-Kohen, "Explanation of the Letters," in *The Early Kabbalah*, trans. Ronald Kiener (New York: Paulist Press, 1986), p. 159.

letter ה is the ד of אֶחָד, which means one, and the ו can be associated
with the six-word exclamation in Deuteronomy:[38]

שְׁמַע יִשְׂרָאֵל יְ־ה־וָ־ה אֱלֹהֵינוּ יְ־ה־וָ־ה אֶחָד

whose direct meaning is Hear! Israel. The Lord is Our God; the Lord
is One, and whose coded esoteric meaning we shall understand when
we study the letter energy intelligence ו as it relates to six Sephirot on
the Tree of Life.

The concealed meaning of the letter energy intelligence ה can be
understood by understanding the function of the א and י. When the
pulsating undifferentiated potential of the letter energy intelligence of
the א is completely thrust into the physical existence of that part of
what we are, there results the י, the letter energy intelligence of Divine
spirituality. And when ה spelled as הֵא is followed by a י, which is
packaged into the cosmic container ר, there results הֵאִיר, which is the
past form of the verb to *light*. We exercise our *power of being* by lighting
candles and shedding light whatever we do and wherever we go. This
light is not light that we ourselves create. This light is the light we
receive from the Divine through the tiny *gap* between the י and the ר
of the ה.

Although we do not create the light, we are able to *form* it and
reveal it. If we selfishly try to keep the light for ourselves, we will
only conceal the light and break the Divine connection by which we
can receive the light. We must choose the desire to receive the light in
order to share it, for the light is a flow and a flow that is held static is no
longer a flow. To participate in the flow, we cannot dam it up. Rather
we must give and surrender what we have to create the metaphysical
condition by which we are able to receive.

The most important word in which ה participates is the Tetragrammaton יְ־ה־וָ־ה.

There is an upper ה and a lower ה.[39]

The first ה is the upper *power of being*. The second ה is the lower
power of being. Each is united by the connection of the ו to permit the

---

38. Ibid., p. 158.
39. *The Bahir*, trans. and comm. Rabbi Aryeh Kaplan (Northvale, NJ: Jason
Aronson, 1995), p. 11.

ה

flow of the Divine spirituality of the י. The first ה corresponds to the giving hand. The second ה corresponds to the receiving hand.[40]

The letter ה is also related to the word *water* in the following verse:

> Let there be a firmament in the midst of the water that it may separate water from water.[41]

The Zohar explains this verse in the following way.

> Thereupon אל (God), the "right cluster" [חֶסֶד, Loving-kindness] אל נָדוֹל (Great God), spread forth from the midst of the water so complete this name אל and to combine with this extension, and so אל was extended into [גְבוּרָה] אֱלֹהִים by the addition of [הים]. These הים extended and became reversed so as to form lower waters יְמה. This extension which took place on the second day is the upper waters. The ה, י, מ form הַיָם (the sea), which is the upper waters. The reversal of these letters יָמָה (seaward), is the lower waters. When they were firmly established, all became one whole, and this name was extended to a number of places. The upper waters are male and the lower waters are female. At first they were commingled, but afterwards they were differentiated into upper and lower waters. This is the meaning of "אֱלֹהִים upper waters," and this is the meaning of "אֲדֹנָי lower waters"; and this is the meaning of upper ה and lower ה. . . . This is the name which is graven with the lettering י־ה־ו־ה to reconcile the upper with the lower waters, the upper with the lower ה; the insertion of the ו between them harmonises the two sides.[42]

We can explore the action of the letter energy ה by seeing how it combines with other letter energy intelligences. When the *power of being* of ה is combined with the archetype container of the letter energy intelligence ב the word הַב forms. This is the imperative form

---

40. Ibid., p. 104.
41. Genesis 1:6.
42. *The Zohar*, vol. 1, trans. Harry Sperling and Maurice Simon (London: Soncino Press, 1978), p. 75.

of the verb to *give*. Living is a giving process. When ה is combined with the letter energy intelligence of material existence ר, there results the word הֵד, which means *echo* or *reverberation*. We reveal the light by being a mirror and reverberating or echoing the light we receive. When ה is combined with the letter energy intelligence of movement ז, there results the root הזה, which means to *prophesy, perceive,* or *behold*. When ה is combined with the letter energy intelligence ט, there results הִטָּה which is the past form of the verb to *divert*. This tells us that it is a diversion to ever think that life can be completed. Since life is never completed, life must always be. Thus our essence, our soul, is eternal.

When ה is combined with the letter energy intelligence of ל, three different verbs form. The first is הלל, which means *praise, commend,* or *glorify*. The second is the root הלל, which means to *shine*, and the third is the root ההל, which means to *give light* or to *shed light*. In addition the word הִלָּה means *halo, crown, glory, radiance,* or *celestial light*. From this we learn that the purpose of הַלֵּל, praise, is to light up the greatness of the one being praised, for the word הַלְלוּיָה, *Hallelujah, Praise ye the Lord*, means הַלְלוּ, shining light on the יָהּ, God.[43] These are the obligations of the *power of being*. These are the ways by which we manifest the letter energy intelligence ה.

The letter energy intelligence מ is the archetype physical existence projected into the world of time and conditioned physical existence. It is the waters of the earth. When ה combines with מ, there results the word הָמַם, which means *frightened, terrified, shocked,* or *confounded*. Therefore, when we center our attention on the waters of the earth, on the emotions, when we put our foundation on the earth we will inevitably become frightened. For *separation* from the Divine leads one to be frightened. This teaches us that we must wrap ourselves around the Divine and become garments for the Divine.

When ה combines with the letter energy intelligence of ס, there results the noun הַס, which means *silence* and is also the imperative verb form of the verb הסה, which means to *be silent*.

> And the Lord is in His holy temple. Let all the earth *be silent* before Him.[44]

---

43. Rabbi Glazerson, *Hebrew: The Source of Languages*, p. 25.
44. Habakkuk 2:20.

Silence in the presence of the Lord God: for the day of the
Lord is at hand. The Lord has prepared a sacrificial feast,
He has bidden his guests purify themselves.[45]

Be silent all flesh before the Lord: for he has roused Himself
out of his holy habitation.[46]

This reminds us that about the ultimate mysteries we must be silent.
For what is revealed to each of us through our experience and understanding cannot be communicated through words to another. We have
no choice but to be silent.

When ה combines with the letter energy intelligence of ר, there
results the word הַר, which means *mountain*. When our *power of being*
is thrust into the cosmic container ר, there is an inevitable *spiritual
elevation*. For that is the way we walk on the mountain.

45. Zephaniah 1:7.
46. Zechariah 2:17.

Vav ו: Connection and Unification

The sixth letter of the Hebrew alphabet is Vav ו, spelled most commonly as וו, but also spelled as ואו and ויו. The letter ו is shaped like a nail, and the word וו is the word for *hook, peg,* or *nail.* It can be used as the conjunctive prefix *and.* It is also a conversive prefix that can time switch or time shift, changing a verb form that is in the past into one that is in the future and, as well a future into a past. Thereby it can be thought of as that letter energy intelligence that makes a *connection* in order to establish a time-transcending eternal *unification* and completion.

There is no vocalization of וו that appears in the Pentateuch or for that matter anywhere in Scripture. וו has the gematria of 12. The word הָבָה also has the gematria of 12 and means *come* in the sense of *get ready* or *prepare.* Rashi explains that every occurrence of הָבָה denotes a preparation of getting together to work for a common purpose, to unite for a common purpose.[1]

The word הָבָה was used by the generation of the people after the flood who had decided to journey from קֶדֶם, from the *east.* Now קֶדֶם also has the meaning of *ancient state, things of old.* This tells us that these people were leaving the God of Noah to establish a separate domain, for they refused to accept the Divinity of God.[2]

> And they said to one another: "*Come,* let us make bricks, and burn them thoroughly." And they had brick for stone, and bitumen they had for mortar. And they said: "*Come* let us build us a city and a tower, whose top may reach to heaven; and let us make us a name lest we be scattered abroad upon the face of the whole earth."[3]

The tower of Babel was intended to physically unify heaven and earth, by establishing a city in which all the people would live together and

---

1. Rashi, *Pentateuch and Rashi's Commentary, Genesis*, vol. 1, trans. Abraham ben Isaiah and Benjamin Sharfman (Brooklyn, NY: S.S. and R. Publishing, 1976), p. 94.
2. *Midrash Rabbah, Genesis*, vol. 1 (38:7) (London: Soncino Press, 1983), p. 306.
3. Genesis 11:3-4.

not be scattered throughout the earth. And what would give rise to this unification? A tower whose top reaches heaven on which they would make themselves a name. Here name means an idol. They were getting ready to build a tower on top of which would be an idol with a sword in its hand to wage war against God.[4] That is, the unification was to be void of God.

But such a unification is impossible. The unification of the energy intelligence of ו is the unification between God and us when we commit ourselves entirely to serve God. So it is no surprise when God says:

> Come, let us go down and there confound their language,
> that they may not understand one another's speech.[5]

This teaches us that any attempted unification, וּן, a unification without the א or without the י, is doomed to physical and spiritual failure.

When unification and connection are parallel to the word וָאן, things are different. Like וָאן, the word הַבוּ has a gematria of 13. It is the second person masculine Kal imperative of the root יהב, which means to *give*. Joseph uses the word הַבוּ in telling the Egyptians that he will give them bread in exchange for their cattle.

> *Give* your cattle and I will sell you food in exchange since
> your money is gone.[6]

When Moses is relating to the Israelites how their numbers had increased and that the burden for him to resolve all their disputes was too much for him to bear by himself, he tells the Israelites:

> *Give* to me wise, understanding, and experienced [respected,
> knowledgeable] men from your tribes and I will set them as
> your heads [over you].[7]

Just before Moses is about to die, he sings a song to the assembly of Israel.

---

4. *Midrash Rabbah, Genesis*, vol. 1 (38:6), p. 305.
5. Genesis 11:7.
6. Genesis 47:16.
7. Deuteronomy 1:13.

For I will proclaim the name of the Lord, *Give* to the greatness of our God.[8]

From these three instances of give, we can learn the dimensions of *unification* and *connection*. What is it that must be given? We must give of our livestock, of our wisdom, understanding, and experience, for the purpose of giving is to give to the greatness of our God, in everything that we do. That is, this unification and connection, this cleaving to God, is not just an affair in prayer. But it must be the essence of the everyday things we do, for the glory of God is revealed in these everyday, ordinary exchanges and relationships.

One of the most important words having gematria 13 is אֶחָד, *one*. The dimensions of one are many.

God called the light Day and the darkness He called Night. And there was evening and there was morning, *one* day.[9]

God said, "Let the water below the sky be gathered into *one* area, that the dry land may appear." And it was so.[10]

Hence the man leaves his father and mother and clings to his wife so that they become *one* flesh.[11]

You shall have *one* law for stranger and citizen alike: for I the Lord am your God.[12]

Hear! Israel. The Lord is our God; the Lord is *one*.[13]

This tells us that in unity we will find one time, the time of the present moment, which when lived to its fullest encompasses the past and the future and is therefore eternal. We have one land, the land where our consciousness has everything. We are one flesh, for we and our neighbor are not separate. We have one law that we are responsible for keeping. And we have one God who is the eternal fountain and rock of our existence. And how does this relate to unification? It is through

---

8. Deuteronomy 32:3.
9. Genesis 1:5.
10. Genesis 1:9.
11. Genesis 2:24.
12. Leviticus 24:22.
13. Deuteronomy 6:4.

the word מִצְוָה, which means *commandment*, *law*, or *precept*. Rabbi Schneerson teaches:

> The word מִצְוָה derives etymologically from a root-word meaning "joining" and "uniting": for one who fulfills God's command becomes united with Him. Such closeness to God surely results in all the Divine emanations of good and blessing necessary to satisfy one's needs.[14]

Now we consider the *unification* and *connection* that is parallel to the word וְיו, a word that has the gematria of 22. When its letters are permuted, there results the word וָוֵי which is the constructive plural of וָו, *hook*. Each of its six uses in the Pentateuch is in conjunction with the building of the tabernacle in the phrase "hooks of the pillars."[15] And in Exodus 27:10 and 38:10 it is the sixth word in the verse. By unification and connection we hook to the pillar of God.

Another word with the gematria of 22 is הַטּוֹב. It means *the good*.

> Observe and hear all these words which I command thee, that it may go well with thee, and with thy children after thee for ever, when thou doest *the good* and the right in the eyes of the Lord thy God.[16]

> And thou shalt rejoice in all *the good* that the Lord thy God has given to thee, and to your household, to thee and the Levite, and the stranger that is among you.[17]

> The Lord shall open to thee his store house of *the good*, the heavens, to send rain on your land in its season and to bless all the work of thy hand.[18]

> See, I have set before thee this day life and *good*, and death and evil; in that I command thee this day to love the Lord

---

14. Rabbi Menachem Schneerson, *Sichos in English*, vol. 7 (Brooklyn, NY: Sichos in English, 1981), p. 34.
15. Exodus 27:10,11; 38:10,11,12,17.
16. Deuteronomy 12:28.
17. Deuteronomy 26:11.
18. Deuteronomy 28:12.

thy God, to walk in his ways, and to keep his commandments and his statutes and his judgments: then thou shalt
live and multiply. And the Lord thy God shall bless thee
in the land into which thou goest to possess it.[19]

Unification and *connection* bring the good, the true nature of which
can be understood through the adjective טוֹבָה, which is the feminine
form for טוֹב, *good*, and which also has the gematria of 22. Half of
the eight occurrences of טוֹבָה in the Pentateuch associate טוֹבָה with
אֶרֶץ טוֹבָה, *good land*.

> And I am come down to deliver them out of the hand of
> the Egyptians, and to bring them up out of that land to a
> *good* and spacious land, into a land flowing with milk and
> honey.[20]

> The land which we passed through to explore is an exceed-
> ingly *good* land. If the Lord delight in us, then he will bring
> us into this land and give it to us; a land which flows with
> milk and honey.[21]

> And they took of the fruit of the land in their hands, and
> brought it down to us, and brought us back word, and said:
> "It is a *good* land which the Lord our God is giving us."[22]

> For the Lord your God is bringing you into a *good* land – a
> land with streams and pools of water, with springs flowing
> in the valleys and hills; a land with wheat and barley, vines
> and fig trees, pomegranates, olive oil and honey; a land
> where bread will not be scarce and you will lack nothing.[23]

Land can be allegorically understood as state of consciousness. By
our unification with and connection to Godliness, our state of consciousness is brought to a good and spacious land, a land flowing with milk
and honey, a land with streams and pools of water, a land with springs

19. Deuteronomy 30:15-16.
20. Exodus 3:8.
21. Numbers 14:7-8.
22. Deuteronomy 1:25.
23. Deuteronomy 8:7-9.

flowing in the valleys and hills, a land where bread is not scarce, and a land where we lack nothing. By our unification with and connection to Godliness,

> All nations shall call you blessed: for you shall be a land of delight.[24]

Hence, *good land* is a state of consciousness in which we have the highest level of delight. We understand and feel that we have everything and that everything has been brought to us by God.

The full gematria of וי is ווי ריו וי, 64. This is the gematria of the word מידי, a plural constructive form meaning *by the hands of*. Jacob uses the word מידי in his blessings for Joseph.

> Joseph is a fruitful vine, a fruitful vine near a spring, whose branches climb over a wall. With bitterness archers attacked him; they shot at him with hostility. Yet his bow stayed taut, and his arms were made firm *by the hands of* the Mighty One of Jacob – There, the Shepherd, the Rock of Israel – The God of your father who helps you, and the Almighty who blesses you with blessings of heaven above, blessings of the deep that couches below, blessings of the breast and womb.[25]

From this we learn that when we live our lives in a state of consciousness arising from unification and connection, a state of consciousness aware that we have everything, aware that everything is being provided by God, then our arms are made firm. God blesses us with the blessings of heaven above, blessings of the deep that crouches below, and blessings of the breast and womb. This is the revealed meaning of ו.

The concealed meaning of ו can be determined from the word או, which means *or*. The word *or* is often used to contrast two things.

> And now, if you mean to treat my master with true kindness, tell me; and if not, tell me also, that I may turn right *or* left.[26]

---

24. Malachi 3:12.
25. Genesis 49:24.
26. Genesis 24:49.

Then Laban and Bethuel answered: "The matter stems from the Lord; we cannot speak to you bad or good."[27]

Here we brought back to you from the land of Canaan the money that we found in the mouths of our bags. How then could we have stolen any silver or gold from your master's house?[28]

When a man or woman commits any wrong toward a fellow man, thus breaking faith with the Lord, and that person realizes his guilt, he shall confess the wrong that he has done.[29]

From the contrasts, we learn that unification transcends the contrasts. Unification transcends the left or the right columns of the Tree of Life, it transcends the good or the bad, it transcends the silver or the gold, and it transcends male or female. In unification, the contrasts that we deal with daily disappear. For example, what we have experienced as wrong done to us, in unification we reexperience as the good coming to us from the hand of God. Everything that comes to us comes from the hand of God. The hand of God brings us only goodness. And what we suffer in our everyday world when unification is absent, we rejoice in when unification is present. Thus, the concealed meaning of ו is that unification transcends contrasts.

The numerical value of ו is six. This is also of particular significance, for the world has six directions: north, south, east, west, above, and below.

For ו is nothing other than the six directions.[30]

These six directions are the physical side of the connection to the spiritual, for the world was sealed with six directions.[31] Also in six days was our world created. The word day in Genesis is a code word for

---

27. Genesis 24:50.
28. Genesis 44:8.
29. Numbers 5:6.
30. The Bahir, trans. and comm. Rabbi Aryeh Kaplan (Northvale, NJ: Jason Aronson, 1995), p. 30.
31. Ibid., p. 12.

Sephirah. Six days refers to the six Sephirot תִּפְאֶרֶת, גְּבוּרָה, חֶסֶד, הוֹד, נֶצַח, and יְסוֹד.

> What are the "six days of בְּרֵאשִׁית" of which the Rabbis speak so often? R. Simeon answered: These are, in truth, "the cedars of Lebanon which he has planted." As the cedars spring from Lebanon, so these six days spring from בְּרֵאשִׁית. These are the six supernal days which are specified in the verse:
>
>> Thine, O Lord, are the Greatness (הַגְּדֻלָּה), the Might (גְּבוּרָה), the Beauty (תִּפְאֶרֶת), the Victory (נֶצַח), and the Majesty (הוֹד) for all in heaven and earth is yours.[32]
>
> The words *for all* refer to the Zaddik (righteous one), who is יְסוֹד (foundation of the world).[33]

The first word of Genesis 1 proclaims six, as the word בְּרֵאשִׁית is composed of the six letters ת, י, שׁ, א, ר, and בּ. From where does our knowledge of this creation begin? Our knowledge begins with the word רֹאשׁ, which is contained in בְּרֵאשִׁית. From this רֹאשׁ, which means *head* and refers to the Sephirah כֶּתֶר, Crown,[34] it continues through the second Sephirah חָכְמָה, Wisdom. This is alluded to by the בּ and flows until ת, which refers to the tenth Sephirah מַלְכוּת, Kingdom.

The first sentence of Genesis is:

בְּרֵאשִׁית בָּרָא אֱלֹהִים אֵת הַשָּׁמַיִם וְאֵת הָאָרֶץ

Notice that ו begins the sixth word and is the twenty-second letter of the verse. Rabbi Ginsburgh teaches that this

> alludes to the power to connect and interrelate all twenty-two individual powers of Creation, the twenty-two letters of the Hebrew alphabet from א to ת. (The word אֵת is

---

32. 1 Chronicles 29:11.
33. *The Zohar*, vol. 1, trans. Harry Sperling and Maurice Simon (London: Soncino Press, 1978), pp. 118-119.
34. Ibid., p. 64.

ן

generally taken to represent all of the letters of the alphabet, from א to ת. Our Sages interpret the word את in this verse to include all of the various objects of Creation present within heaven and earth.)[35]

From this verse we can also conclude why the manifestation of the six Sephirot חֶסֶד, גְּבוּרָה, תִּפְאֶרֶת, נֵצַח, הוֹד, and יְסוֹד is most directly due to the third Sephirah בִּינָה, Understanding. For following בְּרֵאשִׁית are six words that refer to the six Sephirot. Also the word immediately following בְּרֵאשִׁית, is בָּרָא, which is composed of three letters and בִּינָה is the third Sephirah.

Further evidence for this interpretation is found by breaking the word בְּרֵאשִׁית into its two parts: בָּרָא, which means creates and שִׁית, which, in Aramaic, means six. Together the phrase בָּרָא שִׁית means "creates six," six Sephirot.[36]

One of the most sacred of our prayers is the Shema. The esoteric purpose of the prayer is to utilize the letter intelligence of ו to establish a connection for the purpose of unification. Here

> we unite the Name of the Holy One, blessed be He, with a perfect heart and a willing soul.[37]

The Shema begins with the following six-word exclamation which, of course, is in code.

שְׁמַע יִשְׂרָאֵל יְ־ה־וָ־ה אֱלֹהֵינוּ יְ־ה־וָ־ה אֶחָד

The six words again refer to the six Sephirot תִּפְאֶרֶת, גְּבוּרָה, חֶסֶד, נֵצַח, הוֹד, and יְסוֹד. The direct translation of the exclamation is

> Hear! Israel. The Lord is our God; the Lord is One.[38]

Taken as a whole this is the exclamation of the Sephirah חֶסֶד, for in that which is loved, there is no separation, only Oneness. But it has an

---

35. Yitzchak Ginsburgh, *The Hebrew Letters* (Jerusalem: Gal Einai Publications, 1992), p. 94.
36. *The Zohar*, vol. 1, p. 65.
37. Jacob Ben Jacob Ha-Kohen, "Explanation of the Letters," in *The Early Kabbalah*, trans. Ronald Kiener (New York: Paulist Press, 1986), p. 158.
38. Deuteronomy 6:4.

even deeper inner meaning. Each word of the שֶׁמַע can be associated with one Sephirah. The word שֶׁמַע is associated with the Sephirah הוֹד, with אֱלֹהֵינוּ with נֵצַח, יְ־הֹ־וָ־ה with תִּפְאֶרֶת, with יִשְׂרָאֵל, גְּבוּרָה, יְ־הֹ־וָ־ה with יְסוֹד, and אֶחָד with מַלְכוּת. By means of this code, one travels the paths from מַלְכוּת to חֶסֶד, utilizing the letter energy intelligence of ו, the central column, to arise out of the illusion, out of the duality, and understand that in מַלְכוּת, the world of manifestation, there is only Oneness. To participate in this Oneness we need to maintain connection. Thereby we are able to restrict our desire to receive for ourself alone and with our connection we can continuously renew our desire to receive in order to share. When we share, which means love, we give away what we have received and by doing that we create precisely the conditions that enable us to receive. This is what completing the cosmic circuit means.

The Zohar teaches us that the Holy Tetragrammaton יְ־הֹ־וָ־ה is related to some of the verses in Genesis.

> And God said: "Let there be a firmament in the midst of the waters, and let it divide water from water." And God made the firmament, and divided the waters which were under the firmament from the waters which were above the firmament. And it was so. And God called the firmament Heaven. And there was evening and there was morning, a second day.
>
> And God said: "Let the waters from under the heaven be gathered together to one place, and let the dry land appear. And it was so.[39]

The Zohar says:

> The waters: to wit, those that issue from on high, from under the upper ה. From under the heaven: this is the . . . ו. . . . Let the dry land appear. This is the lower ה. This is disclosed and all the rest is undisclosed; from this last we conclude by inference to that which is undisclosed.

---

39. Genesis 1:6-9.

To one place: so called because it is here that the whole of
the upper World is linked into one.[40]

The Zohar is telling us that the upper waters are associated with Sephirah בִּינָה and the first ה. The heaven is associated with the six Sephirot
חֶסֶד, גְּבוּרָה, תִּפְאֶרֶת, נֶצַח, הוֹד, and יְסוֹד and the letter ו. And the
one place, the dry land, is associated with מַלְכוּת, and the second ה.

The letter ו, the third letter of the יְ־הֹ־וָ־ה is situated between the
two הs, the first one for the upper being of the Mother, the Sephirah
בִּינָה, Understanding, and the second one for the lower being of the
Daughter, the Sephirah מַלְכוּת, Kingdom. With respect to the two הs,
the ו harmonizes the two sides.[41] This ו is the Son, associated with the
six Sephirot חֶסֶד, גְּבוּרָה, תִּפְאֶרֶת, נֶצַח, הוֹד, and יְסוֹד. With respect
to the י, the ו acts as the timeless fertilizing agent that by connecting
the Father י to the Mother ה produces the Daughter ה. Here the future
י linked by the ו to the present ה produces the past ה. And read right
to left, the past ה linked by the ו produces the present ה and the future
י.

What does this time-shifting or reversal mean? The actions of
people structure the essence of our universe. No action, no word, no
thought is without consequence at a metaphysical level. Indeed, it is
exactly the thoughts, words, and actions that create these metaphysical energies that are able to connect to and integrate with the whole of
the cosmos. They establish connections with the past and the future,
transcending time and creating eternity.

The Torah states that:

> Whatever goes on its *belly*, and all that goes upon four,
> or whatever has many feet among all creeping things that
> creep on the earth, them you shall not eat: for they are an
> abomination.[42]

The word גָּחוֹן is the Hebrew word for *belly*. And in the Leviticus
11:42 verse, the word גָּחוֹן has a large ו.

---

40. *The Zohar*, vol. 1, p. 77.
41. Ibid., vol. 1, p. 75.
42. Leviticus 11:42.

The word immediately following נָחֹון is the word וְכֹל, meaning *and all.* Permuting the first few letters of these two words and putting the word break after the large ו, we read נוֹכֵל, *swindler,* חוּג, *circle.* The phrase may then be translated as *circle of the swindler.*

> When he drew a *circle* over the surface of the deep.[43]

> But cursed be the *swindler,* who has in his flock a male, and yet vows, and sacrifices to the Lord what is blemished.[44]

For נוכל, we can also read נוּכַל, the first person plural imperfect of the root יכל, meaning to *be able to* or *be capable of.*

Then Laban and Bethuel answered and said:

> This matter comes from the Lord. We are not *able to* speak to thee bad or good. Behold, Rebekah is before thee; take her, and go, and let her be thy master's son's wife as the Lord has spoken.[45]

From this we understand that when we eat that which crawls on its belly, we become connected to the circle (or the circuit) of the able and capable swindler (scoundrel, imposter, rogue, or trickster). This connection to the circuit of the able swindler then closes down our Godly connection. And that is why the Torah states that that which crawls on its belly is not clean.

Consider the word וַדָּאִי, which means *certain.* What is certainty but a cosmic connection that transcends time, extending from the archetype of physical existence ד energized by the pulsation flow of the letter energy intelligence of א and extending to the letter energy intelligence of the Divine י, which is א projected into our universe.

In summary, by the letter intelligence of ו we establish connection and complete the circuits of the Cosmic Intelligence. We participate in the energy of ו to change to a higher state of consciousness, a consciousness that embraces the larger cosmic reality. In this higher state

---

43. Proverbs 8:27.
44. Malachi 1:14.
45. Genesis 25:50-51.

of consciousness, we begin to better understand relationships between people, we begin to better understand the nonmaterial forces that are part of our reality. With this increased wisdom, we become part of the cosmic flow and thereby become connected to the Divinity of the cosmos, to the Divinity of its past, present, and future. This increased wisdom, about which one can only be silent, does not answer the "how" questions of science. Rather, it answers the "why" question. And this is important because until we enter the mystery and are each able to answer the why question, we will be disconnected from the essence of the Divine Cosmic Reality.

דָ֖יָק

Zayin ז : Movement

The seventh letter of the Hebrew alphabet is ז, spelled זין. It has the numerical value of 7. The word זין means *arms* or *weapons*. The letter ז is, after all, shaped like a sword, the top being the hilt and the vertical part being the blade. And what are weapons used for? To bring into being peace or to bring into being that which opposes peace. When arms are used to bring peace into being, the arms are used to oppose that which opposes peace. When arms are used to oppose peace, they initiate destructive actions that break the peace, for when arms are used, they are used to settle a conflict over possession of something material like land, resources, or food. Such conflicts arise from the greed of at least one side, a greed that is associated with the desire to receive for oneself alone. We associate this aspect of ז with the aspect of *movement*, since we arm ourselves to either make movement or prevent movement.

The word זין also has a vulgar slang meaning, to *lie with a woman*. It is cognate to זנן, which means *fornicator*, *lecher*, and *womanizer*. It is also related to זנין, which refers to *sexual intercourse*. To lie with a woman in this sense is to make movement and connection without love. This is precisely what selfish activity is: movement and connection without love.

The word זין does not occur in the Pentateuch, or for that matter anywhere in Scripture. Its gematria is 67 and that is the gematria of ואני, which means *and I*. The first time it is used in the Pentateuch, it is God who says that He will bring the flood. The second time it is used in the Pentateuch, it is God who says that He will establish a convenant.

> *And I*, here, will bring the flood waters upon the earth, to destroy all flesh, in which is the breath of life, from under the heaven; and everything that is on the earth shall die.[1]

> *And I*, here, establish my covenant with you and with your seed after you; and with every living creature that is with

---

1. Genesis 6:17.

> you, of the birds, of the cattle, and of every beast of the
> earth with you; from all that came out of the ark, to every
> beast of the earth.[2]

When God gives the laws to Moses, He uses the word וְאַנִי.

> I have said to you that you shall inherit their land, *and I*
> will give it to you to possess it; a land that flows with milk
> and honey: I am the Lord your God, who has separated
> you from the peoples.[3]

When God tells Moses how Aaron should bless the children of Israel
He uses the word וְאַנִי.

> In this way you shall bless the children of Israel, saying to
> them: The Lord bless thee and keep thee. The Lord make
> His face shine upon thee, and be gracious unto thee. The
> Lord lift up his countenance upon thee and give thee peace.
> And they shall put My name upon the children of Israel,
> *and I* will bless them.[4]

Just before Moses dies, he speaks to the Israelites a long poem that
describes how God acts, stressing that there is no other god. In this
poem He uses the word וְאַנִי.

> See now that I, even I, am He and there is no god with me.
> I kill; I make alive. I wound *and I* heal. Neither is there
> any that can deliver out of my hand.[5]

The full gematria of זין can be determined from זין יוד נון, and
amounts to 193. The word בְּמָצַאֲכֶם, *when ye find*, also has the gematria 193. Jacob uses the word בְּמָצַאֲכֶם after he leaves Laban and he
realizes that Esau is going to meet him with 400 men. Jacob handles
this by sending four messengers each with a drove of animals for gifts
and each separated from the next by some distance.

---

2. Genesis 9:9-10.
3. Leviticus 20:24.
4. Numbers 6:23-27.
5. Deuteronomy 32:39.

ז

And he commanded the first [messenger], saying:

> When Esau my brother meeteth thee, and asketh thee, saying:
>
> > Whose art thou? and whither goest thou? and whose are these before thee?
>
> Then thou shalt say:
>
> > They are thy servant Jacob's, it is a present sent unto my lord, unto Esau; and behold he also is behind us.

And he commanded also the second and the third, and all that followed the droves, saying:

> In this manner shall ye speak unto Esau *when ye find* him;

and ye shall say:

> Moreover, behold thy servant Jacob is behind us.

For he said [to himself]:

> I will gain his favor with the present that goeth before me, and afterwards I will see his face; perhaps he will accept me.[6]

From this we learn another aspect of using our weapons to make movement and bring peace into being. Our weapon, the sword, can take a direct approach and do physical battle, or as in this case, the sword may take an indirect approach and propitiate with a present. So today when we are faced with defending ourselves against aggression from Esau's descendants, we should realize that we have two approaches. And we might consider using the indirect application of the sword, especially in cases when the aggression is motivated by greed and the direct alternative is not feasible.[7]

---

6. Genesis 32:18-21.
7. *Bereishis*, vol. 4, trans. and comm. Meir Zlotowitz (Brooklyn, NY: Mesorah Publications, 1983), pp. 1431-1432.

When the Godly force of the letter energy intelligence of א flows through us, it causes *movement*, either bringing into being the flood waters to destroy our earth or bringing into being the land of milk and honey that we shall possess. One kind of movement wounds, the other heals. One kind of movement kills, the other makes alive. This is our covenant: that we utilize our freedom to become perfect before God. In this way God will bless us and keep us. His face will shine upon us and be gracious to us. He will lift up his countenance upon us and give us peace.

It is this movement or flow that opens all possibility and choice to us. As such, it has a twofold nature. On the one side, its nature is associated with peace and rest. The kabbalistic meaning of rest is associated with the Sabbath. The Sabbath is the seventh day, a day we are told to remember, זָכוֹר.

Remember the Sabbath day, to keep it holy.[8]

Rabbi Glazerson explains that the Gaon of Vilna connects many of the symbols of Sabbath with the number 7, which is the numerical value of ז.[9] The gematria of נֵר, candle, is 250, which when reduced to its small gematria is 7. The gematria of יַיִן, wine, is 70, which when reduced to its small gematria is 7. The gematria of חַלָּה, challah, is 43, which when reduced to its small gematria is 7. The gematria of בָּשָׂר, meat, is 502, which when reduced to its small gematria is 7. Finally, the gematria of דָּג, fish, is 7.

True rest occurs when the desire to receive for ourself alone is at rest. For work can be viewed as the activity we do to fulfill and feed the desire to receive for ourself alone. When the work activity ceases, that is, when the desire to receive for ourself alone is put to rest, a stress-free state emerges. In this stress-free state we are able to take a cosmic view, seeing ourselves as part of and connected to and identified with Godliness rather than separated and fragmented from Godliness.[10]

---

8. Exodus 20:8.
9. Rabbi Matityahu Glazerson, *Letters of Fire*, trans. S. Fuchs (Jerusalem: Feldheim, 1991), p. 140.
10. Phillip S. Berg, *Power of Aleph Beth*, vol. 2 (Jerusalem: Research Centre of Kabbalah, 1988), p. 116.

This separation is the inevitable consequence of activating the desire to receive for ourself alone.

When at rest, we are connected and not separated. We can feel the Godliness in us. Thereby the circuit is complete and the energy intelligence of א can flow through us. The letter energy intelligence of ז is this flow.

So the revealed meaning of ז is the flow of א energy through us, which opens the possiblity of connection with love (peace and rest) and the possibility of connection without love (arms and weapons activity). This twofold possibility puts us in a situation in which we constantly have to choose between realizing the possibility of connection with love or realizing the connection without love. And in order to choose, we have to become wise enough to discriminate and to recognize the essence of each choice we make.

The concealed meaning of זין can be found from זי, which does not constitute a Hebrew word. The closest word to it is ייִן, which is the word for *wine*.

He said: "Serve me and let me eat of my son's game that I may give you my innermost blessing." So he served him and he ate, and he brought him *wine* and he drank.[11]

And the Lord spoke to Aaron, saying: "Drink no *wine* or ale, you or your sons with you, when you enter the Tent of Meeting, that you may not die – it is a law for all time throughout your generations – for you must distinguish between the sacred and the profane, and between the unclean and the clean."[12]

The meal offering with it shall be two-tenths of a measure of choice flour with oil mixed in, an offering by fire of pleasing odor to the Lord; and the libation with it shall be of *wine*, a quarter of a hin.[13]

If anyone, man or woman, explicitly utters a Nazirite's vow, to set himself apart for the Lord, he shall abstain from *wine*

11. Genesis 27:25.
12. Leviticus 10:8-10.
13. Leviticus 23:13.

and ale; he shall not drink vinegar of *wine* or ale, neither shall he drink anything in which grapes have been steeped, nor eat grapes fresh or dried.[14]

Come, let us make our father drink *wine*, and let us lie with him, that we may maintain life through our father.[15]

Wisdom has built her house, she has hewn out her seven pillars: she has killed her beasts; she has mingled her *wine*; she has also furnished her table.[16]

The Lord of hosts shall defend them; and they shall devour, and subdue with sling stones; and they shall drink, and be boisterous as through *wine*; and they shall be filled like bowls, and like the corners of the altar.[17]

For in the hand of the Lord there is a cup, with foaming *wine*; it is full of mixture; and he pours out of the same: but its dregs, shall all the wicked of the earth drain and drink.[18]

Thou hast shown thy people hard things: thou hast made us drink the *wine* of staggering.[19]

For thus says the Lord God of Israel to me: "Take this *wine* cup of fury at my hand and cause all the nations, to whom I send thee, to drink it. And they shall drink, and stagger and be crazed, because of the sword that I will send among them."[20]

With wine we celebrate and consecrate the most important and joyful and holy occasions. Here, wine is a symbol of inward refreshment, blessing, or wisdom. However, with wine we can also become drunk and behave badly in an irresponsible drunken stupor. And in the hand of

---

14. Numbers 6:2-3.
15. Genesis 19:32.
16. Proverbs 9:1-2.
17. Zechariah 9:15.
18. Psalms 75:9.
19. Psalms 60:5.
20. Jeremiah 25:15.

God, the cup of wine is a symbol of God's judgment on Israel and other nations.[21] This double nature that wine has can be seen directly from its colors, for it comes in two colors: white and red. White is the color the Zohar associates with the Sephirah חֶסֶד, Loving-kindness; and red is the color the Zohar associates with the Sephirah גְבוּרָה, Strength.[22] So we see that wine reinforces our understanding of the double nature that ז has.

When ז combines with ד, there forms the root דין, which is the root meaning to *judge, sentence, rule, govern, punish, contend, argue, discuss,* or *litigate* and the noun דין, which means *judgment, sentence, verdict, lawsuit, justice, law, rule,* or *quarrel.*

> If there be a matter concealed from thee in judgment, between blood and blood, between *decision* and *decision*, and between plague and plague, even matters of controversy within thy gates; then shalt thou arise, and get thee up unto the place which the Lord thy God shall choose. And thou shalt come unto the priest the Levites, and unto the judge that shall be in those days; and thou shalt inquire; and they shall declare unto thee the sentence of the judgment.[23]

> The righteous man apprehends the *quarrel* of the poor: but the wicked man cannot grasp that knowledge.[24]

> The Lord stands to plead, and He stands to *judge* the peoples.[25]

> A king that sits on the throne of *judgment* scatters away all evil with his eyes.[26]

From these verses we learn that when the sword of ז is in operation, Divine judgment is occurring. This Divine judgment is not a judgment

---

21. R. Laird Harris, Gleason Archer, and Bruce Waltke, eds., *Theological Wordbook of the Old Testament*, vol. 1 (Chicago: Moody Press, 1990), p. 64.
22. *The Zohar, Parashat Pinhas*, vol. 1, trans. and ed. Phillip Berg (Jerusalem: Research Centre of Kabbalah Press, 1987), p. 34.
23. Deuteronomy 17:8.
24. Proverbs 29:7.
25. Isaiah 13:3.
26. Proverbs 20:8.

of punishment. It is a judgment of nourishment. For the purpose of the sword that executes judgment is not punishment. Its purpose is to make us experience the sword so that from this experience we may ascend to higher levels of purity. Thereby it is our nourishment. This is the concealed meaning of ז.

We can gain a further understanding of why the letter energy intelligence of ז is the archetype of *movement* of the א energy through us by seeing how it combines with other letter energy intelligences. When ז combines with itself there forms the word זז, which means to *move* or to *shift*. Also, when the letter energy intelligence ז combines with the archetype container ב there forms זב, which means *pour, drip*, or *ooze out*. When the letter energy intelligence ז combines with the energy of the cosmic container ר, there forms the word זר, which means *crown* or *wreath* or *rim*.[27] In all its usages in the Pentateuch, the word זר refers to the crown of gold to encompass round about the ark, the table, the altar, and the altar of incense. Rashi, in commenting on the crown of gold for the table, explains that the crown is a symbol of royalty, for the table is a symbol of wealth and greatness.[28] In commenting on the crown of gold for the altar, Rashi explains that it is a symbol of the crown of priesthood.[29]

When the letter energy intelligence ז combines with the energy of the cosmic container ר and with the energy of perfection and completion ם, there forms the root זרם, which means to *flow, pour down*, or *stream*.

From this we learn what is a contained flow: it is one that pours down or streams out of its container. When we make the flow occur, it flows in a circle and we live on the crown or rim of being. Thereby we become priests and reveal the royalty and wealth of the Godliness we bring down.

When the letter energy intelligence of ב is projected into time and conditioned physical existence, there results the letter energy intelli-

---

27. Exodus 25:11,24,25; 30:3,4; 37:2,11,12,26,27.
28. Rashi, *Pentateuch and Rashi's Commentary, Exodus*, vol. 2, trans. Abraham ben Isaiah and Benjamin Sharfman (Brooklyn, NY: S. S. and R. Publishing, 1976), Exodus 25:24, p. 298.
29. Ibid., p. 377.

ז

gence of ב. And when the letter energy intelligence of ב combines
with the letter energy intelligence of ז there results זַךְ, which means
pure, clean, or *spotless*, and זֹךְ which means *purity, clarity*, and *trans-
parence*. The Godly light of א can be revealed only if the container or
vessel through which it flows is transparent. From this we learn that
we must be transparent to the transcendent.

When the letter energy intelligence ז combines with ד there results
the root זד, which means to *think evil*, to *scheme*, to *plot*, and the
noun זֵד, which means *wicked, insolent*, and *wanton*. This is a clear
indication that the manifestation of the flow of the pulsating א into
physical existence is not enough to establish a complete connection, a
Oneness. Indeed the separation is strong enough for there to be evil
and wicked consequences. When ז is combined with the letter energy
intelligence of physical existence ד, and the letter energy intelligence
of spirituality י, the word זִיד means to *act wickedly* or *do maliciously*.
This tells us that when the flow of the unbridled pulsating א is devoted
only to the nourishment of physical existence, the long-term result must
inevitably be transgression. In this context, when ז is attached to
the letter energy intelligence of the power of being ה, wrapped in the
container ב and glorified by the spirit י, there results the word זִיבָה,
which is the word for the disease *gonorrhea*.

When the letter energy intelligence ז combines with ה in a positive
context, there results the exclamation זֶה, which means *this* or *that*. To
understand what might be so special about this or that we just need
to see what happens when זה is encased by ב, the archetype container
or ר, the cosmic container. The first case is the word זָהָב, which
means *gold*. The second case is the word זֹהַר, which means *brightness,
light, brilliance, splendor, radiance, glamour*, or *luster*, as well as the
root זהר, which means to *brighten* or *shine*. Give life to the flow and
contain it and what forms is a brilliance and splendor as precious as
gold.

When the letter energy intelligence of ז combines with the letter energy intelligence of ו, which is the archetype of connection, through the
energy intelligence of spirituality י, the word זִיו forms. It means *brilliance, effulgence, luster, resplendence, brightness, scintillation, light,
splendor, glory, bloom*, and *freshness*.

When the letter energy intelligence of ז combines with the letter energy intelligence of מ, which is the archetype of physical existence projected into time and conditioned physical existence and which represents perfection and completion, and the letter energy intelligence of ן, which is the archetype of the power of being projected into physical existence, the word זְמַן forms. It has the meaning of *time* and *date*. The manifestation of the Divine is through time.

When ר replaces the ן, the word זמר results. Here we learn that the sword can be used constructively. For there are two words with the root זמר: the first one is זָמַר, which means to *trim*, *prune*, *clip*, or *cut off*. The second one is זָמַר, which means to *sing*, *praise*, or *play* a musical instrument. By singing we use the sword to cut through the barrier of materialism between our soul and God.[30]

When the letter energy intelligence ז combines with ג there forms the word זָג which means *grapeskin*, *peel*, *rind*, or *husk*. The flow of א when combined with the organic nourishing, producing activity of ג results in a skin that surrounds the fruit that has been produced.

The letter energy intelligence of ה projected into time and conditioned physical existence produces the letter energy intelligence of emergence ג. When the letter energy intelligence of ז combines with the letter energy intelligence of ג there results זָן, which means to *feed*, *nourish*, and *sustain*.

> Blessed are You, Lord our God, King of the universe, who,
> in His goodness, provides *sustenance* for the entire world
> with grace, with kindess and with mercy.[31]

This tells us that we do obtain our sustenance and inward refreshment by engaging in rest and activity, and by moving into union that which we discover to be separated.

---

30. Rabbi Matityahu Glazerson, *Hebrew: The Source of Languages* (Jerusalem: Yerid HaSefarim, 1987), p. 59.
31. *Siddur Tehillat Hashem* (Brooklyn, NY: Merkos L'Inyonei Chinuch, 1979), p. 89.

חֵית

Chet ה : Life

The eighth letter of the Hebrew alphabet is ח, spelled חֵית. It has
the numerical value of 8, which Rabbi Ginsburgh teaches means Divine
essence in physical reality[1] and which Rabbi Munk teaches means our
ability to transcend the limitations of physical existence.[2] Life is that
which contains Divine essence, thereby permitting it to transcend the
limitations inherent in the circumstances of its physical existence.

The word חַיִּ is related to the word חַיַּת, which is the constructive
form of the noun חַיָּה, meaning *animal* or *beast*. On one level, the verses
involving חַיָּה are about animals of the land and beasts of the field. But
there is a deeper level of meaning to the verses having the word חַיָּה.
This level can be understood by allegory. Land corresponds to the state
of our mind. This is where our mind dwells. An animal of the land
is that which roams the land, living off the land. So allegorically, an
animal of the land is the animal desires and thoughts that appear in
our consciousness. They come from our animal soul.[3] Psychologically,
these are the desires and thoughts that can be attributed to our ego.
"A beast of the field" is an idiomatic expression for a wild animal. A
wild animal has the connotation of animal that not only cannot be
domesticated but eats other animals. So allegorically a wild animal
is the wild animal desires and thoughts of the mind. These are the
inclinations and thoughts of the ego that view the world as a jungle
and whose understanding of surviving in the world is based on the law
of the jungle.

> And God made the *animals* of the land of every kind, and
> cattle of every kind, and creeping things of the ground of
> every kind. And God saw that it was good.[4]

---

1. Rabbi Yitzchak Ginsburgh, *The Hebrew Letters* (Jerusalem: Gal Einai Publications, 1992), p. 132.

2. Rabbi Michael Munk, *The Wisdom in the Hebrew Alphabet* (Brooklyn, NY: Mesorah Publications, 1988), p. 112.

3. Rabbi Shneur Zalman, *Likkutei Amarim – Tanya*, bilingual ed. (Brooklyn, NY: Kehot Publication Society, 1993), p. 25.

4. Genesis 1:25.

So at this level, we can understand that God makes animals of every kind that live in our consciousness. That is, God brings into existence the possibility of desires and thoughts of all kinds. These thoughts and desires are given *life* in us by our dwelling on them. Cattle, our livestock, our domesticated animals, correspond to our everyday domesticated thoughts. And creeping things of the ground correspond to our most close-to-ground thoughts, thoughts and desires that cannot rise to heaven.

> And to every *animal* of the land, and to every bird of the sky, and to everything that creeps on the ground, wherein there is a living soul, every green herb shall be for food: and it was so. And God saw that it was very good.[5]

The thinking of thoughts has a component of green plants, which allegorically correspond to the images and patterns of our thought, the underlying basis of our thoughts. A bird of the sky allegorically corresponds to the heavenly thoughts of the mind.

> And the Lord God formed from out of the ground every *beast* of the field, and every bird of the sky and brought them to the man to see what he would call them. And whatever the man called every living creature, that was its name. And the man gave names to all cattle, and to every bird of the sky, and to every *beast* of the field. But for the man there was not found a help to match him.[6]

And the man Adam can be allegorically understood to be our self-conscious. As Adam names every living soul, our self-conscious interprets everything we desire and perceive. Our self-conscious interprets all our thoughts. And this interpretation is with respect to what we consider to be self. It is self-consciousness that had no helper to be its mate.

God makes Eve to be Adam's mate. Eve can be allegorically understood to correspond to our subconscious. The job of the subconscious

---

5. Genesis 1:30.
6. Genesis 2:19-20.

is to build the automatic reactions of our physical body in accordance
with the images and patterns that the self-conscious gives to the subconscious. These images and patterns, in effect, program the subconscious and the subconscious executes the program.

> Now the serpent was craftier than all the *beasts* of the field
> which the Lord God had made.[7]

The serpent being craftier and shrewder corresponds to our rational
mind, our reasoning ability and distinguishing ability. For it is this
aspect of the intellect that makes judgments and interpretations in
every situation we find ourselves. And each interpretation is at its base
an interpretation of *for me*, which we consider to be *good*, or *against
me*, which we consider to be *evil*. But scripture teaches that we must
not stop just at the point of making the distinction.

> For man should be cognizant of both good and evil, and
> turn evil itself into good. This is a deep tenet of faith.[8]

We are taught that it is exactly what we interpret as evil that we must
turn into the good.

> Because thou has done this, thou art cursed above all cattle,
> and above every *beast* of the field. Upon thy belly shalt thou
> crawl, and dust shalt thou eat all the days of thy life.[9]

So here we learn that as the serpent was cursed and made to crawl
on its belly, we must make the rational part of the intellect also crawl
on its belly and not let it be our principal and sole leader. This is
because the rational intellect inevitably understands self in a narrow
and unduly restricted sense. For it is operating at the level of בִּינָה,
Understanding. And although there is part of our intellect that can
operate at the level of חָכְמָה, Wisdom, this part is beyond the rational
and beyond the serpent. And it is from this level of חָכְמָה, Wisdom,
that we can transform the evil into the good.

---

7. Genesis 3:1.
8. *The Zohar*, vol. 3, trans. Harry Sperling, Maurice Simon, and Paul Levertoff
(London: Soncino Press, 1978), p. 109.
9. Genesis 3:14.

> And God blessed Noah and his sons, and said to them: "Be
> fruitful and multiply, and replenish the earth. And the fear
> of you and the dread of you shall be upon every *beast* of the
> land and upon every bird of the sky, upon all that moves
> upon the ground, and upon all the fishes of the sea. Into
> your hand are they delivered.[10]

The animals of the land are delivered into our hand. We are to
rule them. They are to fear us. This means that the self-conscious is
the governor. For in self-consciousness is free will. And it is by the
use of will that we govern what is in our awareness. Whenever the
animals of our awareness scare us, we have a mental health problem
and if it persists we will find ourselves confined to the wards of a mental
hospital. Because the self-conscious is the ruler, it is the self-conscious
that must be fruitful and multiply and replenish the earth.

> And behold, I establish my covenant with thee, and with
> thy seed after thee, and with every living soul that is with
> thee, with the birds, with the cattle, and with every *beast*
> of the earth with thee, from all that came out of the ark,
> to every *animal* of the land.[11]

God establishes a covenant with us. The covenant is that all things
that happen to us come from the beneficence of God to help us perfect
our ways and become perfect and holy before God. This means that
it is possible for us to learn to have the self-conscious ruler become a
perfect ruler of the mind.

> And six years thou shalt sow thy land and shalt gather in
> its fruits, but the seventh year thou shalt let it rest and lie
> fallow, that the poor of thy people may eat. And whatever
> they leave, the *beasts* of the field shall eat.[12]

Six years we should sow the land means that for six units of time, the
self-conscious must maintain control. The seventh year, the seventh

---

10. Genesis 9:1-2.
11. Genesis 9:9-10.
12. Exodus 23:10-11.

ה

119

unit of time, the self-conscious must rest. It must not rule. It must not give more patterns and images to the subconscious. Rather, the self-conscious must rest to reflect upon what it sees the subconscious doing, what it sees the subconscious playing back. And whatever the subconscious plays back, this is what should nourish the poor part of ourselves and this is what should nourish the wild animals in our self-consciousness. That is, we should observe and honor our wild animals. We should observe and honor our poor. At least by recognizing them, we have the opportunity of doing something about them. We have the opportunity of transforming the wild animals and enriching the poor.

> I will not drive them out from before thee in one year, lest the land become desolate and the [wild] *beasts* of the field multiply against thee. Little by little I will drive them out from before thee until thou be increased and inherit the land.[13]

> And the Lord thy God will put out those nations before thee by little and little. Thou mayst not consume them at once, lest the [wild] *beasts* of the field increase upon thee.[14]

The other nations that are driven out of the land stand for that part of our value system and expectations that are not in accord with Godliness. These nations are the same nations spoken of in the following:

> Righteousness exalteth a nation, but the kindness[15] of the

---

13. Exodus 23:29-30.

14. Deuteronomy 7:22.

15. The Hebrew uses the noun וְחֶסֶד, which can mean *and kindness*, relating to the verb חֶסֶד meaning to *do favors, do good*, or *do a kindness*, or it can mean *and disgrace, and shame*, or *and abomination*, relating to the verb חָסַד, meaning to *deprecate, reproach*, or *sneer at*. Many translations use the word *reproach*. However, the Alter Rebbe in *Tanya*, p. 5, quotes *Etz Chayim*, Portal 49, ch. 3, "that all the good that the nations do, is done from selfish motives." And he also quotes the *Gemara, Bava Batra* (10b) "that all the charity and kindness done by the nations of the world is only for their own self-glorification." And since the nations are not acting out of a holy motive, but out of a selfish motive, their seeming deeds of kindnesses are as a sin.

nations is sin.[16]

For our values and expectations that are not in accordance with Godliness are for the purpose of our own selfishness. Our selfish intentions
are to aggrandize ourselves, to show arrogance, to increase our power
or our wealth, or to enlarge our domain of control.[17,18]

Our values that are not in accordance with Godliness, even if we
could know them all at once, we cannot change all at once. For such
a change, removing a block of incorrect values, would leave a part of
our land desolate. There, the ego would completely take over and the
wild beasts would multiply. Since the covenant is that God gives us
situations for the purpose of helping us, guiding us, along the path of
perfection, so that we can become perfect before God, we are assured
that by adopting an attitude that we want to change for the better,
little by little, we will change for the better. Our value system will get
closer and closer to Godliness. And this will be openly manifested, for
our vices will decrease and our virtues will increase.

> And if thou walkest contrary to me, and willst not hearken
> to me, I will bring seven times more plagues upon thee
> according to thy sins. I will also send [wild] *beasts* of the
> field among thee which shall rob thee of thy children, and
> destroy thy cattle, and make thee few in number.[19]

But, if we do not desire to change and to grow and to become more perfect, if we only desire to stay the way we are, then these very situations
that God gives us to help and guide us to become perfect, complete,
and holy before God will be our plagues. Our population of wild beasts
will increase. They will rob our children, that which we creatively produce. Our cattle will be destroyed and the abilities of our mind will
decrease.

The full gematria of חֵית is חֵית יוֹד תָו, which totals 844. This is
the gematria of the word קְדַשְׁתֶּם, which is the second person masculine
plural Piel imperfect of the root קָדַשׁ, meaning to *sanctify, consecrate,*

16. Proverbs 14:34.
17. *Proverbs*, trans. A. Cohen (London: Soncino Press, 1985), p. 94.
18. Rabbi Shneur Zalman, *Likkutei Amarim - Tanya*, p. 5.
19. Leviticus 26:21-22.

make holy, or *revere as holy*. God uses the word קִדַּשְׁתֶּם in telling Moses why he will not live to see the promised land.

> There on the mountain that you have climbed you will die and be gathered to your people, just as your brother Aaron died on Mount Hor and was gathered to his people. [This is] because ye [both of you] trespassed against Me in the presence of the children of Israel at the waters of Meribah Kadesh in the wilderness of Zin and because ye [both of you] did not *sanctify* Me in the presence of the children of Israel.[20]

The lesson we learn from this is the lesson that Rabbi Shneur Zalman teaches.

> For the holy side is nothing but the indwelling and extension of the holiness of the Holy One, blessed be He, and He dwells only on such a thing that abnegates itself completely to Him.[21]

So when we do or think or dwell on something, if this is not dedicated to our service to God, if this is not done with our intention of bringing down Godliness, then it is not done for the purpose of sanctifying God. And those moments that we so live are dead moments for us. They do not encompass eternity. Indeed, they feed the "other side." This is the reason David says:

> I have set the Lord always before me.[22]

But when we forget God and we do not set God before us, we lead ourselves into sin. Interestingly enough, the word תֶּחֱטָא[23] is the third person feminine singular Kal imperfect of the root חטא, which means to *sin*. It has the gematria 418, the gematria of חֵית. And the word חַטָּאת, also with the gematria of 418, is the noun meaning *mistake*, *unintentional sin*, *inadvertent sin*, *transgression*, *guilt*, and *sin offering*. God uses the word חַטָּאת in speaking to Cain.

---

20. Deuteronomy 32:50-51.
21. Rabbi Shneur Zalman, *Likkutei Amarim – Tanya*, p. 23.
22. Psalms 16:8.
23. Leviticus 4:2,27; 5:1,17,21; Numbers 15:27.

If thou doest what is right, willst thou not be accepted?
But if thou doest not do what is right, *sin* is crouching at
thy door; it desires to have thee, but thou must master it.[24]

In sin we do not inherit the promised land. Our consciousness
cannot be שָׁלֵם,[25] *whole, entire, full,* or *perfect,* and תִחְיוּן,[26] the Kal
imperfect second person masculine plural of the verb to *live,* two words
whose gematria totals 844, the gematria of חֵית יוֹד תָו and קְדַשְׁתֶּם.

> Let your heart therefore be *perfect* with the Lord our God,
> to walk in his statutes, and to keep his commandments, as
> at this day.[27]
>
> In all the ways which the Lord your God has commanded
> you, ye shall walk that ye may *live,* and that it may be well
> with you, and that you may prolong your days in the land
> which ye shall possess.[28]
>
> All the commandments which I command thee this day shall
> you observe to do, that ye may *live,* and multiply, and go in
> and possess the land which the Lord swore to your fathers.[29]

The word חֵית is related to the word חָיוֹת, which is the first, second,
or third person feminine plural of the root חיה, meaning to *live,* to
exist, and to the word חַיּוּת, which means *life* and *vitality,* and to the
word חַיּוּת, which means *life, living, animation, vitality,* or *vividness.*
Hence, it is no surprise that the most common words associated with
ח are חַיִּים, which means *life* and חַי, which means *living, alive, lively,
vivacious, active, raw, fresh, strong, healthy, undiluted,* or *unadulterated.*
The word חַיָּה means *full of life, lively, alive, quick, healthy, vigorous,
vivacious,* and the word חַיִל means *power, strength,* or *valor.*
The word for life, חַיִּים, has the gematria of 68, the gematria of
the word חָכָם, which means *wise, intelligent, prudent, experienced,*

24. Genesis 4:7.
25. 1 Kings 8:61.
26. Deuteronomy 5:30.
27. I Kings 8:61.
28. Deuteronomy 5:30.
29. Deuteronomy 8:1.

or *clever*. Both חַיִּים and חָכָם begin with ח and end with ם. The word חַם means *warm* or *hot*, and the word מֹחַ as an adjective means *marrowy, fat, wealthy* and as a noun means *marrow* and *brain*, which is the physical garment of the mind. Living necessitates being warm and using the brain for the purpose of being wise. And for what does the wise one live? The wise one lives for the purpose of bringing Godliness into this world. Godliness involves revealing the Divine essence that is within us and transcending the limitations of our circumstances. This is the level of living of חָכְמָה, Wisdom. This is the revealed meaning of ח.

Like the letter energy intelligence ב, the concealed meaning of ח can be uncovered by an examination of יִת, which by itself is an abbreviation for יִתְבָּרַךְ, which means *May He be blessed* and is the first word in the Kaddish prayer. When combined with ד, יִת becomes יָתֵד, which means a *peg* or *hook*.[30] This reminds us that by loving we fasten ourselves (with a peg or a hook) to the Divine. When combined with ם, יִת becomes יִתֹּם, which means to *make an orphan*. This reminds us that when our loving is so narrow that it encompasses only the ם of מַיִם, water (*emotion*), the loving will orphan us. When combined with ר, יִת becomes יִתֵר, which means to *add* or *overdo*. It can be used as a prefix to make compound words where it then carries the meaning of *over*, *super*, or *hyper*. We can then understand its meaning as *abundance*, *surplus*, or *excess*, for when the light flows through us, we will reveal it by our loving. We put ourselves in a state of abundance, a state in which there is not just fullness but such a surplus or excess of fullness that the abundance is infinite.

The nature of the letter energy intelligence of ח can be understood from its shape, which is composed of a ו standing side by side with a ז, the two being connected at the top.[31] This connection ties together the rest aspect of the letter energy intelligence ו (from the association ו has to וו, the sustainer of the world) with the active enterprise aspect of the letter energy intelligence ז (from the association ז has to זין, "weapon"). This tells us that the letter energy intelligence of ח is the gateway to the balanced and harmonious living together of *rest* and *activity*. Rest

---

30. Isaiah 22:23, Ezekiel 15:3.
31. Rabbi Munk, *The Wisdom in the Hebrew Alphabet*, p. 115.

means reflectively integrating and observing where we are so that we can determine in what way we can grow and move beyond where we are. Activity means dwelling on patterns of thoughts and desires that are indicative of our new state of being so that these patterns of thoughts and desires can program the subconscious to remodel our body, our automatic reactions, in accordance with how we want to change and grow.

We may gain further understanding of the letter energy intelligence of ח by considering how it interacts with other letter energy intelligences. When ח combines with ד, whose energy intelligence is physical existence, there forms the word חַד, which means *one* or *single*. As a prefix it means *mono*. And when חַד combines with ר, whose energy intelligence is cosmic container, there forms the word חֶדֶר, which means *room, chamber,* or *bridal chamber*. It also means *elementary religious school*. And it also carries the meaning of *innermost part,* as in expressions such as בְּחַדְרֵי חֲדָרִים, *in a most hidden place, in a secret place,* or *in the innermost chambers* and the phrase בָּקִי בְּחַדְרֵי תוֹרָה, which means "expert in all the secrets of the Torah." When חד combines with ש there forms חדש, which is the root meaning to *renew, renovate, revive, invest,* or *establish a new interpretation*. The related adjective חָדָשׁ means *fresh* or *new*. The new has both a positive and negative, as we see from the following verses.

> Now there arose a *new* king over Egypt, who did not recognize [know] Joseph.[32]

> And I will turn myself to thee and make thee fruitful and multiply thee, and establish my covenant with thee. And thou shalt be eating last year's harvest when thou shalt have to move it out to make room for the *new*. I will put my dwelling place [tabernacle] among you and my soul shall not abhor thee.[33]

> He brought me up also out of the gruesome pit, out of the miry clay, and set my feet upon a rock, and established my

---

32. Exodus 1:8.
33. Leviticus 26:9-11.

footsteps. And he has put a *new* song in my mouth, a praise to our God.[34]

For behold, I create *new* heavens and a new earth. And the former things shall not be remembered, nor come to mind.[35]

The related noun חֹדֶשׁ means *month* or *new moon*.

The *new moon* shall be unto you the beginning of *months*.[36]

From this we learn that Life must be united with the Divine in all its aspects. In that way our physical existence becomes a bridal chamber in which there is constant renewal and innovation, fertilizing the most secret and inner of all places.

When ח combines with the letter energy intelligence ב, there results the word חַב, which means to *be indebted* and *incur liability*, to *be obligated* and *be beholden*. For what do we incur this liability? We incur this liability to love, for the combination of ח with ב also results in חִבֵּב which is the past form of the verb to *endear, love, honor*, and *cherish* and means to *make beloved*. And when ח combines with ל, the word חָל forms which means to *become due*. Our love becomes due. It must be returned by choosing as its one and only desire to receive the Godly light for the sake of sharing it and revealing it. And when we do love, in the lightning manner of חֵץ, which means *arrow* or *dart*, we bring about חֹם, *warmth*, חֶם, *forbearance*, חֵן,[37] *grace, beauty, favor, charm, loveliness, attractiveness*, and *preciousness*, and חַף, which means *clean, pure*, and *innocence*. Thereby we create חֹר, which means a *hole* or *opening* for our love to return to the Divine. And as well we prevent חַת, *fear* and *dread* and we do not become חַת, *broken* or *terrified*. And we do not commit חֵטְא, which means *unintentional sin*. Furthermore, when the archetype of physical existence ר combines with the forbearance of חֶם, there forms the word חֶסֶר, which means *lovingkindness, benevolence, grace, favor, righteousness*, and *charity*. חֶסֶר

---

34. Psalms 40:3-4.
35. Isaiah 65:17.
36. Exodus 12:2.
37. Genesis 6:8.

has the gematria of 72. This is the gematria of הֹ יֹ הֹ יֹ when spelled out as יוד הי ויו הי. From this we learn that the Divine element in the world manifests as loving-kindness, for we read:

> The world stands on three things: Torah, service, and deeds of loving-kindness.[38]
>
> The loving-kindness of God fills the earth.[39]
>
> The universe will be built by loving-kindness.[40]
>
> Your loving-kindness, O God, fills the earth.[41]

And it is this loving-kindness that we share as we become more perfect and holy before our God. It is this loving-kindness that is the light of our *life*.

---

38. *Ethics of the Fathers* 1:2.
39. Psalms 33:5.
40. Psalms 89:2.
41. Psalms 119:64.

שֵׁית

Tet ט: Goodness

The ninth letter of the Hebrew alphabet is ט, spelled טֵית. It has the numerical value of 9. The shape of the ט is that of a container having a small opening at the top. The small opening is a funnel through which the Divine light can flow into us and thereby share its *goodness* with us.

The gematria of טֵית is 419. This is the gematria of the word תָּבִיאוּ, the second person masculine plural Hiphil imperfect of the root בּוֹא, which means to *come* or *arrive*. The Hiphil form means to *bring* or *put in*.

> But when ye cross the Jordan and settle in the land the Lord thy God is giving thee as an inheritance, where He will give thee rest from all thy enemies around thee so that ye will live in safety. Then there shall be a place which the Lord thy God shall choose to cause His name to dwell there. There ye *shall bring* all that I command thee: thy burnt offerings, and thy sacrifices, thy tithes, and the offering of thy hand, and all thy choice vows which ye vow to the Lord. And ye shall rejoice before the Lord thy God, ye and thy sons, and thy daughters, and thy menservants, and thy maidservants.[1]

The gematria of the word לִשְׁפּוֹט also is 419. It is the infinitive form of the root שׁפט, which means to *judge, bring to judgment, administer justice, adjudicate, execute judgment, rule,* or *govern.*

> Let the heavens be glad and let the earth rejoice. And let it be said among the nations: "The Lord reigns." Let the sea roar and the fulness thereof. Let the field rejoice and all that is in it. Then shall the trees of the wood sing for joy at the presence of the Lord because He comes *to judge* the earth. O give thanks to the Lord, for He is good and His loving-kindness endures forever.[2]

---

1. Deuteronomy 12:10-12.
2. 1 Chronicles 16:31-34.

King Solomon uses the word לִשְׁפּוֹט in asking for an understanding heart.

> I am but a little child. I know not how to go out or come in. And thy servant is in the midst of thy people which thou hast chosen, a great people, that cannot be numbered or counted for multitude. Give therefore thy servant an understanding heart *to judge* thy people, to discern between good and evil: for who is able *to judge* this so great people of thine.[3]

These three passages teach us about three of the dimensions of *goodness*. First, in the presence of God we bring our choicest vows and rejoice. Second, God comes to judge the earth. This judgment is not just a statement of judgment, but it is a judgment with rulership, a rulership that gives us our next set of circumstances and situations designed to best help us on our path of being of service to God. Therefore, with thanks we receive God's judgment and rulership, which is God's beneficence and loving-kindness, for God is good. Finally, we see that when we develop our own understanding heart, able to discern good and evil, this too is good, for this is the way by which we judge in our own situations. With an understanding heart, our judgments also will be our beneficence and loving-kindness, for part of our service to the Divine is to help guide and facilitate others to more and better Divine service. In this manner we can make our actions bear similarity to Divine action and thereby draw ourselves closer to the Divine.

The full gematria of טֵית is טֵית יוֹד תָו, which totals 845. This is the gematria of the word תְּהֹמֹת, which means *depths* or *deeps*. The Pentateuch uses the word תְּהֹמֹת in describing what happened to the Egyptians when they chased after the Israelites crossing the Red Sea.

> The *depths* have covered them. They sank into the bottom like stone. Thy right hand, O Lord, is glorious in power. Thy right hand, O Lord, has dashed the enemy in pieces. And in the greatness of thy majesty thou has overthrown them that rose up against thee. Thou didst send forth thy

---

3. 1 Kings 3:7-9.

anger, which consumed them as stubble. And with the blast of thy nostrils the waters were piled up. The floods stood upright like a heap and the *depths* were congealed in the heart of the sea.[4]

What are these depths that covered the Egyptians, the depths that were congealed in the heart of the sea? These are the depths of Wisdom, the Wisdom for which we read:

The Lord made me as the beginning of His way, The first of His works of old. I was set up from everlasting, from the beginning, before the earth ever was. When there were no *depths*, I was brought forth; When there were no fountains abounding with water.[5]

These are the depths that were

created by God before the universe because He ordained for her a part in His creative work which changed chaos into order. The same principles which the Creator applied in the formation of the universe have to be employed by man in the development of his highest self. In a word, wisdom, i.e., morality, has been appointed by God to be the controlling force of all life, both of the universe and of mankind, individually and collectively.[6]

These depths of Wisdom cause the execution of judgment to take place. This is the judgment whose execution changes chaos and immorality to order and morality. This is the Divine good. We read in Genesis that

God saw that the light was good.[7]

God saw that it was good.[8]

And God saw all that he had made, and it was very good.[9]

---

4. Exodus 15:5-8.
5. Proverbs 8:22-24.
6. *Proverbs*, trans. A. Cohen (London: Soncino Press, 1985), p. 48.
7. Genesis 1:4.
8. Genesis 1:10,12,18,21,25.
9. Genesis 1:31.

There is yet another way in which we can understand this. The word טִיט is related to the word טִיט, *mud*. Mud is symbolic of the physical realm. This is reinforced by the word טִין, which means *mud* and *silt* and by the word טֶבַע, which means *nature*. And what do we know about the physical realm? We know about people's suffering which is as unwanted as mud. And why do people interpret what happens to them in a way that makes them suffer? Because they do not realize the connection between the Divine and the physical realm, nature. אֱלֹהִים, the God name associated with creation and judgment, is numerically equivalent to הַטֶּבַע, *the nature*, both having the gematria of 86. Because the Divine is associated with nature, everything that occurs, occurs for the best *good*.

> It was taught in the name of R. Akiba: A man should always accustom himself to say, "Whatever the All-Merciful does is for the good."[10]

Similarly, Nahum of Gamzu, who was blind in both his eyes, had his two hands and legs amputated, and had his whole body covered with boils, declared whatever befell him:

> This also is for the best.[11,12]

The Talmud teaches us:

> For good tidings one says, who is good and bestows good: For evil tidings one says, blessed be the true judge. . . . Raba said: What it really means is that one must receive the evil with gladness. R. Aha said in the name of R. Levi: Where do we find this in the Scripture?

> I will sing of loving-kindness [חֶסֶד] and justice [וּמִשְׁפָּט], unto Thee O Lord will I sing praises.[13]

---

10. *The Babylonian Talmud, Seder Zeraim, Berakoth* (60b) trans. Maurice Simon (London: Soncino Press, 1978), p. 380.
11. *The Babylonian Talmud, Seder Moed*, vol. 4, *Taanith* (21a), trans. J. Rabbinowitz (London: Soncino Press, 1938), p. 104.
12. See also the story about Rabbi Sussya in Louis Newman's collection *The Hasidic Anthology* (New York: Charles Scribner's Sons, 1938), pp. 125-126.
13. Psalms 101:1.

Whether it is חֶסֶד I will sing, or whether it is וּמִשְׁפָּט I will sing. R. Ramuel b. Nahmani said: We learn it from here:

In God I will praise His word, in the Lord I will praise His word.[14]

"In the Lord I will praise His word": this refers to the good dispensation. "In God I will praise His word": this refers to the dispensation of suffering.[15]

Rabbi Nachman teaches:

When things go well, it is certainly good. But when you have troubles, it is also good. For you know that God will eventually have mercy, and the end will be good. Everything must be good, for it all comes from God.[16]

Rabbi Luzzatto teaches:

God's purpose in creation was to bestow of His good to another. . . .

Since God desired to bestow good, a partial good would not be sufficient. The good that He bestows would have to be the ultimate good that His handiwork could accept. God alone, however, is the only true God, and therefore His beneficent desire would not be satisfied unless it could bestow that very good, namely the perfect good that exists in His intrinsic essence. . . .

His wisdom therefore decreed that the nature of this true benefaction be His giving created things the opportunity to attach themselves to Him to the greatest degree possible for them. . . .

---

14. Psalms 56:11.

15. *The Babylonian Talmud, Seder Zeraim, Berakoth* (60b), trans. Maurice Simon (London: Soncino Press, 1978), p. 380.

16. Rabbi Aryeh Kaplan, *Gems of Rabbi Nachman* (Jerusalem: Yeshivat Chasidei Breslov, 1980), p. 125.

God's wisdom, however, decreed that for such good to be perfect, the one enjoying it must be its master. He must be one who has earned it for himself, and not one associated with it accidentally. . . .

God therefore arranged and decreed the creation of concepts of both perfection and deficiency, as well as a creature with equal access to both. This creature would then be given the means to earn perfection and avoid deficiency.

This creature then stands balanced between perfection and deficiency, which in turn are the result of this illumination or concealment. When he grasps elements of perfection and makes them his inner gains, he actually grasps Him (blessed be His name), as He is their Root and Source. The more elements of perfection he gains, the greater becomes his grasp and bond of closeness to Him. Finally, as he attains the goal of earning perfection, he thereby attains the goal of an ultimate grasp and bond of perfection to Him, and he thus becomes attached to Him, deriving both pleasure and perfection from His goodness, while he is himself the master of his own good and perfection.[17]

This is indeed the best of all possible worlds. From this, we can conclude that the revealed meaning of ט is טוֹב, *goodness*. Hence, whenever something happens that may seem *bad* and cause *suffering*, we must think that this too is for the best. And when we say the Shema:

שְׁמַע יִשְׂרָאֵל יְ-ה-וָ-ה אֱלֹהֵינוּ יְ-ה-וָ-ה אֶחָד

we are asserting that our Lord, יְ-ה-וָ-ה, the unlimited aspect of God that we experience as *mercy*, חֶסֶד, is one with אֱלֹהִים, the limiting aspect of God that we experience as *strength* and *judgment*, גְּבוּרָה.[18,19] For this is the meaning of

---

17. Rabbi Moshe Chayim Luzzatto, *The Way of God*, trans. Rabbi Aryeh Kaplan (Jerusalem: Feldheim, 1988), pp. 37-41.
18. Rabbi Nachman, *Garden of the Souls* (Monsey, NY: Breslov Research Institute, 1990), p. 9.
19. Rabbi DovBer Schneersohn, *To Know God* (Brooklyn, NY: Kehot Publication Society, 1993), p. 1.

Know this day, and lay it to thy heart, that the Lord, He is God.[20]

and the meaning of

On that day, the Lord shall be One and his name One.[21]

And this is why when we understand that everything that happens to us is for the good, we have a glimpse of the world to come.[22]

The gematria of the word טוב is 17. This 17 is the last 17 years that Jacob lived.

Jacob lived in the land of Egypt seventeen years.[23]

Now Egypt is the land of restriction and oppression. How can living seventeen years in the land of restriction and oppression be good? It was good because Jacob was living with all his children in harmony and tranquillity.[24] Not only was it good, but it was the best years of Jacob's life. It was the best years because by living a Torah life in the depravity of Egypt, Jacob was able to express his vitality, his real living. This is the meaning of "Jacob lived." By really living, Jacob transformed darkness into a high quality light.[25] Going to Egypt was Jacob's descent. The purpose of Jacob's descent, as the purpose of all descents, is for the revelation of the light that emerges from the darkness of the descent.[26] So good here means living a Torah life, full of vitality, in harmony with one's children, being a shining light in the land of restriction and oppression.

Joseph, in speaking to his brothers about how it was that his brothers sold him as a slave, says:

---

20. Deuteronomy, 4:39.
21. Zechariah, 14:9.
22. Rabbi Nachman, *Likutey Moharan*, vol. 1 (Monsey NY: Breslov Research Institute, 1989), lesson 4.
23. Genesis 47:28.
24. *Bereishis*, vol. 6, trans. and comm. Meir Zlotowitz (Brooklyn, NY: Mesorah Publications, 1981), p. 2085.
25. Rabbi Menachem Schneerson, *In the Garden of the Torah*, vol. 1 (Brooklyn, NY: Sichos in English, 1994), p. 70.
26. Rabbi Menachem Schneerson, *Sichos in English*, vol. 8 (Brooklyn, NY: Sichos in English, 1981), p. 147.

God meant it for *good*, to bring it to pass at this day that much people should be saved alive.[27]

The *goodness* of God and that which He does is tied very closely to the commandments.

You shall walk in all the ways which the Lord your God has commanded you, that you may live, and that it *may be well* with you, and that you may prolong your days in the land which you shall possess.[28]

And thou shalt do that which is right and *good* in the sight of the Lord: that it may be well with thee, and that thou mayst go in and possess the *good* land which the Lord swore to thy fathers.[29]

And the Lord commanded us to do all these statutes, to have awe of the Lord our God, for our *good* always, that he might preserve us alive, as it is at this day.[30]

Observe and seek out all the commandments of the Lord your God; that you may possess this *good* land, and leave it for an inheritance for your children after you forever.[31]

And thou shalt return and obey the voice of the Lord, and do all his commandments which I command thee this day. And the Lord thy God will make thee plenteous in every work of thy hand, in the fruit of thy body, and in the fruit of thy cattle, and in the fruit of thy land, for *good*: for the Lord will again rejoice over thee for *good*, as he rejoiced over thy fathers.[32]

And now behold, I have brought the first fruits of the land, which Thou, O Lord, hast given me. And thou shalt set it before the Lord thy God, and worship before the Lord thy

27. Genesis 50:20.
28. Deuteronomy 5:30.
29. Deuteronomy 6:18.
30. Deuteronomy 6:24.
31. 1 Chronicles 28:8.
32. Deuteronomy 30:8-9.

God. And thou shalt rejoice in every *good* thing which the Lord thy God has given thee, and thy house, thou, and the Levite, and the stranger that is among you.[33]

And the Lord shall make thee plenteous in *goods*, in the fruit of thy body, and in the fruit of thy cattle, and in the fruit of thy ground, in the land which the Lord swore to thy fathers to give thee. The Lord shall open to thee his *good* treasure, the heaven, to give the rain to thy land in its season and to bless all the work of thy hand.[34]

In singing praises to God, we often affirm the ultimate goodness of God.

O give thanks to the Lord, because He is *good*: for his steadfast love endures forever.[35]

Thou art *good* and doest *good*.[36]

The Lord is *good* to all; and his tender mercies are over all his works.[37]

טוֹב means that God's purpose in creation is to bestow *goodness*, the ultimate goodness, the perfect goodness that is His intrinsic nature.[38] Therefore, טוֹב means not only that whatever happens to us is good, but also that we must do good by engaging in activities that relate to the purpose of creation, which is to establish a dwelling place for God in the physical realm (טיט). We must be compassionate and gracious, always *giving*, always manifesting *love*. By so doing, we live a life in strength, with the full light of the sun shining on every step we take. By this means we stay טָהוֹר, *pure* and *untainted*.

An important aspect of the טיט, can be understood from a companion word יָוֵן, which by itself means *mud, mire, sludge, ooze, muck,* or *sediment*. Together, they form the phrase טיט הַיָוֵן, which has the

---

33. Deuteronomy 26:10-11.
34. Deuteronomy 28:11-12.
35. 1 Chronicles 16:34.
36. Psalms 119:68.
37. Psalms 145:9.
38. Rabbi Luzzatto, *The Way of God*, p. 37.

literal meaning of "deep mire or miry clay," but which has the figurative meaning of *great trouble* and a place of *suffering*. This tells us that living may involve suffering, but this is also good. The seeming contradiction can be dissolved by noting that the energy intelligence consciousness of ט is also in the word טֵאטֵא, which means to *sweep*. For it is the suffering and darkness that we ourselves create, which we ourselves must sweep away. Divinity provides *light*. We conceal it in suffering and *darkness*. We can reveal the light with the *faith* of knowing in our heart of hearts that from God only comes the perfect Divine beneficence and, therefore, everything that happens to us is for our good, in the short term and in the ultimate long term.

The concealed meaning of ט is revealed by יּת, which as we have seen before are the first two letters of the יִתְבָּרַךְ, may He be *blessed*; יְתֵב, an Aramaic word meaning to *dwell*, to *settle* or to *give*, and יְתֵר, which means *remainder*, *rest*, *abundance*, *surplus*, or *excess*. Putting this all together we obtain: for the *goodness* that we receive, in which we dwell, and by which we have abundance, may He be blessed.

יוֹד

Yod י: Spirituality

The tenth letter of the Hebrew alphabet is י, spelled יוֹד and some-times spelled יוֹד. It has the numerical value of 10. יוֹד is related to the word יָד, which has the common meaning of *hand*, but also means *handle, monument, place, power, strength, share,* or *portion*. It is also related to the root ידע (יְדַע), which means to *introduce* or to *specify*, and the root ידע (יָדַע), which means to *know, perceive, understand, discern, comprehend, be aware of,* and to *have sexual intercourse with*. All this tells us that the energy intelligence consciousness of י is that of projecting the unbridled pulsating energy of א into physical manifestation. This is *spirituality*. For the hand is the hand of the craftsman; it is a means of doing and creating. By its power and strength, it specifies and makes definite and by specification we come to know and perceive. By specifying and making definite we express the spiritual and through its expression we come to know the spiritual.

The י is the smallest of all the letters. It is barely larger than a dot. The shape of the י seems to have no component parts and therefore it is a letter that cannot be divided. But upon careful examination, the י is found to have a top point directed upward toward heaven, a bottom point directed downward toward earth and a middle body that unites the two points. The Zohar teaches that the point above is the Sephirah כֶּתֶר, Crown; the point in the middle is the Sephirah חָכְמָה, Wisdom; and the point below is the Sephirah בִּינָה, Understanding.[1]

As the smallest of all the letters, it symbolizes humility and it repre-sents the metaphysical or *spiritual*, for the strength of the hand comes from the metaphysical or spiritual realm of being.

The word יָדוֹ means *his hand* and is spelled with the same letters as יוֹד. The first scriptural use of the word יָדוֹ occurs after the incident of the tree of knowledge of good and evil.

> The Lord God said: "Indeed, the man has become like the unique one among us, knowing good and bad. What if he

---

1. *The Wisdom of the Zohar*, vol. 1, arr. Fischel Lachower and Isaiah Tishby, trans. David Goldstein (London: Oxford University Press, 1991), p. 342.

141

should stretch out *his hand* and take also from the Tree of
Life and eat? He would live forever!"[2]

Here we see that for man to stretch out his hand and take and eat
from the Tree of Life is not existentially allowable. This would lead
to the situation that man, being immortal, might mislead himself into
believing that man was God, for God is immortal. And this possibility
would then close off the possibility of man's spirituality. For *spirituality*
requires a constant moving, changing, growing, and transcending of the
physical that would be, paradoxically, meaningless if the physical were
everlasting and not limited by time. That is, it is our limitation of time
that is the gateway for our *spirituality*.

The first use of יד in Exodus is when God is convincing Moses to
take up the leadership of the Israelites and request Pharaoh to let the
Israelites leave Egypt. Moses does as he is told and takes his rod and
throws it to the ground, where it becomes a snake.

> And the Lord said to Moses: "Put out thy hand, and take
> it by its tail. And he put out *his hand*, and caught it, and
> it became a rod in his hand: that they may believe that the
> Lord God of their fathers, the God of Abraham, the God
> of Isaac, and the God of Jacob, has appeared to thee."[3]

On the surface this verse says that we work the "now you see it, now
you don't" kind of magic with our hands. But this magic is not our
magic. We just follow the instructions. God is the one who makes the
magic happen. On a deeper level, these verses tell us that it is through
the work of our hands that the manifestation of our own *spirituality*
enters into our everyday consciousness. In other words, meditation
alone, however good it may be to help us quiet the mind and discipline
us to concentrate and focus, can only bring us to the door of spirituality. Whatever feelings, visions, insights, or experiences the meditation
process brings on, this must be considered to be only the realization of
an opening. The fulfillment of the spirituality comes about in a deed
that is invested with the meaning that the doing of the deed is connected with the Divine. If we do not do anything with our hands or

---

2. Genesis 3:22.
3. Exodus 4:4.

what is equivalent to our hands, then the full manifestation of our own spirituality will not enter into our everyday consciousness.

> And the Lord said furthermore to him: "Put now thy hand into thy bosom." And he put *his hand* into his bosom. And when he took it out, behold, *his hand* was diseased as white as snow. And he said: "Put thy hand into thy bosom again." And he put *his hand* into his bosom again. And when he took it out of his bosom, behold, it was turned again as his other flesh.[4]

This tells us that what we do with our hands can facilitate our own illness, or can facilitate our own healing: physically, emotionally, or *spiritually*.

As instructed by God, Aaron stretches out his hands to cause the plagues of frogs and then the plague of lice on Egypt.

> And Aaron stretched out *his hand* over the waters of Egypt. And the frogs came up and covered the land of Egypt.[5]

> And the Lord said to Moses: "Say to Aaron: 'Stretch out thy rod and smite the dust of the land that it may turn into lice throughout all the land of Egypt.' " And they did so. For Aaron stretched out *his hand* with his rod, and smote the dust of the earth, and it became lice in man, and in beast. All the dust of the land became lice throughout all the land of Egypt.[6]

It is the hand of Moses that when stretched out over the Red Sea initiates God's action to divide the sea and then to close up the sea.

> And Moses stretched out *his hand* over the sea. And the Lord caused the sea to go back by a strong east wind all that night, and made the sea dry land, and the waters were divided.[7]

---

4. Exodus 4:6-7.
5. Exodus 8:2.
6. Exodus 8:12-13.
7. Exodus 14:21.

And Moses stretched out *his hand* over the sea, and the sea
returned to its strength when the morning appeared.[8]

And when the Israelites are fighting with Amalek, it is Moses' upheld
hand that initiates God's help, making the Israelites prevail.

And it came to pass, when Moses held up *his hand* that
Israel prevailed. And when he let down *his hand*, Amalek
prevailed.[9]

But the Talmud here teaches us that it was not only the physical act of
holding up his hand that initiated God's help. Holding up his hand was
the means by which Moses communicated to the Israelites to keep their
thoughts tuned to the above and to subject their hearts to God. And
it was the tuning of their thoughts to the above, and the subjecting
of their hearts to the will of God that was the direct cause for God's
help.[10]

So we learn from these verses that it is the physical act with our
hand, which is below, coincident with the proper thoughts of our mind
and the feelings of our heart that cause the hand that is above to act.
And when the hand above does act we are told not to forget, but to
know and remember His greatness, the mightiness of His hand, and His
outstretched arm.

And ye (for [I do not speak] with your children who did not
know and who did not see the the lesson of the Lord your
God) know this day His greatness, the mightiness of *His
hand*, and His outstretched arm.[11]

The gematria of the יוד is 20. The word הָאָבִיב has the gematria of
20 and is the biblical name for the month initiating spring, the month
celebrating the feast of the unleavened bread.

---

8. Exodus 14:27.
9. Exodus 17:11.
10. *The Babylonian Talmud, Seder Moed*, vol. 4, *Rosh Hashanah* (29a), trans.
Maurice Simon (London: Soncino Press, 1938), p. 134.
11. Deuteronomy 11:2.

And Moses said unto the people: "Remember this day, in which you went out from Egypt, out of the house of bondage; for by the strength of the hand the Lord brought you out from here. And no leavened bread shall be eaten. This day you go forth in the month of *Aviv*."[12]

The feast of unleavened bread shalt thou keep; seven days thou shalt eat unleavened bread, as I commanded thee, at the time appointed in the month of *Aviv*.[13]

The feast of unleavened bread shalt thou keep. Seven days thou shalt eat unleavened bread, as I commanded thee, at the time appointed in the month of *Aviv*, for in the month of *Aviv* thou camest out of Egypt.[14]

Observe the month of *Aviv*, and keep the passover to the Lord thy God: for in the month of *Aviv* the Lord thy God brought thee forth out of Egypt by night.[15]

It is in our periodic spring that we transcend the wilderness and night where we are. This is the night that previously had been day, for today's limitations are actually put in place by yesterday's transcending. This means that when the transcending is over the wilderness comes into being. And when the transcending begins the wilderness disappears.

The full gematria of יוד is יוד וָיו דָלֶת, which totals 476. This is the gematria of the word לָמוּת, the infinitive of the root מות, which means *to die*. When the Israelites are at the Red Sea and they see that the Egyptians have pursued them, they say sarcastically to Moses:

[Is it] because there are no graves in Egypt that you took us away *to die* in the wilderness?[16]

And when the Israelites have no water and they quarrel with Moses they ask:

---

12. Exodus 13:3-4.
13. Exodus 23:15.
14. Exodus 34:18.
15. Deuteronomy 16:1.
16. Exodus 14:11.

And why have you brought up the congregation of the Lord
into this wilderness, *to die* here, we and our cattle?[17]

After Aaron dies, and after the Israelites destroy the Kenanites, the
Israelites are discouraged and they speak against God and Moses:

Why have you brought us up out of Egypt *to die* in the
wilderness? for there is no [real] bread, nor is there any
water; and our soul loathes this miserable bread.[18]

Another word with the gematria of 476 is עָבַדְתָּ, the second person
masculine singular Kal perfect of the root עבד, which means to *work*,
labor, *till*, or *serve*. The word עָבַדְתָּ is used when Moses is summa-
rizing to the Israelites the blessings for obedience and the curses for
disobedience to God's commandments.

All these curses will come upon you. They will pursue you
and overtake you until you are destroyed, because you did
not obey the Lord your God and observe the commands and
decrees he gave you. They will be a sign and a wonder to
you and your descendants forever. Because you *served* not
the Lord your God joyfully and with gladness of heart for
the abundance of all things, therefore in hunger and thirst,
in nakedness and in dire poverty, you will serve the enemies
the Lord sends against you.[19]

This teaches us about the very depths of *spirituality*. We bring the
spiritual to life when we endow each of our everyday situations with
holy meaning. Holy meaning means that we acknowledge, recognize,
and bless the connection that the everyday situation has to the Divine.
We fully receive our everyday situations. If there were no death, then
the urgency to establish this connection with the time we are given
would not be there. Our endowment of the everyday with holiness is
what transcends the limitation of time, the limitation of death, for the
transcending makes each moment eternal.

---

17. Numbers 20:4.
18. Numbers 21:5.
19. Deuteronomy 28:45-48.

When we do not make each of our everyday situations sacred, then we are in the wilderness, the desert. In the desert, we find that there is no water and what bread there may be we grow tired of and find deficient. The Israelites asking Moses why were they brought up to the desert did not have the understanding that the wandering in the desert is the interface between the slavery in Egypt, in limitation, and the freedom in the land of milk and honey. And this interface is not deficient. The wilderness too has the abundance of all things. For the wilderness, paradoxically, is an opening. If we did not experience the deficiency of the wilderness, we would not have the urge to go on and to change ourselves, thereby transcending ourselves. We would just be content to stay where we are. And this means we die spiritually. Therefore, even in what appears to be the wilderness, we serve God joyfully and with gladness of heart. But if we do not recognize the connection our wilderness has with the Divine, who gives to us all our openings, then we will interpret the wilderness as our enemy. And we will be in hunger and thirst and we will have great deficiency: our lives will be in poverty.

So the revealed meaning of ' is that *spirituality* is the transcendence of death by our endowment with sacredness of even what appears to be our wilderness. Spirituality is the triumph and celebration of the transcendence of the physical, the transcendence of the limitations of time and space.

The concealed meaning of ' is revealed by וד, the first two letters of the verb וְדָא, which is the past form of the root meaning to *ascertain, certify, ensure, verify, confirm,* or *authenticate.* Humble ' certifies and authenticates physical existence by providing the pathway through which physical existence can be elevated and *spiritually* escalated. This elevation is what establishes the dwelling place of God in the physical realm. This elevation, which is the creation and formation of Godliness in our lives, is what produces the light. And with the establishment of the dwelling place of God in the physical realm comes information that we can obtain in no other way but by the experience of physical existence. That information is a key factor in the elevation can be understood by the fact that וד are also the first two letters of the word וֶדַע, which means *information.* We also learn that the possibility of this elevation is absolutely certain, for ‏וי‎ are also the first two letters of the word ‏וַדָּאוּת‎, which means *certainty* and ‏וַדָּאִי‎, which means *certain* and *sure*.

We can learn more about the letter energy intelligence of ‏י‎ by seeing how it combines with other letters. When the letter energy intelligence of ‏י‎ combines with the letter energy intelligence of ‏ד‎, which is the archetype for physical existence, there results the root ‏ידד‎, which means to *become friends*, to *get to like*, to *strike up a friendship with*, to *fraternize*, to *make friends*, and to *be on friendly terms with*. When the form ‏יד‎ combines with the letter energy intelligence of ‏ה‎, which stands for power of being, there results the root ‏ידה‎, which means to *throw, cast, hurl*, or *fling*. It also carries the alternate meaning of to *admit, confess, acknowledge, think, glorify*, and *praise*. This notion of throw is further reinforced when we see the combination of the form ‏יד‎ with the letter energy intelligence of ‏ו‎, which is the archetype for connection. The word ‏ידוי‎ forms which means *throwing* or *hurling*.

When the form ‏יד‎ combines with the letter energy intelligence of ‏ח‎, which stands for life, there results the root ‏יחד‎, meaning to *be united* or *joined* or *attached*. When the form ‏יד‎ combines with the letter energy intelligence of ‏ס‎, which stands for support, there results the root ‏יסד‎, which is the root to *found, establish, base, form*, or *organize*.

> By wisdom the Lord *founded* the earth. By understanding
> He set the heavens in place. By knowledge the deeps were
> divided and the clouds let drop the dew.[20]

When the form ‏יד‎ combines with the letter energy intelligence of ‏ע‎, which stands for insight and consciousness, a number of words are formed. Among them are ‏ידע‎, which is the root meaning to *punish* and which is also the root meaning to *know, learn to know, perceive, consider, care for, regard, be acquainted with, be skillful*, or *have sexual intercourse with*, and ‏יֶדַע‎, which means *knowledge, know-how*, or *expertise*.

And Adam *knew* his wife Eve and she conceived.[21]

---

20. Proverbs 3:19.
21. Genesis 4:1.

Jacob awoke from his sleep and said: "Surely there is the Lord in this place, and I did not *know* it!"[22]

Know therefore this day, and consider it in thy heart, that the Lord is God in heaven above, and upon the earth beneath: there is no other. Thou shalt keep, therefore, His statutes and His commandments which I command thee this day, that it may go well with thee and with thy children after thee and that thou mayst prolong thy days upon the earth, which the Lord thy God gives thee, for ever.[23]

This I *know*: for God is for me. In God, I will praise His word. In the Lord, I will praise His word. In God have I put my trust. I will not be afraid. What can man do to me?[24]

Trust in the Lord with all thy heart and do not lean upon thy own understanding. In all thy ways *acknowledge* Him, and He shall direct thy paths.[25]

When ד׳ combines with ע there also forms יעד, which is the root meaning to *appoint, assign, designate, earmark, betroth,* or *engage,* and יֵעָד, which means *mission, purpose, aim, destination, target,* or *objective.*

So it appears that we are flung in physical existence and punished. But when we utilize the energy intelligence of י, physical existence becomes a friendly place, a place to which we are united and betrothed. It is a place in which we utilize our knowledge to organize and establish our creations, our formations. It is a place in which we can accomplish our mission and purpose. It is a place we glorify and praise, for it is the place in which we make Divine connection. It is the place where God dwells.

When the letter energy intelligence of י combines with the letter energy intelligence of ם, which stands for perfection and completion, there results the word יָם, which means *sea, ocean, lake,* or *large basin.*

22. Genesis 28:16.
23. Deuteronomy 4:39-40.
24. Psalms 56:11-12.
25. Proverbs 3:6.

The word **ם֫** also carries the meaning of the direction *west*. When the form **ם֫** combines with the letter energy intelligence of **ו**, which is the archetype for the flow of **א**, there results the word **ם֫י֫**, which means *initiator*.

When the letter energy intelligence of **י** combines with the letter energy intelligence of **שׁ**, the letter energy intelligence of cosmic nourishment, there results the word **שׁי֫**, which means *existence, substance, being, reality, possessions*, or *assets*.

> Jacob awoke from his sleep and said: "Surely there *is* the Lord in this place, and I did not know it!"[26]

> And he called the name of the place Massa and Meriva, because of the strife of the children of Israel, and because they tempted the Lord, saying: "Does the Lord *exist* among us, or not?"[27]

Wisdom says of herself:

> That I may cause those who love me to inherit *substance*: and I will fill their treasures.[28]

And when the form **שׁי֫** is wrapped in the archetype container **ב**, there results the root **בשׁי֫**, which means to *sit, dwell, inhabit, live, stay, reside*, or *abide*.

> And ye shall do My statutes and keep My judgments and do them. And ye shall *dwell* in the land in safety. And the land shall yield her fruit, and ye shall eat your fill, and dwell in safety.[29]

> If you walk in my statutes and keep my commandments and do them, then I will give you rain in due season and the land shall yield its increase, and the trees of the field shall yield their fruit. And your threshing shall reach to the vintage and the vintage shall reach to the sowing time.

---

26. Genesis 28:16.
27. Exodus 17:7.
28. Proverbs 8:21.
29. Leviticus 25:18.

And you shall eat your bread to the full and *dwell* in your land safely.[30]

When the form יָשׁ is wrapped in the letter energy intelligence ר, the cosmic container, there results the word ירשׁ, which is the root to *inherit, take possession of,* or *succeed,* and the word יָשָׁר, which means *straightness, righteousness, equity, honesty, fairness, integrity, sincerity, purpose,* or *straightforwardness.* Our inheritance is existence in which the physical part of us resides and that we must approach as an initiator, having an attitude of righteousness, integrity, honesty, and sincerity. From this we see that Israel, יִשְׂרָאֵל, means יָשָׁר אֵל, the straightforwardness, honesty, and sincerity of God and as well means the inheritance or possession of God. Hence the land of Israel, אֶרֶץ יִשְׂרָאֵל, is that place, that state of consciousness whose substance is filled with the straightforwardness, honesty, sincerity, and inheritance of God.

אֶרֶץ is related to אֶרְצֶה, which is the first person future of the root רצה, meaning to *will.* From this point of view, אֶרֶץ יִשְׂרָאֵל means "I will go straight to God. I will to possess in me the presence of God. I will to make my will whatever God's will might be."[31]

When the letter energy intelligence י combines with the letter energy of פ, which means speech and freedom, the word יְפִי forms which means *beauty, splendor,* or *loveliness.* And when the form יְפִ is invested with the power of being of ה, there results the word יָפֶה, which means *beautiful, pretty, fair, nice, lovely, handsome, good-looking, good, worthy,* or *wholesome* and the word יָפָה, which means to *be beautiful, pretty, lovely, handsome, fair, good-looking,* or *nice.*

When the letter energy intelligence י combines with the letter energy intelligence of צ, which stands for righteousness and humility, a variety of interesting combinations results. When the form יצ combines with the letter energy intelligence of א, the unbridled pulsating force, there results the root יצא, which means to *go out, come out, go away, emerge, depart, leave, appear,* or *rise.* God tells Abram, who was in the

---

30. Leviticus 26:5.
31. See a related discussion to this in *Midrash Rabbah*, vol. 1, *Genesis* (5:8), trans. H. Freedman (London, Soncino Press, 1983), p. 38.

land of Haran, to leave Haran and go to the land that God will show him.

> Abram was seventy-five years old when he *departed* from Haran.[32]

Immediately after the Israelites leave Egypt, Moses says to the Israelites:

> Remember this day, in which you *went out* from Egypt, out of the house of bondage; for by the strength of the hand the Lord *brought you out* from here.[33]

God tells Moses to tell the Israelites:

> On that day, tell your son:
>
>> I do this because of what the Lord did for me when I *came out* of Egypt.[34]

In Deuteronomy we are told:

> Remember what the Amalekites did to you along the way when you *came out* of Egypt.[35]

When Moses is ready to die he tells the Israelites:

> I am now one hundred and twenty years old and I am no longer able to *go out* and to come in.[36]

To go out or depart means to transcend where we are. And if we are in the process of transcending when doubt (Amalek) enters into us, we must remember what the Amalekites did to us when we came out of Egypt, the land of limitation, for if we do not remember and doubt stays within us, then we will not be able to transcend. When we no longer are able to go out and transcend, then our time to die has come.

---

32. Genesis 12:4.
33. Exodus 13:3.
34. Exodus 13:8.
35. Deuteronomy 25:17.
36. Deuteronomy 31:2.

53

When the form is then wrapped in the cosmic container ר, there results the root יצר, which means to *manufacture, fashion, form, produce, devise,* or *contrive,* and the word יֵצֶר, which means *instinct, inclination, impulse, nature, will, desire, drive,* or *lust.* When the form יצר combines with the letter energy intelligence of ה there results the word יְצִירָה, which means *creation, formation, production, deed, word, composition, creativeness.*

> And the Lord God *formed* man of the dust of the ground and breathed into his nostrils the breath of life; and man became a living soul. And the Lord God planted a garden eastward in Eden. And there he put the man whom he had *formed.*[37]

> I am the Lord, and there is none else. I *form* the light and create darkness.[38]

> For thus says the Lord that created the heavens: God Himself *formed* the earth and made it; He has established it. He did not create it a waste land. He *formed* it to be inhabited. I am the Lord; and there is none else.[39]

> The sea is His and He made it. And His hands *formed* the dry land.[40]

From this we learn that our forming must be like God's forming. It must be to make our world more and more inhabitable.

When the letter energy intelligence י combines with the letter energy intelligence of ק, which stands for cosmic unbridled force and is then wrapped in the cosmic container, which is the letter energy intelligence of ר, there result the words יָקָר and יְקָר. The word יָקָר means *dear, expensive, precious, scarce,* or *rare.* The word יְקָר means *honor, respect, value, dignity, splendor,* and *precious thing.*

When the cosmic unbridled force of ק is replaced with א, there results the root ירא, which means to *threaten, frighten, intimidate,*

---

37. Genesis 2:7-8.
38. Isaiah 45:6-7.
39. Isaiah 45:18.
40. Psalms 95:5.

or *terrify* and the word יָרֵא, which means *fearful, dreading, fearing, apprehensive, timid, respecting,* or *revering.* And when the form יִרְא combines with the letter energy intelligence of ה, there results the word יִרְאָה, which has the meaning of *fear, terror, dread, awe,* and *reverence.*

From these combinations, we learn that we make use of the letter energy intelligence of י when we transcend ourselves, making a change within, that facilitates our creating and forming new things on a higher and more moral, practical, or aesthetic level, creating new ideas, forming new situations or policies that are more effective in making the world a place for God's dwelling. We accomplish this creation and formation by our use of will in a context of awe and reverence. Our actions, which are what result, are precious, honorable, and beautiful. These actions are a manifestation of יָצָא, a going out, יָרַד, a coming down, and יָצַר, a forming of that essence that we really are.

In a verse in Moses' poem, Moses says:

> Thou art unmindful of the Rock that begot thee and thou
> hast forgotten God who brought thee forth.[41]

The Hebrew word for "thou art unmindful" is תֶּשִׁי. This is the second person masculine singular of the root שׁיה, to *forsake* or *be unmindful.* The י of תֶּשִׁי is a small י. *Pesikta Rabbati* renders the translation

> The Artist who begot thee thou dost weaken.[42]

Here, the word צוּר, *rock,* is taken to be related to צָר, *artist* and the word תֶּשִׁי, is taken as a form of the root תשׁשׁ, to *become weak* or *become feeble.* This may be interpreted as follows: When we become unmindful of God, we weaken the י, the projection into time and physical existence of the unbridled timeless energy of א. And that is why the י of תֶּשִׁי is small. By forgetting God, we weaken Godliness in the physical world. In effect, we weaken God's strength as God manifests to us.[43]

---

41. Deuteronomy 32:18.
42. *Pesikta Rabbati*, Piska 24, trans. William G. Braude (New Haven and London: Yale University Press, 1968), p. 507.
43. Rashi, *Pentateuch and Rashi's Commentary, Deuteronomy*, vol. 5, trans. Abraham ben Isaiah and Benjamin Sharfman (Brooklyn, NY: S. S. and R. Publishing, 1976), Deuteronomy 32:18, p. 297.

When Israel settled in Schittim, the Israelites committed harlotry with the daughters of Moab.[44] The Ramban explains that the elders of Midian and the Moabites took counsel together. The Midian elders encouraged the Moabite daughters to first prostitute themselves with the Israelites so that they could lead the Israelites to commit idolatry by worshiping Baal-peor.[45] The consequence of this was that God put a plague among the Israelites.

While this plague is occurring, Pinchas sees a Midianite woman and a prince of Israel engaging in immoral sex within the sight of the congregation of Israel.[46] Pinchas gets very zealous, takes a spear and thrusts the spear into the two of them. And this stays the plague among the Israelites for their immoral behavior and idol worship.[47]

What is interesting is that the next time the name Pinchas is mentioned, the ' in Pinchas, פִּינְחָס, is a small yod.

> And the Lord spoke to Moses, saying, *Pinchas*, son of Eleazar, son of Aaron the priest, has turned my wrath away from the children of Israel, in that he was zealous for my sake among them, that I consumed not the children of Israel in my jealousy.[48]

Rabbi Hirsch explains that פִּינְחָס should be read as פִּי נֵחַס, where נֵחַס is similar to נַחַץ, to *urge on* and פִּי means *my mouth*. The name Pinchas thereby meaning, my mouth urged me on. My mouth, the mouth of God, urged me to it.[49]

Another interpretation is to include the word following Pinchas: פִּינְחָס בֶּן. Leaving the פִּי as before and permuting the remaining letters we obtain: פִּי חָנֵן סָב. The word פִּי means *my mouth*. The word חָנֵן is a verb one of whose meanings is to *ask for mercy*. And the word סָב means *grandfather*. This hints that at the time Pinchas was

---

44. Numbers 25:1.
45. Rabbi Moshe ben Nachman, *Ramban Commentary on the Torah, Numbers*, trans. Charles Chavel (New York: Shilo Publishing House, 1971), p. 291.
46. Numbers 25:6.
47. Numbers 25:8.
48. Numbers 25:10-11.
49. Samson Raphael Hirsch, *The Pentateuch, Numbers*, vol. 4, trans. Isaac Levy (Gateshead: Judaica Press, 1989), p. 431.

thrusting his spear, committing murder, he was thinking that the soul of his grandfather Aaron, the high priest, the peacemaker, might not understand what Pinchas was doing and that he should understand that Pinchas was being zealous only for God. Therefore, his mouth pleaded that his grandfather should give him mercy rather than judge him harshly. And in the very next verse, we read that it was mercy that Pinchas received. For God says:

> Wherefore say: Behold, I give unto him [Pinchas] My covenant
> of peace; and it shall be unto him and to his seed after him,
> a covenant of an everlasting priesthood; because he was
> zealous for his God, and made atonement for the children
> of Israel.[50]

The most important word beginning with a ' is the Tetragrammaton יְהֹוָה. The Zohar teaches that

> the ' is the symbol of the head of all creatures; the two הs
> represent the five fingers of the right hand and the left; the
> ו is the symbol of the body.[51]

The thorn that is the tip of the ' represents God's Supreme Will, which is the source of the benevolence issuing from His Name.[52] The ' itself represents God's Wisdom.

Rabbi Shneur Zalman teaches that the wisdom of ' is

> the state of concealment and obscurity, before it develops
> into a state of expansion and revelation in comprehension
> and understanding. When the "point" evolves into a state
> of expansion and revelation of comprehension and under-
> standing in the concealed worlds, it is then contained and
> represented in the letter ה. The shape of the letter [ה] has
> dimension, expansion in breadth, which implies the breadth

50. Numbers 25:12-13.
51. *The Zohar*, vol. 3, trans. Harry Sperling, Maurice Simon, and Paul Levertoff (London: Soncino Press, 1978), p. 130.
52. Rabbi Shneur Zalman, "*Igeret Hateshuvah*," in *Likkutei Amarim – Tanya*, bi-lingual ed. (Brooklyn NY: Kehot Publication Society, 1993), p. 363.

of explanation and understanding, and expansion in length, to indicate extension and flow downward into the concealed worlds.

In the next stage this extension and flow are drawn still lower into the revealed worlds. . . . This stage of extension is contained and represented in the final letters ו and ה.

ו, in shape a vertical line, indicates downward extension. Also this flow downward is effected through the divine traits of benevolence and goodness and His other sacred traits, included in general terms in the six attributes in the verse:

> Thine, O Lord is the greatness, the strength, the beauty, the victory, the glory, all that is in heaven and earth.[53]

His seventh attribute

> Thine, O Lord, is the dominion.[54]

. . . This attribute of dominion is contained and represented in the final ה of the Tetragrammaton.[55]

The meaning of the Tetragrammaton can now be understood from an analysis of the energy intelligence consciousness of the letters that make up the Tetragrammaton. י is the projection into time and physical existence of the unbridled timeless energy of the א. Hence י brings into physical manifestation and being that which unites heaven and earth. ה is the eternal life above, the life in the spiritual realm, and this is our true identity. ו is the connection between above and below. And the final ה is the transitory life below, the life in the physical realm. Thus,

יְהֹוָה is the source which brings into being all existence.[56]

53. 1 Chronicles 29:11.
54. Ibid.
55. Rabbi Zalman, "Igeret Hateshuvah," in *Likkutei Amarim - Tanya*, p. 359.
56. Rabbi Menachem Schneerson, *Sichos in English*, vol. 51 (Brooklyn, NY: Sichos in English, 1992), p. 214.

Thus it is above and

beyond the limits of existence.[57]

"God" is a translation of the name (ה־יָ־הָ־יְ *Havayah*), which refers to His transcendent dimension, the aspect of Godliness that is above the limits of existence.[58]

The four Divine worlds of *Emanation*, *Creation*, *Formation*, and *Action* are created by the spiritual energy intelligences of ה־יְ־הָ־יְ. Rabbi Krakovsky teaches that the י,

> which is named Wisdom and is called the World of Emanation, desires to receive its bounty from the Infinite, in order to meet the demands of the ה, or Intelligence, called the World of Creation. This World of Creation is just beneath the . . . . י . . . which is the World of Emanation. . . .
>
> The ה, or Intelligence, wishes to obtain its essential life sustenance from its precedent phase of wisdom, in order to fulfill the requisite cravings of its so-called child, the ו, or the World of Formation. . . .
>
> The ו, or the World of Formation, is necessarily of the same purport, to pursue and pray for bounty in order to fulfill the cravings of the ה which is beneath the ו, and which is the only complete receptacle established in its full dimension called the World of Action, or Kingdom. . . .
>
> The last ה, . . . exerts an active desire in demanding its abundance in order to distribute this to all the nether worlds, including the angels, souls, and at last to humanity as a whole.[59]

Rabbi Luzzatto and Rabbi Krakovsky teach that these worlds correspond to the four different ways the Tetragrammaton ה־יְ־הָ־יְ can

---

57. Rabbi Schneerson, *Sichos in English*, vol. 50, p. 33.
58. Rabbi Schneerson, *Sichos in English*, vol. 49, p. 235.
59. Rabbi Levi I. Krakovsky, *The Omnipotent Light Revealed* (Hollywood, CA: Kabbalah Culture Society of America, 1939), p. 69.

be spelled out. The first way spells out יְהֹוָה as יוֹד הֵי וִיו הֵי. This spelling has a total value of 72 and corresponds to the world of *Emanation* and is associated with the Sephirah חָכְמָה, Wisdom. The second way spells out יְהֹוָה as יוֹד הֵי וָאו הֵי. This spelling has a total value of 63 and corresponds to the world of *Creation* and is associated with the Sephirah בִּינָה, Understanding. The third way spells out יְהֹוָה as יוֹד הֵא וָאו הֵא. This spelling has a total value of 45 and corresponds to the world of *Formation* and is associated with the six Sephirot חֶסֶד, Loving-kindness, גְבוּרָה, Strength, תִפְאֶרֶת, Beauty, נֶצַח, Victory, הוֹד, Glory, and יְסוֹד, Foundation. The fourth way spells out יְהֹוָה as יוֹד הֵה וו הֵה. This spelling has a total value of 52 and corresponds to the world of *Action* and is associated with the Sephirah מַלְכוּת, Kingdom.[60,61]

Rabbi Kaplan explains that the Tetragrammaton contains the mystery of benevolence and charity.[62] The first letter, י, denotes the coin that is given. It is the coin because the letter י is small and simple like a coin. As the letter י has the numerical value of 10 the coin has the spiritual value of the ten Sephirot. The second letter, ה, denotes the hand that gives the coin. The hand has five fingers just as the letter ה has the numerical value of 5. The third letter, ו, denotes the arm reaching out, giving the coin. The arm connects the hand to the body, moving the hand in any of the six directions of physical space, for the letter ו has the numerical value of 6. The fourth letter, ה, denotes the hand that receives the coin. That hand has five fingers just as the letter ה also has the numerical value of 5. The five that receives and the five that gives constitute the ten of the י. In this there is a deep *spiritual* kabbalistic lesson.

---

60. Rabbi Moshe Chayim Luzzatto, *General Principles of the Kabbalah* (Jerusalem: Research Centre of Kabbalah, 1984), p. 55, p. 100.
61. Rabbi Levi Krakovsky, *Kabbalah: The Light of Redemption* (Jerusalem: Research Centre of Kabbalah, 1970), pp. 162-163.
62. Rabbi Aryeh Kaplan, *Jewish Meditation* (New York: Schocken Books, 1985), pp. 73-74.

Caph כֹ: The Crowning Achievement

The eleventh letter of the Hebrew alphabet is כ, spelled כַּף. Numerically כ has the value of 20. It has a final form ך, which can take the value of either 20 or 500. Now 20 is the value of יוֹד, the spelling of the letter י. Thereby, we learn that כ is responsible for holding, covering, and letting flow the light of י, the energy intelligence of spirituality. Since it has the numerical value of 20, כ is the projection of the energy consciousness of ב, the energy intelligence of container, into time and conditioned physical existence. Thus, כ is the flow of spirituality within the container.

As a prefix כ means *as*, *like*, *when*, *at*, *about*, or *according to*. The word כַּף means the curved or *hollow of the hand*, the *palm*, or the *hollow of the foot*, the *sole*. As well it can mean *spoon*, *handle*, *pan*, *dish*, or *container full of valuable contents*. The word כַּף is cognate to the word כֵּף, which means *cliff*, *rock*, *cape*, or *promontory*. The letter energy intelligence of כ is the high point of land or rock projecting into the sea beyond the line of the coast.

The first use of כַּף occurs in the incident where an angel wrestles with Jacob until the breaking of the dawn.

> And when he [the angel] saw that he prevailed not against him [Jacob], he touched [reached into] the hollow of his thigh and the *hollow* of Jacob's thigh was strained, as he wrestled with him. And he said: "Let me go for the dawn breaketh." And he said: "I will not let thee go, except thou bless me." And he said unto him: "What is thy name?" And he said: "Jacob." And he said: "Not Jacob shall any more be called thy name, but Israel."[1]

This wrestling incident occurs in the night. The night is darkness, without light. This is the time of concealment. In the time of concealment each of us wrestles with the man. Each of us wrestles with desires that

1. Genesis 32:26-29.

163

are not worthy. Each of us wrestles with our evil inclination. For these desires reach and extend into us and strike us in the hollow, in the כַּף, of our thigh. As Rashi tells us, this is the place where

> the thighbone is lodged in the hipbone . . . because the
> flesh which is above it is like the ladle [כַּף] of a pot.[2]

The word for *his thigh* is יְרֵכוֹ. This is the same word that is used to describe the descendants of Jacob who came to Egypt with him.

> All the souls belonging to Jacob that came into Egypt, that
> came out of *his thigh*, besides the wives of Jacob's sons, all
> these souls were sixty six.[3]

We will our own desires to be. And it is these desires that come out of our thighs and become our progeny as they are enclothed in our thoughts, speech, and actions. Our unworthy desires are enclothed in unworthy thoughts, speech, and actions. This in turn strains or dislocates our hip bone, moving it from the place of its joint. But if our first desire is Godliness, then our name is no longer Jacob, but Israel. Israel, יִשְׂרָאֵל, can be understood to mean אֵל, God, combined with the root יָשַׁר, which means *to be straight, to go straight, to be right*, or *to be level*. So our *crowning achievement* is Jacob's achievement. Jacob prevailed. And we prevail by so deeply and consistently desiring to bring down Godliness that our name too is Israel, "straight to God."

This interpretation is reinforced by another verse using the word כַּף, in the sense of sole:

> For if you shall diligently keep all these commandments
> which I command you to do them, to love the Lord your
> God, to walk in all His ways, and to cleave to Him, then
> will the Lord drive out all these nations from before you
> and you shall possess greater nations and mightier than
> yourselves. Every place whereon the *sole* of your foot shall

---

2. Rashi, *Pentateuch and Rashi's Commentary, Genesis* vol. 1, trans. Abraham ben Isaiah and Benjamin Sharfman (Brooklyn, NY: S.S. and R. Publishing, 1976), p. 330.
3. Genesis 46:26.

tread shall be yours: from the wilderness to Lebanon, from
the river, the river Euphrates, to the uttermost sea shall be
your border. There shall be no man able to stand against
you.[4]

From this we learn that the *crowning achievement* is to love the
Lord our God, to walk in all His ways, and to cleave to Him. To
walk in all His ways means to be close to God by being similar to
Him. God acts with loving-kindness, so in crowning achievement we
act with loving-kindness. God acts mercifully, so in crowning achievement we act mercifully. God is charitable, so in crowning achievement
we are charitable. God is true, so in crowning achievement we are true.
To cleave to God means to have faith in God and to follow the wise
ones. Then God will drive out nations greater than ourselves. Nations
here means ungodly thoughts. In our crowning achievement, ungodly
thoughts will no longer linger in our land, our consciousness. Every
place where we put our attention and become conscious of, every situation from the wilderness to Lebanon, from the south to the north,
from the Euphrates to the uttermost sea, from the east to the west, all
these places where we set our consciousness will have no lingering ungodly thoughts. Everything we experience, we experience as the hand
of God. We receive it completely and we bring out and develop the
good in it. Therefore, there is nothing that can stand against us.

The word כָּף has the gematria of 100. The word מִמֶּךָ, which means
of you or *from you*, also has gematria of 100. God uses the word מִמֶּךָ
in telling Abraham how he will be a patriarch of many nations.

And I will make thee exceedingly fruitful, and I will make
thee nations, and kings shall come out *of thee* and thy seed
after thee in their generations for an everlasting covenant,
to be a God to thee, and to thy seed after thee.[5]

God again uses the word מִמֶּךָ in telling Jacob that he too will be a
patriarch of many nations.

---

4. Deuteronomy 11:22-25.
5. Genesis 17:6.

> I am God Almighty: be fruitful and multiply. A nation and
> a company of nations shall be *of thee*, and kings shall come
> out of thy loins. And the land which I gave to Abraham
> and Isaac, to thee I will give it, and to thy seed after thee
> will I give the land.[6]

This reinforces the interpretation that from us come many nations,
many thoughts. These thoughts dwell in our land, our consciousness.

The word מַלְכֵי is the constructive plural of the word מֶלֶךְ, which
means *king*. It too has the gematria of 100. God uses the word מַלְכֵי
in telling Abraham how he blesses Sarah.

> And I will bless her, and give thee a son also of her. And
> I will bless her, and she shall be a mother of nations: *kings*
> of peoples shall issue from her.[7]

Here we see that when our will for Godliness, כֶּתֶר, clothes itself through
wisdom, חָכְמָה, and into understanding, בִּינָה, which is mother, what
issue are not just nations, not just ordinary thoughts, but royal thoughts,
thoughts worthy of a king.

The word יִמְלֹךְ, the Kal third person masculine singular imperfect
of the root מלך, which means to *reign*, to *rule*, or to *be king* or to
become king, also has the gematria of 100. Moses and the Israelites
use it in the song they sing when they cross the Red Sea. They sing
that God brings them, the Israelites, into the mountain of God's inheritance. God brings us, we who are spiritual cultivators, into a land, a
consciousness, that is not a flat land, but to a mountain, the height of
all the land, the height of all consciousness.

> Thou bringest them in, and plantest them in the mountain
> of Thine inheritance, the place which Thou hast made for
> Thee to dwell in, O Lord. The sanctuary, O Lord which
> Thy hands have established. The Lord shall *reign* for ever
> and ever.[8]

---

6. Genesis 35:11-12.
7. Genesis 17:16.
8. Exodus 15:17-18.

When we become spiritual cultivators, putting Godliness first, our consciousness becomes a place in which God can dwell, our consciousness becomes a sanctuary for God. And there God reigns. And when God reigns in us, when the King, who is above, reigns in us, then we, who are below, become a king (queen) below. And this is the *crowning achievement*, the revealed meaning of כ.

The full gematria of כ is כַּף פֵּ, which totals 185. The word לְהָקִים is the infinitive Hiphil constructive form of the root קוּם. The Hiphil form means to *cause to stand up, raise up, establish,* or to *set up.*

> And it came to pass on the day that Moses had finished
> *setting up* the tabernacle, and had anointed it, and sanc-
> tified it, and all its instruments, both the altar and all its
> vessels, and had anointed them, and sanctified them that
> the princes of Israel, heads of the house of their fathers,
> who were the princes of the tribes and were over them that
> were numbered, offered. And they brought them before the
> tabernacle.[9]

This tells us that we must set up our own tabernacle and there our princes, our heads of houses, will offer. The tabernacle is a temple. A temple is a holy place, a place where we come to commune with God. The temple is external and can be thought of as representing the external physical world. The real temple is inside each of us. It represents the spiritual world. And at the next higher level of understanding, the two temples are one temple. For the spiritual resides and manifests in the physical. And what we do when we enter the temple and pray is to shed our consciousness of the appearance of the physical and concentrate on the essence of the spiritual. This shedding is a giving up of our consciousness of the appearance aspect. It is our sacrifice. Filled with love and reverence, we sacrifice our unworthy inclinations. These are the inclinations always associated with the purely appearance aspect of our reality.

The Hebrew word for *offering* or *sacrificial gift* is קָרְבָּן. It is related to the root קרב meaning to *approach, draw near, appear before God, come near,* or *advance.* The purpose of the temple sacrifices is to

---

9. Numbers 7:1-3.

approach God, to be closer to God. It is our daily rededication to God. The offering is the physical act corresponding to the unconditional surrendering of our will to God's will.[10] The offering is then the conquest of our nature, for it is the slaughtering of our evil inclination.[11] Hence, the animal sacrifice in the temple was not just an offering of an animal.

The sacrifices were also a means of atonement. For the sacrifice service entailed a confession of transgressions. And before the animal of the sacrifice was killed, the offerer had to put his two hands on the animal's head. This is symbolic of the sacrificer saying that the sacrificer is offering to God his animal soul, the seat of what had been his unworthy inclinations, inclinations he no longer wants to be part of himself, inclinations for which he separates himself and thereby returns to a state of purity.[12]

For there to be a temple, the temple must be established. It must be set up, for the setting up of the temple does not happen on its own. To move our consciousness so that it is increasingly filled with the consciousness of the Godliness in all things, we must set up our temple. And having set it up, we must use it. And this is the concealed meaning of כ, the *crowning achievement*.

The shape of the letter כ is curved and bent. That כ has an important meaning relating to being bent can be learned from the fact that כָּפוּף means *bent, bowed, hunched up* and to *subordinate,* כְּפוּף means *bent, bowing, subordination*, and the root כָּפַף means to *bend* or *incline*. The root כָּפַן means to *bend* or *incline* and has the alternate meaning of to *be hungry*. To satisfy our hunger for Godliness, we must bend and subordinate our will to God's will.

כ is the first letter of the word כָּבוֹד, which means *honor, respect, glory, splendor, majesty, reverence, distinction, importance, wealth, riches,* or *ambition*. It has a gematria of 32; these are the 32 wondrous (mystical) paths of wisdom discussed in *Sefer Yetzirah*.[13] These

---

10. Rabbi Elie Munk, *The World of Prayer*, vol. 1, trans. Henry Biberfeld and Leonard Oschry (Jerusalem: Feldheim, 1961), p. 50.
11. Ibid., p. 53.
12. Nissan Mindel, *My Prayer* (Brooklyn, NY: Merkos L'Inyonei Chinuch, 1984). p. 84.
13. *Sefer Yetzirah*, trans. and comm. Rabbi Aryeh Kaplan (York Beach, ME: Samuel Weiser, 1990), p. 5.

are the 32 teeth of the mouth.[14] Rabbi Nachman teaches that

> When כָּבוֹד is complete – with its ו – it is, "So that glory
> may sing praise to You, and not remain silent." Otherwise,
> when כָּבוֹד is without the ו (כָּבֹד), the Thirty-Two Paths
> of Wisdom are incomplete. This is כְבַד פֶּה faltering speech
> and a corrupted mouth.[15]

Although the word כָּבוֹד does not occur in the Pentateuch, its
constructive form, כְּבוֹד, occurs exactly ten times in the Pentateuch in
the phrase כְּבוֹד יְ־הֹ־וָ־ה,[16] or the phrase כְבוֹד יְ־הֹ־וָ־ה,[17] glory of
the Lord.

> And Moses and Aaron said to all the children of Israel: "At
> evening you shall know that the Lord has brought you out
> from the land of Egypt. And in the morning, you shall
> see the *glory* of the Lord when he hears your murmurings
> against the Lord."[18]

> And it came to pass, as Aaron spoke to the whole congre-
> gation of the children of Israel, that they looked toward the
> wilderness, and behold, the *glory* of the Lord appeared in
> the cloud.[19]

> And the *glory* of the Lord rested upon mount Sinai, and the
> cloud covered it for six days. On the seventh day He called
> to Moses out of the midst of the cloud. And the sight of
> the *glory* of the Lord was like a devouring fire on the top of
> the mountain in the eyes of the children of Israel.[20]

> And Moses said: "This is the thing which the Lord com-
> manded you to do. And the *glory* of the Lord shall appear

---

14. Rabbi Nachman, *Likutey Moharan*, vol. 1B, trans. Moshe Mykoff, ann. Chaim
Kramer (Jerusalem: Breslov Research Institute, 1989), p. 170.
15. Ibid., p. 171.
16. Exodus 16:7,10; 24:16,17; Leviticus 9:6; Numbers 17:7.
17. Leviticus 9:23; Numbers 14:20; 16:19; 20:6.
18. Exodus 16:6-7.
19. Exodus 16:10.
20. Exodus 24:16-17.

to you."[21]

And Moses and Aaron went into the Tent of Meeting and came out and blessed the people. And the *glory* of the Lord appeared to all the people.[22]

And the Lord said: "I have pardoned according to thy word. Nevertheless, as all the earth is filled with the *glory* of the Lord, surely, all those men who have seen my glory, and my miracles, which I did in Egypt, and in the wilderness, and yet have tempted me now these ten times, and have not hearkened to my voice: surely, they shall not see the land which I swore to their forefathers. Nor shall any of those who provoked me see it. But my servant Caleb, because he had another spirit with him and followed me fully, him will I bring into the land into which he went and his seed shall possess it."[23]

And Korah gathered all the congregation against them to the door of the Tent of Meeting. And the *glory* of the Lord appeared to all the congregation.[24]

And it came to pass when the congregation was gathered against Moses and against Aaron, that they looked toward the Tent of Meeting and behold, the cloud covered it, and the *glory* of the Lord appeared.[25]

And Moses and Aaron went from the presence of the assembly to the door of the Tent of Meeting, and they fell upon their faces. And the *glory* of the Lord appeared to them.[26]

From this we learn that *glory of the Lord* means the revealed presence of God, a presence that is not only a presence of splendor, but a presence that is openly apprehendable to the worthy and unworthy

---

21. Leviticus 9:6.
22. Leviticus 9:23.
23. Numbers 14:20-24.
24. Numbers 16:19.
25. Numbers 17:7.
26. Numbers 20:6.

alike. It is a presence that fills all the earth. Yet it is a presence that can be in the midst of a cloud that covers it. And it is a presence that can be on the top of a mountain, appearing like a devouring fire. Maimonides teaches us that glory

> is sometimes intended to signify the created light that God causes to descend in a particular place in order to confer honor upon it in a miraculous way.[27]

This Divinely created light

> is that primordial light, which, as the direct emanation of the Deity, represents the initial stage of the creation, the first step in the transition from the metaphysical to the material world. Its supernatural splendor is too great for the human eye, bounded by the limits of time, to bear. It is therefore hidden away in the "storehouse of life" . . . to be kept there till man reaches a higher level of spiritual existence, and to be given to him as the crowning reward for this ethical perfection.[28]

Our *crowning achievement* is associated with seeing the glory of God wherever we look, for there is no place devoid of the presence of God. To see it, we have to believe that the entire earth is filled with His glory. And we have to live in a way that our every thought, word, and action is focused on revealing this presence, the immanence of God within nature, within the material world. And this is why we say in our daily prayers:

> Blessed be the glory of the Lord from its place.[29,30]

For with this statement we affirm that we completely receive God's immanence in the world.

---

27. Moses Maimonides, *The Guide of the Perplexed*, vol. 1, trans. Shlomo Pines (Chicago: University of Chicago Press, 1963), p. 156.
28. Rabbi Munk, *The World of Prayer*, vol 1, p. 96.
29. Ezekiel 3:12.
30. *Siddur Tehillat Hashem* (Brooklyn, NY: Merkos L'Inyonei Chinuch, 1979), p. 44.

כ has a final form ך. When used as a suffix on a noun, final caph, ך, has the meaning *your*. The shape of caph final, ך, is very different from כ. ך is straight and extends below the line. Any Hebrew letter that goes below the line symbolizes some sort of connection between upper and lower. Here the meaning is that in order to connect to the upper, the lower must bend. The primitive impulses of the ego must yield to the higher mission of the soul. And this is the way in which we become king, for final caph, ך, is the last letter of the word מֶלֶךְ, which means *king*.

That this connection is an intrinsic part of the כ can be learned from the fact that כרך is the root to *be bound* or *connected*. The kind of connection is learned from the word כָּנַף, which means *surround* or to *hide oneself*.

Many of the words that relate to covering and concealment begin with the letters כס, which itself forms the word כֵס, meaning *throne*. The root כסה means to *cover, conceal,* or *hide*; כְּסוּי means a *cover*; כָּסוּי means *cover, covering* or *hiding*; כְּסָיָה means a *covering*; כָּמוּס means *hidden, concealed, secret, latent, occult*; from the root כמן, to *hide*, כְּמִינָה means *hiding, concealing*; and the root כמס means to *hide, conceal, lay up,* or *store*.

Why does covering relate to throne? Because throne is the seat of the highest holiness, for

> God sits on the throne of his holiness.[31]

This throne is כִּסֵּא כָבוֹד,[32] the throne of God, literally, a *throne of glory*. This is the seat of power, of omnipotence, and it is this omnipotence and power that is concealed in the palm, כַף, the instrument of doing, when we allow the Divine light to flow through us.

The word כֹּחַ means *power* or *strength*.

> But they that wait upon the Lord shall renew [exchange] strength.[33]

The Berditschever Rabbi teaches that

---

31. Psalms 47:9.
32. Jeremiah 17:12.
33. Isaiah 40:31.

this means that those who seek the Lord give their strength unto Him, and receive in return from Him new strength to serve Him further.[34]

There is an interesting instance in which כ is used as an indication of covering. It occurs in the word וְלִבְכֹּתָהּ, which means *and to weep for her*. The letter כ is smaller in this word.

> And Sarah died in Kiriat Arba, that is Hebron, in the land of Canaan, and Abraham went to mourn for Sarah, and to *weep* for her.[35]

Since the letter כ is smaller in the word וְלִבְכֹּתָהּ, this suggests that we examine these letters for an additional meaning. The letters לֵב constitute the word *heart*. The letters הֻכַּת constitute the word meaning to *be smitten* or *crushed*. The letter ו is the prefix meaning *and*. Therefore, we can construct: and [Abraham's] heart was crushed. And even though Abraham's heart was crushed, beaten, and pulverized, he nevertheless went to the Hittites and negotiated the sale of the cave of Machpelah for the burial of Sarah.

The totality of the Divine energy intelligence that we can be aware of resides in the upper cosmic realm named Atzilut, the realm of emanation. The code name for the energy intelligence there is the Sephirah חָכְמָה, Wisdom. This energy intelligence consciousness gradually transforms to more concrete fixed and limited forms. The next lower cosmic realm is the realm of Briah, the realm of creation. Here the energy intelligence consciousness takes on a new code name that is the Sephirah בִּינָה, Understanding. The next lower cosmic realm is the realm of Yetzirah, the realm of formation. This realm contains six energy intelligence consciousnesses whose code names are the Sephirot חֶסֶד, Loving-kindness, גְּבוּרָה, Strength, תִּפְאֶרֶת, Beauty, נֶצַח, Victory, הוֹד, Glory, and יְסוֹד, Foundation. It is ך that provides the connection from Briah to Yetzirah.[36] It does so by being the מַלְכוּת, Kingdom, of Briah and the כֶּתֶר, Crown, of Yetzirah.

---

34. Louis Newman, *The Hasidic Anthology* (New York: Charles Scribner's Sons, 1938), p. 132.

35. Genesis 23:2.

36. Phillip Berg, *Power of Aleph Beth*, vol. 2 (Jerusalem: Research Centre of Kabbalah Press, 1988), pp. 26-27.

This connection, ‏ד‎, provides the transformation for the light that is purely spiritual to begin to change its dominant characteristic of abstractness to concreteness. In this sense, ‏ד‎ relates to the root ‏כלה‎, which means to *be completed, finished, ready,* to *be at an end,* to *be destroyed,* to *vanish,* and related to the associated noun ‏כָּלָה‎, which means *extinction, extermination, annihilation, destruction,* or *determination.*

> But the house of Israel rebelled against Me in the wilderness; they walked not in My statues, and they despised My ordinances, which, if a man keep, he will live through them, and My Sabbaths they desecrated exceedingly. Then I said to pour out My wrath upon them in the wilderness, to *make an end* to them.[37]

> Indeed, I also lifted up my hand to them in the wilderness, that I would not bring them into the land which I had given them, one flowing with milk and honey, which is the ornament of all the lands; because they rejected my judgments, and did not follow my statutes, but profaned my Sabbaths. For their heart went after their idols. Nevertheless, my eye spared them, and I did not destroy them, neither did I *make an end* of them in the wilderness.[38]

> And the Lord thy God will put out those nations before thee by little and little. Thou mayst not *consume* them at once, lest the wild beasts of the field increase upon thee.[39]

‏ד‎ is related to the noun ‏כַּלָה‎, which means *bride,* and to the root ‏כלא‎, to *lock up, shut, detain, restrain,* or *confine.* To form from that which is created requires making a place for it as well as destroying, in the sense of transforming, the abstract form of that which is created. And to make a place for it means destroying what had been at that place. But forming and putting that which is formed in its place means finishing and completing it. So the hidden character of ‏כ‎ is in the

---

37. Ezekiel 20:13-14.
38. Ezekiel 20:15-18.
39. Deuteronomy 7:22.

connection ר, which has the dual role of destroying and completing. In this way, ר makes it possible for us to welcome the bride.

> Come, my Beloved, to meet the Bride; let us welcome the Shabbat.[40]

This dual role occurs both in the inner and in the outer. The role in the outer is obvious. The inner must be explained further.

The important part of the action of a cosmic connection is always inner. In the case of ר, that which is to be formed is perfect happiness, for this in itself is completeness and perfection. That which is to be exterminated is anything the ego holds on to that makes our state of being anything less than perfect happiness. In other words, the structure that the ego holds on to conceals the light. Perfect happiness coincides with the revealment of the light. It is the energy intelligence of ב, which when utilized, frees the ego from its hold on the light. We use this energy intelligence when we use our power to do for the sake and joy of the doing, without attaching ourselves to what is done. That is, we detach ourselves from the results. This detachment frees the light.

When the light is freed, it flows and something new has the possibility to be formed. The ego will want to attach itself to this possibility. A transitory attachment then creates the physical conditions for something new to be formed again. But the formation cannot be completed, in the lower and upper senses, until the ego again detaches itself. So when the light is not frozen, this spiritual cycle can repeat itself endlessly, rising, descending, achieving higher and higher levels, yet ever remaining the same; and this we call the *crowning achievement*.

---

40. *Siddur Tehillat Hashem*, p. 131.

Lamed ל: Learning, Teaching, and Purpose

The twelfth letter of the Hebrew alphabet is ל, spelled לָמֶד. It has the numerical value of 30. As a prefix, ל can mean *to, unto, into, toward, during, for, about, according to, at, by, of, with, in, within, each, every, as,* or *belonging to.* All of these establish ל as providing in the physical realm a directed association or connection of one thing to or with another. The root למד means to *learn, study,* or *become familiar with.* In the Piel form it means to *teach.*

The energy intelligence of ל is *learning, teaching,* and *purpose.* It is the energy intelligence of נ projected into time and conditioned existence. The energy intelligence of נ has to do with the organic activity of nourishing until completely ripe. How is the activity of conditioned existence nourished until completely ripe? The activity is prepared for. Everything that we need to control in the activity, we need to learn about and become familiar with until it becomes second nature to us. We establish a connection first in the realm of Atzilut, then in the realm of Briah, then in the realm of Yetzirah before engaging in the activity in the realm of Assiah. Thus the learning of the energy intelligence of ל is for the purpose of bringing "exalted values down into the world of action."[1]

The letter ל is the tallest of all the letters. This suggests that learning and teaching are among the highest capabilities we have.[2] But learning here means more than intellectual learning of secular matters. Learning here means learning that connects to the heart, לֵב. This is the kind of learning in which we transform our heart to do and desire more and more always in connection with Godliness. That is the reason the shape of the letter ל is composed of a ו on the top, constituting the tower, and a כ for the body. The ו is the connection to Godliness. And with the connection to Godliness learned and taught

---

1. Rabbi Matityahu Glazerson, *Letters of Fire,* trans. S. Fuchs (Jerusalem: Feldheim, 1991), p. 50.
2. Rabbi Michael Munk, *The Wisdom in the Hebrew Alphabet* (Brooklyn, NY: Mesorah Publications, 1988), p. 139.

there is always lasting purpose in what we desire, think, say, and do. This leads us to כ, the energy intelligence of the crowning achievement. Hence it is no surprise that the ו and the כ total 26, the gematria of the Tetragrammaton, יְ־הֹ־וָ־הֹ.

Neither the word לָמַד nor any of its cognates occur in the Pentateuch. However, it does have cognates that occur in other biblical Scripture. The word לָמַד is the Kal perfect third person masculine singular of the root לֹמד.

> Shall the wicked be favored, who did not *learn* righteousness?[3]

The word לָמֹד is the Kal infinitive absolute of the root לֹמד.

> And it shall come to pass, after I have plucked them out I will return, and have compassion on them, and will bring them back, every man to his heritage, and every man to his land. And it shall come to pass, if they will diligently *learn* the ways of my people, to swear by my name.[4]

The word לִמַּד is the Piel perfect third person masculine form of the root לֹמד.

> And besides being wise, Koheleth [Teacher] also *taught* the people knowledge; for he weighed and sought out and set in order many proverbs.[5]

From these verses we see that what is to be learned and what is to be taught is the wisdom associated with being righteous. We can learn what it means to be righteous from the following:

> The righteous shall inherit the land, and abide forever in it. The mouth of the righteous utters wisdom, and his tongue speaks what is right. The teaching of God is in his heart; his feet do not slip.[6]

---

3. Isaiah 26:10.
4. Jeremiah 12:16.
5. Ecclesiastes 12:9.
6. Psalms 37:29-31.

More explicitly, no matter what our role is in life, from white-collar to blue-collar worker, from homemaker or parent to tradesman or professional, no matter how much or little training we had to have to acquire the experience and knowledge to do our job well, our life in this role only provides a context for us to learn how to be better at being righteous. Being righteous here means being in the world, doing in the world, knowing that everything is connected to God, knowing that there is nothing separated from God. And this means that we understand that everything that happens has a Godly purpose. Such doing in the world leads to living a life full of goodness, Godliness, and lasting purpose. This kind of *learning* is the most important kind of learning. This kind of teaching is the most important kind of teaching. And this kind of learning and teaching is what we associate with real knowledge: wisdom.

We read in *Midrash Rabbah*:

It says:

> Surely oppression (*'oshek*) turneth a wise man
> into a fool; and a gift destroyeth the understanding.[7]

When a wise man busies himself (*mit-'asek*) with many matters, then his wisdom becomes confused.[8]

Here there is a play on words: עוֹשֶׁק, which is related to the root עשׁק, meaning to *oppress* or *maltreat*, and עסק, which is the root meaning to *deal with, attend to, engage in, occupy oneself with busy trade,* or *practice.* Thus by becoming busy with many affairs like business deals and other affairs of the world, a wise person turns into a fool. For such business so fills our mind that we forget what has been learned: that the purpose behind everything is its connection to God.

With a direct interpretation, עוֹשֶׁק means *quarrels* or *strives.* When students, instead of learning and delighting in what is to be learned, become more interested in quarrelling with each other about what it is that they each have learned, the quarrelling, which is the instigation

---

7. Ecclesiastes 8:7.

8. *Midrash Rabbah*, vol. 3, *Exodus* (6:2), trans. S. M. Lehrman (London: Soncino Press, 1983), pp. 105-106.

of the ego, so dominates the mind that the learned student becomes a
fool.[9]

The gematria of לָמֵד is 74. The gematria of the word חָכְמוּ, the
Kal perfect third person plural of the root חכם, which means to *be
wise*, also is 74. Moses uses the word חָכְמוּ in his poem.

> Oh that they *were wise*, that they understood this, that
> they would consider their latter end! How should one man
> chase a thousand and two put ten thousand to flight, unless
> their Rock had sold them and the Lord had shut them up?[10]

The word וְחָכָם, *and wise*, also has the gematria of 74. Joseph uses
the word וְחָכָם in explaining to Pharaoh how to handle the upcoming
years of plenty and the following years of famine. Then Pharaoh uses
the word וְחָכָם in choosing Joseph to fulfill the role of the wise man.

> Now therefore let Pharaoh seek out a man discreet *and wise*,
> and set him over the land of Egypt. Let Pharaoh do this
> and let him appoint officers over the land and take up the
> fifth part of the land of Egypt in the seven years of plenty.
> And let them gather all the food of those good years that
> come, and lay up corn under the hand of Pharaoh, and let
> them keep food in the cities.[11]

> And Pharaoh said to Joseph, since God has shown thee all
> this, there is none so discreet *and wise* as thou art: thou
> shalt be over my house, and according to thy word shall all
> my people be ruled.[12]

Pharaoh, פַּרְעֹה, can be understood as רַע, "evil or wickedness,"
within פֶּה, "opening, mouth, gateway, or entranceway" and with פֹּה,
here, in this place. In modern Hebrew פֶּה רַע is translated as *bad mouth*.
But esoterically, we understand it as the gateway to wickedness. This
is what Pharaoh is. Here wickedness must be understood as being

---

9. *Midrash Rabbah*, vol. 8, *Ecclesiastes* (7:1), trans. A. Cohen (London: Soncino
Press, 1983), p. 180.
10. Deuteronomy 32:29-30.
11. Genesis 41:33-35.
12. Genesis 41:39-40.

opposite to righteousness. And since righteousness is associated with behaving with an understanding that everything is connected to God, it must be that פַּרְעֹה symbolizes he whose doing in the world is sometimes predicated on forgetting that everything has a connection to God.

The gematria of פַּרְעֹה, Pharaoh, is 355. This is the gematria of the word וַיִּשְׁכָּחֵהוּ,[13] which means *and he forgot him*. Pharaoh is he who can on occasion forget God. And it is precisely on these occasions when instead of choosing a discreet and wise man, as Pharaoh does in this passage, Pharaoh chooses to "deal wisely with them,"[14] wisely there meaning shrewdly. And these later actions of Pharaoh lead to the enslavement of the Israelites, the spiritual seekers.

Pharaoh is not the personification of wickedness. Pharaoh is the personification of the gateway to wickedness. What is the difference between the personification of wickedness and the gateway to wickedness? The personification of wickedness is he who always and necessarily acts wickedly. The gateway to wickedness is he who, having a gateway to wickedness, becomes wicked on the occasions when he walks through the gateway. This passage is instructive because it depicts Pharaoh standing outside the gateway to wickedness and engaging in an action to choose a discreet and wise man for a Godly purpose, where he himself is not fully aware of the extent of the Godliness of his choice.

The gematria of the word וְלַהֲבִיאֲךָ is 74. It means *and to bring you*.

> Behold, I send an angel before thee, to keep thee in the way, and *to bring thee* to the place which I have prepared.[15]

Here we discover where *learning* and *teaching* righteousness lead. They lead to the place God prepares for us. This is a holy place, a place filled with cosmic purpose. It is a place that nurtures our soul. It is a place we love to be, a place of fulfillment. We are led to this place by learning in accordance with our angel, that silent inner voice by which we become aware and learn of the way. When we listen to it, this inner voice keeps us in God's way, on the path of Godliness. And

---

13. Genesis 40:23.
14. Exodus 1:10.
15. Exodus 23:20.

when we follow this path, which means living righteously, we are led to the place that God has prepared for us. This place is the purpose of creation.

In conjunction with this we note that in Deuteronomy 29:27 the word וַיַּשְׁלִכֵם, which means *and cast them*, has a large לֹ.

> Therefore the anger of the Lord was kindled against this land, to bring upon it all the curse that is written in this book. [16]

> And the Lord rooted them out of their land in anger and in wrath, and in great indignation, *and cast them* into another land, as at this day.[17]

The large לֹ makes this verse require another interpretation. We may parse the word וַיַּשְׁלִכֵם as וְיֵשׁ לָכֶם, *existence for you*. Thereby we may read: existence for you is in another land. Land refers to our consciousness. So in the full context of these two verses we understand that when existence is for us in another state of consciousness, separated from God, then as it is written in this book, God puts a curse on our land. And for what purpose is the curse put? In order for us to experience the consequence of this choice of state of consciousness. Because experiencing its consequences will create for us the opportunity to learn; and by learning we change, thereby activating the process of repentance.

The gematria of the word בְּעַב is 74 and it means *in the thickness* or *in the denseness*.

> And the Lord said to Moses: "Lo I come to thee *in the thickness* of the cloud, that the people may hear when I speak with thee, and believe thee for ever."[18]

God's presence is not revealed to us as a presence of a thing that can be heard, seen, or touched directly. What can be heard, seen, or touched directly is only appearance. We hear what God has to say

---

16. Deuteronomy 29:26.
17. Deuteronomy 29:27.
18. Exodus 19:9.

through the thickness of the cloud. What God has to say is always of essence and essence is always the inner layer of appearance. Deep within every appearance is its essence. And no matter what our frame of reference or level of understanding, there is always an inside, an essence, that is just beyond what we understand, hear, see, or touch. This essence is in the thickness of the cloud and is the cause of and the motivation for the appearance that we perceive.

The gematria of the word הָאֶבְיוֹן is 74. It is an adjective and it means *the needy, the poor, the miserable,* or *the wretched.*

> If there be among you a poor man, one of thy brethren within any of thy gates in thy land which the Lord thy God gives thee, thou shalt not harden thy heart, nor shut thy hand from thy *poor* brother: but thou shalt open thy hand wide to him and shalt surely lend him sufficient for his need in that which he lacks. Beware that there be not an unworthy thought, saying: The seventh year, the year of release, is at hand and thy eye be evil against thy *poor* brother and thou give him nothing; and he cry to the Lord against thee: for it shall be reckoned to you as sin.[19]

Finally, we learn here what is required of us in the way of action. Our actions must always be giving actions, actions that provide for the poor around us. Here providing for the poor means much more than just giving charity. It means to nourish the poor, to teach the poor. To give a gift that facilitates the poor learning how to nourish themselves. And from this giving, we ourselves receive nourishment, for by giving we receive.

Here "unworthy thought" refers to giving with the expectation that we give for the purpose of getting a return on the investment of our giving. By giving in a way that does not expect that there will be a return on the giving, we truly give. And that is when we truly receive: when our giving is entirely free, a giving without expectations of any return compensation.

The full gematria of ל can be determined by adding up the numerical values of each of the spelled-out letters of לָמֶד. Adding up

---

19. Deuteronomy 15:7-9.

the numerical values of לָמֶד מֵם דָּלֶת, we obtain 588. And 588 is the gematria of the word וּבְשֵׂעִיר, which means *and in Seir*.

> *And in Seir* dwelt the Horites aforetime, but the children of Esau dispossessed them; and they destroyed them from before them, and dwelt in their stead; as Israel did unto the land of his possession, which the Lord gave unto them.[20]

Now the land of Seir is the dominion of Esau.[21] And the power and strength of Esau is Samael.[22] And in the land of Seir means in a consciousness brought on by the desires and values of a person like Esau. And these desires and values are described by Isaac's blessing to Esau:

> Behold, thy dwelling shall be of the fatness of the earth, and of the dew of heaven above: and by thy sword shalt thou live, and thou shalt serve thy brother.[23]

The Zohar explains:

> Isaac thus blessed him with worldly goods; he surveyed his grade and said, "And by thy sword shalt thou live," as much as to say: "This is just what suits you, to shed blood and to make war."[24]

The Zohar further interprets the meaning of "thy dwelling shall be of the fatness of the earth, and of the dew of heaven above." This wording is the opposite order from the corresponding part of the blessing given Jacob, where the dew of the heaven comes first and the fatness of the earth comes second.

> The difference between the two goes very deep. For the "dew of heaven" promised to Jacob is the supernal dew

---

20. Deuteronomy 2:12.
21. *The Zohar*, vol. 2, trans. Harry Sperling and Maurice Simon (London: Soncino Press, 1978), p. 64.
22. Ibid., p. 65.
23. Genesis 27:39-40.
24. *The Zohar*, vol. 2, p. 67.

that flows from the Ancient of Days, and is therefore called "dew of heaven," namely, of the upper heaven, dew that flows through the grade of heaven, to fall on the "field of consecrated apples." Also, the earth mentioned in Jacob's blessing alludes to the supernal "earth of the living." Jacob thus inherited the fruit of the supernal earth and the supernal heaven. Esau, on the other hand, was given his blessings on earth here below and in heaven here below. Jacob obtained a portion in the highest realm, but Esau only in the lowest. Further, Jacob was given a portion both above and below, but Esau only here below.[25]

Thus we learn that by having the values of Esau, our state of consciousness shall be in the land of Seir. We shall shed blood and make war. And our inheritance shall be only the earth below and the heaven below.

The concealed meaning of ל can be learned from the meaning of מַד. מַד has the meaning of *garment, coat,* or *covering* as well as the meaning of a *measure* and *meter* or *instrument gauge.* This concept of garment is reinforced by the root לבש, which means to *put on,* to *wear.* From this we learn that actions are a garment and covering, what we put on, to reveal our true purpose and intentions, and we learn that we can measure these intentions through our actions.

There is the related word מִדָּה, which means *measure, measurement, attribute, nature, character,* or *quality.* The plural form, מִדּוֹת, is used in Kabbalah to refer to the seven lower Sephirot: תִּפְאֶרֶת, גְבוּרָה, חֶסֶד, נֶצַח, הוֹד, יְסוֹד, and מַלְכוּת. These are the emotional traits. The purpose of *learning* and *teaching* is to form these emotional traits in each of us so that the energy-light coming through them is the light of Godliness and not the darkness of ungodliness.

Additional words that reinforce the notion of teaching are the word לְמִידָה, *learning* or *study* and the word לָמִיד, *teachable,* לִמֵּד to *teach, instruct, train, prove, practice,* לֻמַּד, to *be trained, taught, schooled,* and לָמֵד, *learned, learning, accustomed to,* or *taught.*

It may be surprising, but there is a relation between the connection that ל as a prefix establishes and the Hebrew word for bread. The

---

·Hebrew word for *bread* is לֶחֶם. The third person singular Kal perfect form of the verb to *eat bread* is לָחַם and the causative form of this verb is הִלְחִים, whose meaning is to *solder*, to *join together*. By eating bread we join together body and spirit. The connection is for the purpose of elevation and the connection is established by action. The action comes about because we have learned to perform the action to accomplish the elevation of endowing physical reality with Godliness. The action comes about because we have taught someone to perform the action to accomplish this purpose.

The root of the Hebrew verb to *take* is לקח. The root of the Hebrew verb to *pick up*, to *gather up* is לקט. This tells us how the action accomplishes the purpose of elevation. By taking, picking, and gathering up the empty shells we encounter, we endow them with the holiness of our purpose. How do we do the action? With a singing and caressing, with a uniting and blending, for the root of the Hebrew verb to *sing* is לחן, and the root of the verb to *caress, pet, fondle* is לטף, and the root of the verb to *unite*, which is also the musical term to *blend*, is לכד.

The energy intelligence consciousness of ל is in the word לב, which can mean *heart, understanding, mind, thought, conscience, center, middle, midst, will, bosom,* or *core*. From the moral point of view, it is our heart that controls what we bring into manifestation, the heart being associated with the seven מדות. And when our learning is not complete, what we bring into manifestation through our behavior does not ascend. There is a passage in the Zohar that discusses light that does not ascend.

> Wood whose light does not ascend[26] – they strike it and it shines. A body in which the light of the soul does not ascend – they strike it and the light of the soul ascends,[27] and they become interdependent and shine.[28]

Rabbi Shneur Zalman translates this passage as follows:

26. Which does not burn properly.
27. They afflict the body, and so enable the light of the soul to be kindled within it, through repentance and good deeds.
28. *The Wisdom of the Zohar*, vol. 2, arr. Fischel Lachower and Isaiah Tishby, trans. David Goldstein (London: Oxford University Press, 1991), pp. 784-785.

A wooden beam that will not catch fire should be splintered.
. . . ; a body into which the light of the soul does not
penetrate should be crushed.[29]

Rabbi Shneur Zalman writes about this light of the soul that the
Zohar discusses:

> The reference to the "Light of the soul" is that the light of
> the soul and of the intellect does not illuminate to such an
> extent as to prevail over the coarseness of the body. For,
> although he understands and contemplates in his mind on
> the greatness of God, this is not apprehended and implanted
> in his mind to a degree that would enable him to prevail over
> the coarseness of the heart because of [the nature of] this
> coarseness and crassness, the cause being the arrogance of
> the kelipah, which exalts itself above the light of the holiness
> of the divine soul, obscuring and darkening the light thereof.
> Therefore one must crush it and cast it down to the ground,
> that is to say, by setting aside appointed times for humbling
> oneself. . . .[30]

Here we learn that intellectual understanding is not the same as full
apprehension. For that which is learned to the extent that it is fully
apprehended will find its way to prevail over the coarseness of the heart.
Learning that does not result in action is learning that is neither deep
nor permanent. It is learning without true understanding. What is
fully learned fully manifests in the the realms of Atzilut, Briah, Yetzirah, and Asiyah. Conversely whatever is not fully manifested by our
actions in Asiyah is not fully learned. This is not fully apprehended.
To get what we have not fully understood, fully apprehended, requires
that we humble ourselves. The hardness of our heart must be splintered, breaking its outside shell, thereby permitting an opening for the
learning to take root and become fully understood. Learning that is
through the heart, penetrating into the heart, is learning that lasts.

---

29. Rabbi Shneur Zalman, *Likkutei Amarim – Tanya*, bi-lingual ed. (Brooklyn, NY:
Kehot Publication Society, 1993), p. 125.
30. Ibid., p. 125.

This is deep understanding. For *learning* that is through the heart results in action for a sacred *purpose*.

Mem מֵם : Perfection and Completion

The thirteenth letter of the Hebrew alphabet is Mem, spelled מֵם. It has the numerical value 40 and it has a final form ם that can also carry the value of 40 or alternatively can carry the value of 600. Since ד has the value 4 and מ has the value 40, the letter energy intelligence מ is the projection of the letter energy intelligence ד, the archetype of physical existence, into time and conditioned physical existence. This projection is *perfection* and *completion*.

There is no vocalization of מם that occurs in the Pentateuch or for that matter anywhere in Scripture. The gematria of מם is 80. This is also the gematria of the word נְטוּיָה, which is the Kal feminine singular passive participle of the root נטה, meaning to *stretch out*, *extend*, *incline*, or *bend*. Each instance of its use in the Pentateuch is when God's outstretched arm brings deliverance to the Israelites.

> I am the Lord and I will bring you out from under the burdens of Egypt and I will deliver you out of their bondage, and I will redeem you with an *outstretched* arm, and with great judgments. And I will take you to me for a people, and I will be to you a God. And you shall know that I am the Lord your God, who brings you out from under the burdens of Egypt. And I will bring you into the land which I swore to give to Abraham, to Isaac, and to Jacob. And I will give it to you for a heritage. I am the Lord.[1]

> Ask now about the former days, long before your time, from the day God created man on the earth. Ask from one side of heaven to the other whether there has been any happening so great as this or whether anything like this has been heard of? Has any other people heard the voice of God speaking out of fire as you have and lived? Has any god ever tried to take for himself one nation out of another nation by trials, by signs, and by wonders, and by war, and by a mighty hand, and by an *outstretched* arm, and by great terrors,

---

1. Exodus 6:6-8.

> according to all that the Lord your God did for you in
> Egypt before your eyes?[2]
>
> And remember that thou wast a servant in the land of
> Egypt, and that the Lord thy God brought thee out from
> there with a mighty hand and an *outstretched* arm.[3]
>
> And the Lord brought us out of Egypt with a mighty hand,
> and with an *outstretched* arm, and with great terribleness,
> and with signs and with wonders. And he brought us to
> this place and gave us this land, a land flowing with milk
> and honey.[4]

These passages give us the meaning for *outstretched* arm. When we
are in bondage to limitation because we live in a way that does not
transcend where we are and how we are, and when we realize that we
are indeed in slavery and are miserable because of this slavery, then God
will hear our cry and deliver us out of slavery with an outstretched arm.
God will deliver us to the land of milk and honey. God will deliver us to
a state of consciousness full of milk and honey, a state of consciousness
that is *perfect* and *complete*.

What initiates this deliverance with an outstretched arm is our cry,
our desire from the bottom of our broken hearts to be delivered. This
cry is our desire from the level of חָכְמָה, Wisdom, to break through the
shell of the heart, thereby shattering the ego in which there is no space
for God.

Like מֵם, the word הַלַּיְלָה, *the night*, has the gematria of 80. Moses,
his heart breaking when he finds the Israelites worshiping the golden
calf, cries out to God, imploring God to forgive the Israelites.

> Thus I fell down before the Lord. The forty days and the
> forty *nights* I fell down because the Lord said He would
> destroy you.[5]

---

2. Deuteronomy 4:32-34.
3. Deuteronomy 5:15.
4. Deuteronomy 26:8-10.
5. Deuteronomy 9:25. Note that the Hebrew construction for the forty nights
is אַרְבָּעִים הַלַּיְלָה, literally "the forty night." This is a common biblical con-

This cry is the response to a broken heart.

A broken heart is very dear and precious to God.[6]

Sacrifice to God is a broken spirit; God, you will not despise a broken and contrite heart.[7]

When the shell of the heart is broken, then the pure heart forms. God fills the pure heart and with an outstretched arm God creates the openings through which we are delivered. And this is the meaning of this verse:

Arise, cry out in the night: in the beginning of the watches pour out thy heart like water before the face of the Lord.[8]

The deliverance with the outstretched arm is not something that happens once in our lives. Rather, it happens once each cycle of our lives. The cycle begins when we go down to sojourn in Egypt just as Abraham did and just as Joseph did. We immerse ourselves in limitation and in physicality in order to express ourselves. Express means to push out from our essence something of our essence. We do this by the garments of thought, speech, and action. Once our expression is complete, which happens when we have repeated the expression in all its variations for all the different circumstances in which it is appropriate, we often mindlessly continue the repetition of the expression. We repeat because of habit, laziness, or lack of watchfulness. Then the expression becomes solely limitation. And this is how we become slaves in the land of Egypt, the land of constriction. We are held in bondage by our evil inclination, which is naturally lazy about understanding or finding new, more meaningful ways of being and doing. Our evil inclination

---

struction. However, it can also be understood to indicate that the forty days and the forty nights should be not be viewed as a sequence of forty individual days and forty individual nights. Rather, it should be viewed as a totality that includes forty days and forty nights.

6. Rabbi Aryeh Kaplan, *Gems of Rabbi Nachman* (Jerusalem: Yeshivat Chasidei Breslov, 1980), p. 134.

7. Psalms 51:19.

8. Lamentations, 2:19.

literally renders a man so blind that he becomes like one that gropes in the dark and stumbles over the obstacles which he does not see.[9]

When we realize that we have enslaved ourselves, our heart becomes broken,[10] and we cry out for deliverance from the burden of slavery; we cry

out to God, searching and waiting to discover God's glory.[11]

The outstretched arm of the blessed Holy One delivers us. And we find ourselves wandering in the wilderness. In the wilderness, the place of

the vast and dreadful desert, that thirsty and waterless land, with its venomous snakes and scorpions.[12]

In the wilderness, we are given water, the Torah. We are led to the land of milk and honey, the land of our inheritance. What perfection! What completion! Then soon after we arrive in the land of our inheritance, we express ourselves at the next higher level, and when we are not careful enough about the mindless repetition of our expression, we begin the cycle again, enslaved in another Egypt.

Egypt is not a land where we must necessarily become slaves. Joseph, for example, did not enslave himself. Our actual situation in Egypt always is that we have completed a level of transcending and in Egypt there are hidden sparks of Godliness waiting for us to reveal them by our expression, an expression that can no longer be merely a repetition. The revelation of the hidden sparks of Godliness by our expression is our transcendence.

---

9. Rabbi Moshe Chayim Luzzatto, *Mesillat Yesharim: The Path of the Upright*, trans. Mordecai Kaplan (Philadelphia: Jewish Publication Society, 1966), p. 50.

10. Rabbi Nachman teaches: "There is a vast difference between depression and a broken heart. When one has a broken heart, he can be standing in the middle of a crowd, and turn around and say, 'Master of the world . . . .' " (Rabbi Nachman, *Outpouring of the Soul*, trans. Rabbi Aryeh Kaplan, Jerusalem: Breslov Research Institute, 1980, p. 44).

11. *The Bahir*, trans. and comm. Aryeh Kaplan (Northvale, NJ: Jason Aronson, 1995), p. 23.

12. Deuteronomy 8:15.

The word יָמֶיךָ means *thy days* and also has a gematria of 80. We are commanded that for all our days, our expressions must be directed to:

> Honor thy father and thy mother: that *thy days* may be long in the land which the Lord thy God gives thee.[13]

> That thou mightest be in awe of the Lord thy God, to keep all his statutes and his commandments, which I command thee, thou, and thy son, and thy son's son, all the days of thy life, that *thy days* may be prolonged.[14]

> Take heed that thou forsake not the Levite all *thy days* in thy land.[15]

> Thou shalt have a perfect and just weight, a perfect and just measure shalt thou have: that *thy days* may be lengthened in the land which the Lord thy God gives thee.[16]

> To love the Lord thy God and to obey His voice that thou mayst cleave to him: for He is thy life and the length of *thy days*, that thou mayst dwell in the land which the Lord swore to thy fathers, to Abraham, to Isaac, and to Jacob.[17]

The full gematria of מֵ can be determined from מֵם מֵם, a total of 160. The word עֵינֶיךָ, which means *your eyes*, has the gematria of 160. After Lot separated from Abraham, God said to Abraham:

> Now, lift up thy eyes and look from the place where thou art, northward, and southward, and eastward, and westward: for all the land which thou seest, to thee will I give it, and to thy seed for ever.[18]

Just before Jacob left Laban, God spoke to Jacob in a dream and said:

---

13. Exodus 20:12.
14. Deuteronomy 6:2.
15. Deuteronomy 12:19.
16. Deuteronomy 25:15.
17. Deuteronomy 30:20.
18. Genesis 13:14.

> Now lift up thy eyes and see all the rams which leap upon
> the flock are streaked, speckled and grizzled: for I have seen
> all that Laban does to thee. I am the God of Bet-el, where
> thou didst anoint a pillar, and where thou didst vow a vow
> to me. Now arise, get out of this land, and return to the
> land of thy birth.[19]

From this we learn that to receive the perfection and completeness
of this world, a perfection and completeness created by God, we must
lift up our eyes toward God. This lifting up our eyes is not just on
occasion. But our eyes must continually be toward God in order to
continuously receive the perfection and completeness.

A further aspect of the revealed meaning of מ can be found from
the closest word to the spelling of מ. This word is the root מים, which
means to *water*. The word מַיִם means *water*. Water sandwiches a י
between the initial מ and the final ם. From this we learn that water is
the carrier of י, which is the projection of the timeless pulsating energy
of א into time and conditioned physical existence. Water is the life-
sustaining liquid. It flows freely. It is formless and takes the shape of
its container. When there is a *confluence of water*, a מִקְוָה, there is
trust and hope. This is a מָקוֹר, a *source*. From the source there forms
מַבּוּעַ, a *spring* and *fountain* whose *fullness*, מְלֵאוּת, makes possible all
actions arising from the root מלא. Those actions from מלא are to *be
full*, to *fill*, to *fulfill*, to be *filled*, and to *be fulfilled*.

> Naftali: abounding with satisfaction and *full* with the blessing
> of the Lord.[20]
>
> The earth is *full* of the loving-kindness of the Lord.[21]
>
> All the earth is *filled* with the glory of the Lord.[22]

We can further understand how מ is a source by identifying the
wetness of water with the wetness in the *womb*, רֶחֶם, a word whose
gematria is 248, the gematria of אַבְרָהָם, the patriarch associated with

---

19. Genesis 31:12-13.
20. Deuteronomy 33:23.
21. Psalms 33:6.
22. Numbers 14:21.

the Sephirah חֶסֶד, Loving-kindness. מם is the womb. מ is the female aspect. It has an opening at the bottom through which it can give birth. And since מ is the balancing point of all manifestation, it must have a male aspect. The male aspect of מ is its final form ם. ם and מ are married by the י. They are parents of the future children, for מ is the womb of בִּינָה,[23] the womb of the future, and ם is the womb of חָכְמָה, the womb of the past.

The concealed meaning of מ can be understood through its use as a prefix and as an interrogative pronoun. As a prefix מ can mean *from, out of, away from, apart from, part of, since, after,* or *because of.* As an interrogative pronoun, מִי means *who* and מַה means *what.* The energy intelligence consciousness מ constantly bathes us in a kingdom, מַלְכוּת, in which our thoughts, words, and actions answer its query: From what? From whom? Out of what? Out of whom? Away from what? Away from whom? Apart from what? Apart from whom? Because of what? Because of whom? מ keenly listens to our answer, which embodies the manifestation of the *king,* מֶלֶךְ. For it is our answer that establishes whether we become a מְקַבֵּל, a *recipient* or *receiver,* or a מַבְדִּיל, *separator* or *differentiator.*

From the letter energy intelligence consciousness מ comes a deep *mystery,* מִסְתּוֹרִין. It is that the creation of man and woman completes the channel uniting the upper and lower worlds. The upper extremity of heaven is called מִי and the lower extremity of heaven is called מַה. This can be understood when the letters of מִי and מַה are spelled out. When מִי is spelled out we have: מם יוד. The total of this is 100 and 100 corresponds to the numerical value of the letter ק, whose energy intelligence is holiness and growth. Holiness and growth constitute the upper heavens. When the letters of מַה are spelled out we have: מם הא. The total of this is 86. This is the same as the gematria of אלהים, the name for that aspect of God's manifestion having to do with the continual creation of the physical world.[24] From this we understand that the openings are created for us in the physical world. Our task is to see them and utilize them.

The מִי can be sought, but only the מַה can be known. The Zohar

23. *The Bahir,* pp. 14, 114.
24. Genesis, chapter 1.

says:

> It is the mysterious Ancient One, whose essence can be
> sought, but not found, that created these: to wit, מִי, the
> same who is called from, מ, the extremity of heaven on high
> because everything is in His power, and because He is ever
> to be sought, though mysterious and unrevealable, since fur-
> ther we cannot enquire. That extremity of heaven is called
> מִי, but there is another lower extremity which is called מָה.
> The difference between the two is this. The first is the real
> subject of enquiry, but after a man by means of enquiry
> and reflection has reached the utmost limit of knowledge,
> he stops at מָה, as if to say, what knowest thou? What have
> thy searchings achieved? Everything is as baffling as at the
> beginning.[25]

The Zohar continues:

> When the most Mysterious wished to reveal Himself, He
> first produced a single point which was transmuted into a
> thought, and in this He executed innumerable designs, and
> engraved innumerable gravings. He further graved with the
> sacred and mystic lamp a mystic and most holy design,
> which was a wondrous edifice issuing from the midst of
> thought. This is called מִי, and was the beginning of the
> edifice, existent and non-existent, deepburied, unknowable
> by name. It was only called מִי. It desired to become mani-
> fest and to be called by a name. It therefore clothed itself in
> a refulgent and precious garment and created אֵלֶּה [which
> means these], and אֵלֶּה acquired a name. The letters of the
> two words intermingled, [the מִי reflected itself] forming the
> complete name אֱלֹהִים.[26]

> The heavens and their hosts were created through the medium
> of מָה . . . God is above the heavens in respect of His

25. *The Zohar*, vol. 1, trans. Harry Sperling and Maurice Simon (London: Soncino
Press, 1978), pp. 4-5.
26. Ibid., p. 6.

name, for He created a light for His light, and one formed a vestment to the other, and so He ascended into the higher name; hence "In the beginning אֱלֹהִים created," that is the supernal אֱלֹהִים. Whereas מַה was not so, nor was it built up until these letters אֵלֶּה (from the name אֱלֹהִים) were drawn from above below, and the Mother lent the Daughter her garments and decked her out gracefully with her own adornments.[27]

And who are the daughters? The daughters are the *queens* or *princesses*, מְלָכוֹת which constitute our *kingdom*, מַלְכוּת. This is the mystery held by מ.

מ is the energy intelligence consciousness by which *East*, מִזְרָח, and *West*, מַעֲרָב, come into being, מְצִיאוּת. מ provides energy for מִזּוּג, which means *joining, harmonizing, synthesis*, as well as מָזוֹן, which means *food* and *sustenance*. מ is the energy intelligence consciousness of מִכְלוֹל, *totality, entirety*, or *wholeness*, מִכְלָל, *perfection*, and מַהוּת, *being* or *essence*.

מ questions whether we are aware of the *luminary*, מָאוֹר. Are we an *entrance*, מָבוֹא, for the light? Are we acting in a way, always doing *good deeds*, מִצְווֹת, that binds us to the *king*, מֶלֶךְ? Our *dwelling place*, מִשְׁכָּן, carries those things we do life to life. By them we bring to *concreteness* and *reality*, מַמָּשׁוּת, *sweetness*, מְתִיקוּת, or *bitterness, sorrow*, and *affliction* מֶמֶר,[28] or מְרִירוּת, in the *kingdom*, מַלְכוּת, over which we *rule*, מְמֻשָּׁלִים.

The shape of the letter מ can be seen as a ו on the left married to a כ on the right. The ו is leaning over to the right, the head of the ו touching the כ on its upper leftmost point. And on the bottom, the ו leaves a tiny opening between its base and the base of the כ. The numerical sum of a ו and a כ is 26, the same as the Tetragrammaton י-ה-ו-ה. This tells us that the manifestation of the transcendent י-ה-ו-ה in physical existence is through the מ, which is the middle letter of the Hebrew alphabet. מ is therefore the balancing point of all manifestation.

---

27. Ibid., p. 7.
28. Proverbs 17:25.

Final mem ם, the closed mem, can be seen to consist of two ד s that can be put together and form a square. The square is the womb,[29] the male aspect of the womb. In the female aspect of the womb, מ, the offspring is nourished until it is ready to be born. And from

He did not shut up the doors of my mother's womb[30]

we understand that there are two doors to our womb: an entrance door and an exit door. The entrance is opened when we cry out. Then we are delivered by God's outstretched arm. Our womb becomes fertile and nourishes our offspring as we wander in the wilderness. Then our offspring leaves the womb through the exit door and we come to the promised land. The exit door is the opening at the bottom of the מ.

מ has the gematria of 40. The number 40 is four tens. The tens represent the ten steps of the four. The four steps represent כֶּתֶר, חָכְמָה, and בִּינָה, which lead to דַּעַת, knowledge. This forty is the forty days and nights Moses was on the mountain to receive the Torah.[31] And forty is four times ten. There are four worlds and ten Sephirot in each world for a total of forty Sephirot.[32]

> This is the law of the burnt-offering: such burnt offering shall remain on the *hearth* upon the altar all night unto morning; and the fire of the altar shall be kept burning thereby.[33]

In this verse, the word for *firewood*, מוֹקְדָה, begins with a smaller-sized mem. Whenever a letter of a word of the Pentateuch is larger or smaller than the other letters it is significant. In this case, the phrase "on the hearth," עַל מוֹקְדָה, can be rearranged as עלם וקדה. The root עלם means to *hide* or *conceal* and as well means to *surround, tie up,* and to *be strong.* The noun עֶלֶם means *secret* and it means *vigorous lad.* And the noun עָלַם means *eternity* or it means *world.* The root קדה means

---

29. Rabbi Nachman, *Likutey Moharan*, vol. 4, trans. Moshe Mykoff (Jerusalem: Breslov Research Institute, 1993), p. 41.

30. Job 3:9.

31. Exodus 24:18.

32. Rabbi Nachman, *Likutey Moharan*, vol. 3, p. 69.

33. Leviticus, 6:2.

to *bow* or *bend* and as well it is the abbreviation for קְדוּשׁ הַשֵׁם, which means *sanctification of the Holy Name.*

This can be allegorically interpreted. First, recall that in a blast furnace, the hearth is the lower part of the furnace on which the charge of the raw ore is placed. This is the area where the charge is melted down and refined. Thus the verse means: Upon the altar, all night until the morning, we vigorously sacrifice with all our strength that part of ourselves that thinks itself to be separate from God. For that is the part that has to be melted down (transformed) and refined. Our essence knows that the world forever surrounds Godliness, effectively concealing it. And the fire of our sacrifice, our refinement, is the fire that lights the night. This is the inner light. It burns in our heart. We refine ourselves with joy and ecstasy, an inner ecstasy that is surrounded by and concealed within our bodies.[34] The small מ hints that we can do this refinement, no matter how great, scholarly, or pious we are, only by making ourselves sufficiently humble.[35] It also hints that our zeal in refining ourselves must not be publicly displayed, but must be kept within our heart.[36]

We can understand more about the letter energy intelligence of מ through those words that begin with מ and end with final ם. In these words, and the words associated with them, the beginning מ has an opening at the bottom. This alludes to the fact that from below we can perceive God through the functioning of the universe. The final ם is closed. This alludes to the fact that although we perceive God, the *king*, מֶלֶךְ, through the functioning of the universe, ultimately God remains unknowable and hidden.

מָקוֹם means *place, stand, abode.* The place of God is in the kingdom and also:

God is the place of the world.[37]

---

34. Rabbi Michael Munk, *The Wisdom in the Hebrew Alphabet* (Brooklyn, NY: Mesorah Publications, 1988), p. 145.

35. Zalman Sorotzkin, *Insights in the Torah, Vayikra,* trans. Raphael Blumberg (Brooklyn, NY: Mesorah Publications, 1993), p. 76.

36. Alexander Friedman, *Wellsprings of Torah,* vol. 1 (New York: Judaica Press, 1974), pp. 205-206.

37. *The Bahir,* p. 6.

And because God is the place of the world, God is omnipresent and is there as a מֵאַד,[38] a *power* or a *force*, a *strength*. The kingdom is a מַרְאָה, a *mirror*, by which we can see the מַרְאֶה, the *appearance*, of our true selves. And upon seeing our true selves, it is a kingdom in which we can *change*, מוּר, ourselves. As well, the kingdom is a place of *magic*, מְקְסָם, a place of the *magician*, מָג, a place in which one can be *deceived*, מִרְמָה, and *die*, מֵת. Yet for all this, the kingdom is a place of מְתֹם, *soundness, wholeness, completeness*. It is a *mountain peak*, a *heaven*, מָרוֹם. It is a *cover*, מִכְסֶה, a *mask* or *covering* מַסֵּכָה, by which God becomes manifest. It is a reality that is מוּפְלָא, *marvelous* and *wonderful*, a reality for which we are מוֹדִים, *thankful* and *grateful*. It is a place that is מֻשְׁלָם, *perfect* and *complete*.

38. Deuteronomy 6:5, 2 Kings 23:25.

נָוָן

Nun נ ן: Emergence

The fourteenth letter of the Hebrew alphabet is נ, spelled נון. It carries the numerical value of 50. It has a final form ן, which, like the regular form, carries the numerical value of 50 and can carry the numerical value of 700. In Aramaic, the word נון means *fish*. In Hebrew, the word נון is the root to *sprout, spread, propagate,* or *shine* and the root נונן means to *flourish* or *blossom*. The word נון is cognate to the root נון, to *generate*, and is cognate to the root נון, to *decline*, to *become decadent*, or to *cause to degenerate*. Also the word נונן means *degeneration, degeneracy, decadence, decline,* or *disintegration*. From this it is clear that נ has a twofold nature of flourishing and degenerating. We can understand this twofold nature by understanding נ as the power of being of ה projected into time and conditioned physical existence. In physical existence our power of being pulsates with a beginning, a birth, then a growth that is a flourishing, a blossoming, a spreading, then a peak followed by a decline, degeneration, and disintegration. This is then followed by a new flourishing.

The twofold nature of נ can also be understood from the point of view that when something emerges and flourishes, it takes space and nourishment. The space it takes makes that which was previously there decline. The food that it takes in order to emerge, grow, and flourish while being a nourishment to it is a total decline and disintegration of the food itself.

Every instance of the word נון in the Pentateuch is in the phrase בן נון,[1] which means *son of Nun*. Joshua, who led the Israelites after Moses, was the son of Nun. The Ramban associates נון with the word ינין,[2] which is usually translated as *endures* or *continues*.

> May his name be forever. As long as the sun lasts, may his name *endure*. May men bless themselves by him. Let all nations call him happy.[3]

---

1. Exodus 33:11; Numbers 11:28; 13:8,16; 14:6,30,38; 26:65; 27:18; 32:12,28; 34:17; Deuteronomy 1:38; 31:23; 32:44; 34:9.
2. Rabbi Moshe ben Nachman, *Ramban Commentary on the Torah, Exodus*, trans. Charles Chavel (New York: Shilo Publishing House, 1971), p. 579.
3. Psalms 72:17.

From this we can infer that the holy that emerges and flourishes shall endure.

There are three verses about the son of Nun that are appropriate to review.

> And he gave Joshua, the son of *Nun*, a charge, and said: "Be strong and of good courage, for thou shalt bring the children of Israel into the land of which I swore to them. And I will be with thee."[4]

> But Joshua, the son of *Nun*, who stands before thee, he shall go in there. Encourage him, for he shall cause Israel to inherit it.[5]

> And Joshua, the son of *Nun*, was full of the spirit of wisdom, for Moses had laid his hands upon him and the children of Israel hearkened to him and did as the Lord commanded Moses.[6]

That which is in *emergence* does not immediately accomplish what is to be accomplished, for what is to be accomplished takes place later in time. It is the son of Nun, Joshua, the offspring of Nun, who goes into the land and causes us to inherit it. The father, Nun, emergence, does not go into the promised land. Therefore, when we are engaging in emergence we are charged to be strong and of good courage for it will take time for our emergence to produce something seeable. And in emerging we shall be full of the spirit of wisdom.

The son of Nun, נוּן בֶּן, if put together as one word where the double נ is reduced to one נ, is close to the word בִּנְיָן, which is the word meaning *building, structure, construction,* or *edifice*. It is the construction of the building, which is a container for the essence, that is accomplished by emergence.

The word נוּן has the gematria of 106. The word יְצַו is the Piel third person masculine singular of the root צוה, which means to *command, order,* or *ordain*. It also has the gematria of 106. Moses uses the word יְצַו in one of his last teachings to the Israelites.

---

4. Deuteronomy 31:23.
5. Deuteronomy 1:38.
6. Deuteronomy 34:9.

The Lord *shall command* the blessing upon thee in thy barns, and in all that thou settest thy hand unto; and He shall bless thee in the land which the Lord thy God gives thee.[7]

The word כֻּלָּנוּ, which means *all of us*, has the gematria of 106. Moses uses the word כֻּלָּנוּ in reviewing with the Israelites the laws that God gave them.

The Lord made not this covenant with our fathers, but with us, even us, who are *all of us* here alive this day.[8]

In the wilderness of Paran, the Israelites are ready to go into the promised land. God commands Moses to send men to search out the land. As before, *land* here means *state of consciousness*. Moses chooses the heads of the children of Israel, one prince from each of the twelve tribes, to search out the land. These are the most respected and renowned men of each tribe. And in telling them their mission, Moses uses the word עֲלוּ, which means *go up*. As נוּג, the word עֲלוּ has the gematria of 106.

And Moses sent them to explore Canaan and he said to them: "*Go up* through the Negev and on into the hill country. And see the country, what it is and the people who dwell in it, whether they are strong or weak, few or many, and what the land is that they dwell in, whether it is good or bad and what cities they dwell in, whether in tents, or in strongholds, and what the land is, whether fat or lean, whether there are trees in it or not. And be of good courage and bring of the fruit of the land."[9]

Here we understand that Moses tells them to go through the Negev, which is the desert of the south and the worst part of the land[10] and

---

7. Deuteronomy 28:8.
8. Deuteronomy 5:3.
9. Numbers 13:17-20.
10. Rashi, *Pentateuch and Rashi's Commentary, Numbers*, vol. 4, trans. Abraham ben Isaiah and Benjamin Sharfman (Brooklyn, NY: S.S. and R. Publishing, 1976), Numbers 13:17, p. 128.

then go to the high country, which is fertile. First see the *worst* and then see the *best*, for our consciousness has the capacity to contain within it the worst and the best. Know what the worst is, but retain only the best. Then see the people in the land. Determine if they are strong or weak. Here people means *will*. See what kind of will dwells in consciousness. Is it a strong will or a weak will? See the state of consciousness that the will has created in this land. See whether this state of consciousness is good or bad. See the cities. Report back about the centers of creative and cultural activities. Tell us whether it is good, having wells and deep waters,[11] or whether it is dry, having no water. Tell us whether the land has trees, whether this state of consciousness can support honorable, proper people,[12] people who can adapt and work with zeal and conscientiousness.

And when you find all this out, be of good courage. Regardless of how you interpret the bad things you see, the difficult things you see, be of good courage. For the possibility of the bad must exist in order for the good to exist. So be of good courage and bring back the fruit of the land. Bring back some of the milk and honey.

When this group of twelve come back after exploring the land for forty days, they bring back with them one cluster of grapes so large that they had to carry it on a pole between two of them. They brought back pomegranates and figs. And when they came back, they showed the Israelites the fruit of the land and said to them that the land "flows with milk and honey."[13] This state of consciousness flows with *milk and honey*.

And then they said אֶפֶס: *but, however*.[14] Then they said that the people are strong and the cities are fortified and very great. Allegorically this means that the will that is required to make this consciousness endure in us must be a strong will. And they observed that "they are stronger than we."[15] Their wills are stronger than our wills. To be in this state of consciousness we will have to build fortified structures

---

11. Ibid., Numbers 13:19, p. 129.
12. Ibid.
13. Numbers 13:27.
14. Numbers 13:28.
15. Numbers 13:31.

as they built fortified structures. Do you realize how much work this is going to require? Do you know how hard it is to live so zealously, always trying to maintain our connection to God? Do you realize what it means to be constantly working on developing and refining our character traits? Every day we will have to face the children of Anak living within us. We will have to confront the Anak, that in us that inclines us to ostentatiousness,[16] the Amalekites, that in us that inclines us to doubt God,[17] the Hittites, that in us that inclines us to frighten others,[18] the Jebusite, that in us that inclines us to despise others,[19] the Amorite, that in us that inclines us to boast about ourselves,[20] and the Canaanite, that in us that inclines us to oppress ourselves.[21,22] None of it can be hidden. Constantly will we be engaged in sacrificing these parts of ourselves. Constantly we will be transforming ourselves. And when we transform one aspect, nullifying it at one level, we will proceed to a higher level and then again face a higher-level Amalekite, a higher-level Hittite, and so forth. "Would it not be better for us to return to Egypt?"[23] Slavery in the land of constriction is not so much work. At least it is identical day after day. We do not have to confront new things. We are not required to grow or change.

Then Caleb, one of the twelve who explored the land, spoke to the Israelites and used the word נוּכַל, which means *well able* or *can*, and like נוֹן has the gematria of 106.

---

16. Anak in Hebrew is עֲנָק. The root ענק, in addition to meaning "giant," means to *wear*, to *decorate, tie*, to *put ornaments around the neck*.

17. Amalekite in Hebrew is עֲמָלֵק. Its gematria is 240, the gematria of the root ספק, which means to *doubt*.

18. Hittite in Hebrew is חִתִּי. This is related to the word חִתִּית, which means *fright* or *terror*.

19. Jebusite in Hebrew is יְבוּסִי. This is related to the root בוס, meaning to *tread underfoot*, to *trample, crush, despise, loathe*, or *detest*.

20. Amorite in Hebrew is אֱמֹרִי. This is related to the root אמר, which means to *say*. The Hitpael form of this root is הִתְאַמֵּר, which means to *boast* or to be *overproud*.

21. Canaanite in Hebrew is כְּנַעֲנִי. This is cognate to the root כנע, which means to *oppress ourselves*, to be *depressed*, or *mournful*.

22. Numbers 13:28-29.

23. Numbers 14:4.

> And Caleb stilled the people before Moses and said: "Let
> us go up at once, and possess it: for we are *well able* to
> overcome it."[24]

Caleb said to pay no attention to the work that we will have to do to
dwell in this land, in this state of consciousness. This work is our service
to God. We can do it. We can do it joyously. It is the holiness we are
called upon to fulfill. It is the only thing that is meaningful to do. And
whatever we have to confront, we can confront it and overcome it. We
can possess this land. We can dwell in this state of consciousness. We
can be in emergence.

The full gematria of גֻּן can be determined from נֻן וָיו גִּימֶל, which
totals 234. This is the gematria of the word וַאֲבָרְכָה, the first person
singular imperfect with conjunctive prefix of the root בָּרַךְ, which means
to *bless*. God uses the word וַאֲבָרְכָה in telling Abraham to get out of
his country.

> I *will bless* them that bless thee and curse him that curses
> thee. And in thee shall all the families of the earth be
> blessed.[25]

After Abraham rescues his brother's son Lot, Melchizedek, the king
of Shalem, blesses God using the word וּבָרוּךְ, which means *and blessed
be*. The word וּבָרוּךְ also has a gematria of 234.

> *And blessed be* the most high God, who has delivered thy
> enemies into thy hand.[26]

Moses uses the word וּבָרוּךְ in his last set of teachings to the Israelites. He says:

> And it shall come to pass, if thou shalt hearken diligently to
> the voice of the Lord thy God, to observe and to do all his
> commandments which I command thee this day, that the
> Lord thy God will set thee on high above all the nations of

---

24. Numbers 13:30.
25. Genesis 12:3.
26. Genesis 14:20.

the earth: and all these blessings shall come on thee, and overtake thee, if thou shalt hearken to the voice of the Lord thy God. Blessed shalt thou be in the city, *and blessed* shalt thou be in the field. Blessed shall be the fruit of thy body, and the fruit of thy ground, and the fruit of thy beasts, the increase of thy cattle, and the flocks of thy sheep. Blessed shall be thy basket and thy store. Blessed shalt thou be when thou comest in *and blessed* shalt thou be when thou goest out.[27]

So when we engage *emergence*, we engage in building the container to house our future essence. In emerging we sprout and blossom. And God blesses us. This is the revealed meaning of ב.

The concealed meaning of בון is contained in the form ון, which by itself is not any Hebrew word. However, the form ון occurs combined with other letters in a variety of words, all of which begin with ב. The word בון means *tune* or *melody*. But it does not carry only the meaning of an ordinary melody. It carries the meaning of a melody of Divine celebration. One who sings or plays a בון becomes so focused on the joy, happiness, and delight in the melody that the melody creates a connection ו between the ב above and the ן below, a connection that nourishes ב, the singer, and opens the doorway for the singer to participate in the cosmic Oneness of the Divinity. In this manner, the energy intelligence of the bent ב becomes the energy intelligence of the straight final form ן. The *wise* and *understanding*, the בונ, know this.

When the nourishment ב of בון changes to the door ד of בוד, the meaning melody changes to the meaning *topic*. The Hebrew word בוד means topic or *subject under discussion*. When the heart and mind are fully focused on a subject under discussion, the speech and utterances of the discussion help form a new physical reality, thereby opening the doorway for a manifestation of Godliness. Thus it is no surprise that when the door ד of בוד changes to ז, the flow of א, the Hebrew root בוז forms, carrying the meaning of to *be maintained*. Both the melody and doorway connecting upper to lower must be maintained. By this maintenance, the letter energy intelligence of ', the projection of א

---

27. Deuteronomy 28:1-6.

into physical existence, is added to the root נְבוֹן. Thereby the Arabic word נְבִיוֹם forms, with the meaning of *governor*. By maintaining the connection between above and below, we fully become governors of ourselves and the cosmos. All becomes נָכֹון, which means *correct, true, sound, right, certain, clear, proper,* and *appropriate*. The root of the Hebrew word for *giving* is נְתַן. The word נְתַן reads the same from right to left or from left to right. In this there is a lesson, for when we give, we receive.[28] And this is what is *given*, נָתוּן, as the revealed meaning of נ.

The letter energy intelligence of נ is associated with נֵס, *miracle, wonder, marvel,* or *providential event*. But נֵס also has the meaning of *flag, banner,* or *standard*. About this relation Rabbi Schneerson teaches:

> The word miracle, נֵס, also has the meaning of *uplifted* or *raised*. It is used in the context of raising a banner high so that it can be seen by those far away. A miracle involves elevating the world and lifting it up so that its Godly nature can be perceived by all, even those far removed from Godliness. They see something that goes beyond the rules of nature and they realize that it could only be accomplished by God's power. That, in turn, allows them to appreciate how even nature's rules are controlled by God.[29]

The letter energy intelligence of נ is also associated with נֵר, *candle, light,* or *ancient lamp*, נִיר, *candle, light,* or *splendor*, נוּר, the Aramaic word for *fire*, נֶאֱור, the word for *enlightened, cultured, illumined,* and *glorious*, and נָהַר, to *shine light*. By shining light there results נַחַת, which means *contentment, peace, quiet, rest, calm,* and *satisfaction*. We recognize that our true identity is not with any particular physical flourishing and declining, but with the Godliness within. Our essence is spiritual, for we have נֶפֶשׁ, which means *soul, spirit, life,* and *breath*. The gematria of נֶפֶשׁ is $300 + 80 + 50 = 430 = 7$. And when the letter

---

28. Rabbi Matityahu Glazerson, *From Hinduism to Judaism* (Jerusalem: Himelsein Glazerson, 1984), p. 46.
29. Rabbi Menachem Schneerson, *Sichos in English*, vol. 23 (Brooklyn, NY: Sichos in English, 1985), p. 168.

energy intelligence of פ changes to the letter energy intelligence of ח, נֶפֶשׁ changes to נָחָשׁ, which means *snake* or *serpent* and also has the value of 300 + 8 + 50 = 358 = 16 = 7. נָחָשׁ is cognate to נַחַשׁ, which means *magic*, *sorcery*, and *enchantment* and is cognate to נָחָשׁ, which means *diviner*, *enchanter*, *sorcerer*. This is the occult meaning of נ.

The letter energy intelligence of נ carries some other important meanings. The aspect of נון that means to propagate gives rise to נִין, which means *offspring* or *descendant*, when the connection of ו changes to י, the projection of א into physical existence. The aspect of נון that means degeneration gives rise to the word נְפִילָה, which means *fall*, *falling*, *collapse*, *downfall*, *defeat*, *degradation*, which we all must go through. But by being נֶאֱמָן, by being *faithful*, *trustworthy*, *loyal*, *reliable*, *firm*, and *sure* we can surrender all through the fall and still maintain the connection between the upper and the lower, knowing that there will come another pulsation of the letter energy intelligence of א by which we will again flourish and blossom.

Samek ס: Support

The fifteenth letter of the Hebrew alphabet is ס, spelled סָמֶךְ. The letter energy intelligence of ס is that of ו projected into time and conditioned physical existence. Thus, it has the numerical value of 60. The letter energy intelligence of ו has the meaning of connection, so it comes as no surprise when we learn that סָמֶךְ is cognate to the root סמך, which is the verb having the meaning to *rely on, trust in, support, aid, assist, lay hands on, draw near, make close, encourage,* or to *be supported.* The character sequence סמך occurs as the word סָמַךְ exactly once in the Pentateuch. There it has the meaning "to lay hands on." To lay hands on is a spiritual anointing. This tells us that ס relates to spiritual *support.*

> And Joshua, the son of Nun, was full of the spirit of wisdom for Moses had *laid* his hands upon him. And the children of Israel listened to him and did what the Lord had commanded Moses.[1]

Nouns cognate to the root סמך include סֶמֶךְ, which means *support* or *fullness,* סָמָךְ, which means *reference* (a reference is, after all, a support for a concept), and סֹמֶךְ, which means *consistence.* The act of connecting to the Divine source on the spiritual plane manifests in a resulting support or act of support on the physical plane. This act of support can be an act of trust, an act of assistance, an act of encouragement, an act of drawing near and making close, or an act of ordaining. All acts done with the goal of Divine service, of becoming one with God, or of doing the will of God are acts that become endowed with a holiness whose physical manifestation is a support structure that functions to facilitate other such acts of holiness such as supporting the poor.[2] The revealed meaning of ס is, therefore, *support.*

The gematria of the word סָמַךְ is 120. Other words with the gematria of 120 include עַמּוּד, which means *pillar.* Every instance of its use

---

1. Deuteronomy 34:9.
2. *The Babylonian Talmud, Seder Moed,* vol. 1, *Shabbat,* trans. H. Freedman (London: Soncino Press, 1938), p. 500.

in the Pentateuch is with respect to the pillar of the cloud of God. This pillar of the cloud supported the Hebrews as they wandered in the desert.

> He did not take away the *pillar* of the cloud by day, nor the pillar of fire by night, from before the people.[3]

> And the *pillar* of the cloud went from before their face, and stood behind them.[4]

> And it came to pass, as Moses entered the Tent, the *pillar* of the cloud descended and stood at the door of the Tent while the Lord talked to Moses. And all the people saw the *pillar* of the cloud stand at the door of the Tent.[5]

> And the Lord appeared in the Tent in a pillar of a cloud; and the *pillar* of the cloud stood over the door of the Tent.[6]

Another word with the gematria of 120 is עוֹמֵד. It means *stands* and appears exactly once in the Pentateuch, when God speaks to Moses at the burning bush.

> And He said: "Do not come near. Put off thy shoes from off thy feet, for the place on which thou dost *stand* is holy ground."[7]

God supports us by graciousness. The word וְחַנּוּן means *and gracious* and also has the gematria of 120. It occurs exactly once in the Pentateuch, after Moses receives the two tablets the second time.

> The Lord passed by him and proclaimed: "The Lord, is a compassionate *and gracious* God, slow to anger, abounding in loving-kindness and truth; maintaining mercy unto the thousandth generation, forgiving iniquity, and transgression and sin.[8]

---

3. Exodus 13:22.
4. Exodus 14:19.
5. Exodus 33:9-10.
6. Deuteronomy 31:15.
7. Exodus 3:5.
8. Exodus 34:6-7.

And God supports us by supplying us with water. The word מֵימֶיךָ means *your water* and also has the gematria of 120.

> And thou shalt serve the Lord your God and He will bless thy bread and thy water.[9]

And God supports us with His strong hand. The word חֲזָקָה means *strong* or *mighty* and has the gematria of 120.

> And I know that the king of Egypt will not give you leave to go, except by a *mighty* hand.[10]

> And the Lord said unto Moses: "Now shalt thou see what I will do to Pharaoh; for by a *strong* Hand shall he let them go, and by a *strong* hand shall he drive them out of his land."[11]

> And it shall be to thee for a sign upon thy hand, and for a memorial between thine eyes; in order that the Law of the Lord may be in thy mouth; for with a *strong* hand hath the Lord brought thee out from Egypt.[12]

> And Moses besought the Lord his God, and he said: "Why O Lord, doth Thy wrath wax hot against Thy people, whom Thou hast brought forth out of the land of Egypt with great power and with a *mighty* hand?[13]

> Or has God tried to go to take Him a nation from the midst of another nation by trials, by signs and by wonder, and by wars, and by a *mighty* hand, and by an outstretched arm, and by great terrors, according to all that the Lord your God did for you in Egypt before thine eyes?[14]

> And thou shalt remember that thou wast a servant in the land of Egypt, and the Lord thy God brought thee out thence by a *mighty* hand and by an outstretched arm.[15]

---

9. Exodus 23:25.
10. Exodus 3:19.
11. Exodus 6:1.
12. Exodus 13:9.
13. Exodus 32:11.
14. Deuteronomy 4:34.
15. Deuteronomy 5:15.

Then thou shalt say unto thy son: "We were Pharaoh's slaves in Egypt; and the Lord brought us out of Egypt with a *mighty* hand.[16]

But because the Lord loved you and because He would keep the oath which he swore unto your fathers, hath the Lord brought you out with a *mighty* hand, and redeemed you out of the house of bondage, from the hand of Pharaoh king of Egypt.[17]

And I prayed unto the Lord, and I said: "O Lord God, destroy not Thy people and Thine inheritance, that thou hast brought forth out of Egypt with a *mighty* hand."[18]

And the Lord brought us forth out of Egypt with a *mighty* hand, and with an outstretched arm, and with great terribleness, and with signs and with wonders.[19]

When the word סָמֶךְ is completely spelled out, there results סָמֶךְ מֶם כַּף, which has a total gematria of 300. The word יָצַר is the third person masculine singular past of the root יצר, meaning to *form, shape, fashion, devise, produce,* or *create.* It has the gematria of 300. The related noun יֵצֶר means *formation, frame, pattern, image, fiction, thought, device, formation of thoughts, bent of desire, inclination,* or *desire.*

And the Lord God planted a garden eastward in Eden; and there he put the man whom he had *formed.*[20]

Whose *mind [thoughts, inclinations]* are steadfast [on Thee], Thou wilt keep in perfect peace.[21]

And the Lord saw that the wickedness of man was great in the earth, and that all the *inclination* of the thoughts of his heart was only evil continually.[22]

---

16. Deuteronomy 6:21.
17. Deuteronomy 7:8.
18. Deuteronomy 9:26.
19. Deuteronomy 26:8.
20. Genesis 2:8.
21. Isaiah 26:3.
22. Genesis 6:5.

ס 223

And the Lord smelled the sweet savor; and the Lord said in his heart I will not again curse the ground any more for man's sake; for the *inclination* of man's heart is evil from his youth.[23]

And thou, Solomon, my son, know thou the God of thy father, and serve Him with a perfect heart and with a willing mind [soul] for the Lord searches all hearts, and understands every *inclination* [*imagination, motive*] of the thoughts; if thou seek him, he will be found by thee, but if thou forsake Him, He will cast thee off forever.[24]

The concealed meaning of ס can be understood from the meaning of מָס. This form is similar to the root מס, which means to *become poor* and to *be depressed* and to the noun מָס, which means *poor* or *humble*. The form is also similar to the prefix מְ, which means *infra*. If we do not make connection with the Divine source, support will not manifest and we will become poor and depressed. Furthermore, the only way in which connection can be made is with an attitude of humbleness. And when we make a connection and are humble, we help create an infrastructure that supports us in the best and in the most troublesome of circumstances.

Combinations of the letter energy intelligence of ס with the other letter energy intelligences give further insights to the character of the support associated with ס. When the letter energy intelligence of ס combines with the letter energy intelligence of ב, which is the archetype for container, there results a container for support. The word סָב means *old man, grandfather, ancestor,* or *scholar,* each of which is a container for a kind of support. The word סֹב is the imperative form of the root סָבַב, meaning to *turn about, go around, surround, encompass, circle, encircle, rotate, revolve, spin,* or *gyrate*.

You have *gone around* this mountain long enough. Now face to the north.[25]

---

23. Genesis 8:21.
24. 1 Chronicles 28:9.
25. Deuteronomy 2:3.

Until the day breaks and the shadows flee, *turn about*, my lover, and be like a gazelle or like a young stag on the rugged hills.[26]

And the present form סוֹבֵב or סֹבֵב occurs in verses like these:

Going to the south and turning to the north,
Round and round the wind goes,
The wind ever returning on its course.[27]

The shape of the letter ס is related to the circle, encircle, surround, or encompass meaning of סבב. For the interior of the letter ס is like a disk surrounded by a circle. The empty inside stands for the spiritual nature of *support* related to ס. The circular perimeter stands for the infinity of God, who has no beginning or end, and for the Glory of God that fills and surrounds the earth.[28] Thus, wherever we are we can be in contact with the omnipresent Being of the Divine.

There also results the related verb סבֵּב, which means to *cause, alter, bring about*, or to *change*. Support is not a static structure. The very dynamics of life involve changes that we bring about by our acts of will. These changes when done in the context of receiving the Divine love and returning the light, when done in the context of learning, growing, and changing in response to the changing circumstances in which we find ourselves, produce a structure that *supports* a dynamic equilibrium. The nature of the dynamics for support can be learned from the root סבב. Finally, when the letter energy intelligence of ס combines with the letter intelligence of ר, which means cosmic container, there results the word סָר, which means to *move* or *turn aside*. When we turn aside from where we are supposed to be focusing our attention, we separate ourselves from the Divine and we become סַר, which means *sullen* or *ill-humored*, and *dispirited*.

And the King of Israel went to his house *sullen* and displeased.[29]

---

26. Song of Songs 2:17.
27. Ecclesiastes 1:6.
28. Rabbi Michael Munk, *The Wisdom in the Hebrew Alphabet* (New York: Mesorah, 1988), p. 160.
29. 1 Kings 20:43.

Here we see *support* involves motion. But the motion is not translational motion. It is rotational motion, motion that after one complete revolution brings us back to where we started. And from where do we start but from the Divine will that seeks to create a dwelling place, an abode in the physical world for God? It is our job to make manifest this dwelling place by our thoughts, words, and actions, which follow the law: love is the law, love under will. And by so doing we transform and move our physical reality to a spiritual reality, making the two one: God is one. There is only one true identity or essence. And this Godly essence is our essence. We have no other true identity besides this essence.

When the letter energy intelligence of ס combines with the letter energy intelligence of ר, which is the archetype for physical existence, there results the root סר, which means to *whitewash*, and the word סַד, which means the *stocks* used for torturing.[30] Physical existence in its own way is a double-edged sword. On the one hand it can be perceived to be a dwelling place for God. On the other hand it can be perceived to be only a place in which physical material things happen without Divine connection. This latter occurs whenever we pay attention only to physical reality, when we pay attention only to the outer surface of the situation. In these cases, we are just whitewashing. The structure whitewashed will eventually fall to pieces and thereby become a torturing stock to our ego, whose involvement in the whitewashing constitutes a narrow selfish involvement, an involvement separated from God. These kinds of involvements lead to evil deeds, sins, and transgression, which is the meaning of the word סַס.

When the letter energy intelligence of ס combines with the letter energy intelligence of ג, which is the archetype for nourishment, we might think that there would be created a nourishing support. However, the word סַג carries the meaning of *backsliding* and *moving away*. To understand this we must recall the nature of the letter energy intelligence of א, which is the pulsating unbridled force. One moment it is here, in the sense of being revealed, and the next it is not, in the sense of being concealed. One week it is here, the next not. Sometimes we think that the most direct way to a goal is monotonic motion toward the goal.

---

30. Job 13:27, 33:11.

But our evolution and growth are not like that. There are apparent times of slippage, of backsliding. There are times of readjustment and rebalancing. These times permit attributes, values, perspectives, and actions that had been supressed in the prior monotonic motion to be revealed. The word סֻן reminds us that seemingly backward motion is in a global and local sense also a source of nourishing support, for our descent is for the purpose of our ascent.

> The descent is itself a phase in the ascent. Every descent is in essence for the purpose of ascent, and is capable of bringing one to a level higher than that enjoyed before the ascent.[31]
>
> "Always ascend higher in holy matters; never descend." Although on a revealed level there is less light, inwardly, a process of ascent is taking place.[32]

---

31. Rabbi Menachem Schneerson, *Sichos in English*, vol. 47 (Brooklyn, NY: Sichos in English, 1990), p. 187.
32. Rabbi Schneerson, *Sichos in English*, vol. 50, pp. 251-252.

עַיִן

Ayin ע: Insight and Consciousness

The sixteenth letter of the Hebrew alphabet is ע, spelled עין. The numerical value of ע is 70, which means that ע is the energy intelligence of ז, whose numerical value is 7, projected into existence. The energy intelligence of ז is movement, which here means the flow of א. Hence the energy intelligence of ע is that of the flow of א projected into existence, and this flow is *insight* and *consciousness*.

The word עין, sometimes spelled עין, has the meaning of *eye, face, look, appearance, sight, aperture, bud, sparkle,* or *gleam.* And when we know the eye we realize that the eye is more than the eye. We become conscious of something deeper, for

> The *eye* is not satisfied with just seeing.[1]

This is because it is by the light of the *eye* that we can see and follow the correct path.[2] Therefore, the eye is deep and protected.

> Guard me like the apple of Thine *eye.*[3]

And where shall our eyes be?

> For the *eyes* of mankind, as of all the tribes of Israel shall be towards the Lord.[4]

> Mine *eyes* are ever toward the Lord.[5]

> Lift up thine *eyes* on high, and behold who has created these things, that brings out their host by number.[6]

And when we turn our *eyes* to God, what do we see? As Rabbi Menachem Mendel Hager of Kossov teaches, we see with our intellect and intuition.[7] We see eye to eye.

---

1. Ecclesiastes 1:8.
2. Moshe Alshech, *Book of Psalms,* vol. 1, trans. Rabbi Eliyahu Munk (Brooklyn, NY: Moriah Offset, 1976), p. 93.
3. Psalms 17:8.
4. Zechariah 9:1.
5. Psalms 25:15.
6. Isaiah 40:26.
7. Avraham Yaakov Finkel, *The Great Chasidic Masters* (Northvale, NJ: Jason Aronson, 1992), p. 112.

They have already heard that Thou, O Lord, art with these
people. That Thou, O Lord, art seen *face to face* [*eye to
eye*].[8]

Together they shall sing: for they shall see *eye to eye*, the
Lord returning to Zion.[9]

And when we turn our eyes to each other, what happens?

And Isaac went out to meditate in the field before the
evening; and he lifted up his *eyes* and saw. And behold,
there were camels coming. And Rebekah lifted up her *eyes*,
and when she saw Isaac, she alighted from the camel.[10]

And what is the eye? The eye is the window through which our
character may be discerned.

Eat thou not the bread of him that hath an evil *eye*. Neither
desire thou his dainties.[11]

He that hath an evil *eye* hasteneth after riches. And knoweth
not that want shall come upon him.[12]

He that hath a bountiful *eye* shall be blessed; For he giveth
of his bread to the poor.[13]

The word עַיִן (its constructive form being עֵין) has the meaning of
spring or *fountain*. A fountain is a subterranean reservoir that feeds
the oceans and rivers.[14]

And an angel of the Lord found her by a *spring* in the
wilderness.[15]

---

8. Numbers 14:14.
9. Isaiah 52:8.
10. Genesis 24:63.
11. Proverbs 23:6.
12. Proverbs 28:22.
13. Proverbs 22:9.
14. *Proverbs*, trans. A. Cohen (London: Soncino Press, 1985), p. 49.
15. Genesis 16:7.

Behold, I stand here by the *spring* of water where the daughters of the men of the city come out to draw water. And let it come to pass, that the girl to whom I shall say, "Let down thy pitcher, I pray thee, that I may drink," and she shall say, "Drink, and I will give thy camels drink also." Let her be she that thou hast appointed for thy servant Isaac.[16]

For the Lord thy God brings thee into a good land, a land of water courses, of *fountains* and depths that spring out of valleys and hills; a land of wheat, and barley, and vines, and fig trees, and pomegranates; a land of olive oil, and honey; a land in which thou shalt eat bread without scarceness, thou shalt not lack any thing in it.[17]

עַיִן is related to the verb עַיִן, which means to *consider, go into the matter, think over, peruse, weigh carefully, reflect, study, meditate, ponder,* and the verb עַיִן, which means to *be balanced.*

The gematria of עַיִן is 130. The word סֻלָּם has the gematria of 130 and means *ladder.* Our eye is our ladder; for the rays emanating from God are seen by our eyes, that is, by our *insight.* Rabbi Yosef Yitzchak Schneersohn of Lubavitch teaches that this connection from earth to heaven is bonded by the praises in our prayer.[18]

And behold a *ladder* set up on the earth, and the top of it reaching heaven.[19]

Rabbi Menachem Mendel Hager of Kossov teaches that when our evil inclination tells us that like the ladder, we are just standing on the ground and are unworthy of aspiring toward holiness, it is our insight that reminds us that the top of the ladder reaches toward heaven. When our evil inclination tells us that we have reached the loftiest spiritual heights, our insight reminds us that like the ladder, we are just standing on the ground.[20]

---

16. Genesis 24:13-14.
17. Deuteronomy 8:7.
18. Rabbi Yosef Yitzchak Schneersohn, *Likkutei Dibburim,* vol. 1, trans. Uri Kaploun (Brooklyn, NY: Kehot Publication Society, 1987), p. 164.
19. Genesis 28:12.
20. Finkel, *The Great Chasidic Masters,* p. 112.

The word סִינָי also has the gematria of 130 and means *Sinai*.

> And afterwards all the children of Israel came near. And he gave them all the commands that the Lord had spoken with him on Mount *Sinai*.[21]

From this we are taught by Rabbi Yaakov Yosef of Polnoye that our ladder, the means by which we become closer to God, is the Torah, which was what was given on Mount Sinai.[22]

When the word עַיִן is spelled out there results עַיִן יוֹד נוּן, and this has a total gematria of 256. The word נִרְאָה means *has appeared* or *has been seen* and also has the gematria of 256. It is the third person masculine singular past Niphal form of the root רָאָה, which means to *see*, or *perceive*. Thus from to see we go to to be seen, to be seeable, to appear. From the usages of נִרְאָה, we can see to what ע ultimately relates.

> And Jacob said to Joseph: God Almighty *appeared* to me at Luz in the land of Canaan and blessed me, and said to me, "Behold, I will make thee fruitful, and multiply thee."[23]

> Go and gather the elders of Israel together, and say to them: The Lord God of your fathers, the God of Abraham, of Isaac, of Jacob, has *appeared* to me saying "I have surely visited you, and seen that which is done to you in Egypt."[24]

> But behold they will not believe me, nor hearken to my voice: for they will say: "The Lord has not *appeared* to thee."[25]

> That they may believe that the Lord God of their fathers, the God of Abraham, the God of Isaac, and the God of Jacob, has *appeared* to thee.[26]

---

21. Exodus 34:32.
22. Finkel, *The Great Chasidic Masters*, p. 15.
23. Genesis 48:3.
24. Exodus 3:16.
25. Exodus 4:1.
26. Exodus 4:5.

And it came to pass as Aaron spoke to the whole congregation of the children of Israel, that they looked toward the wilderness, and behold, the glory of the Lord *appeared* in the cloud.[27]

For today the Lord will *appear* to you.[28]

And the Glory of the Lord *appeared* in the Tent of Meeting before all the children of Israel.[29]

They have already heard that Thou, O Lord, art with these people. That Thou, O Lord, art *seen* face to face [eye to eye].[30]

Words that end in עִין include מַעְיָן, which means *spring, fountain, source,* or *well* [31] and has the alternate meaning of *thought, attention,* or *consideration,* מְעֻיָן, which means *balanced, evenly balanced,* or *poised* as well as *rhombus* or *diamond shaped.* The spring or fountain or well of sight and balance is *insight* and *consciousness.* This is the revealed meaning of ע.

The shape of the letter ע is like two eyes attached to a pipe that faces leftward. On our left side is our heart. This shows that our eyes, our insight, and consciousness will influence our heart.[32] Our job is to set our eyes, our insight, our consciousness on what is appropriate. In this way our heart can be purified, enabling us to love God with all our heart.

The concealed meaning of עִין can be found from the study of the form יִן, which itself has no literal meaning. In this case we must look for related forms. The word יַיִן means *wine* and the word יַיָּן means *winemaker* or *wine expert.* When the form יִן combines with ה, the letter energy intelligence of power of being, there results the form יָנה, which is the root meaning to *oppress,* to *tread down,* to *trample*

---

27. Exodus 16:10.
28. Leviticus 9:4.
29. Numbers 14:10.
30. Numbers 14:14.
31. Leviticus 11:36, Psalms 84:7.
32. Rabbi Matityahu Glazerson, *Hebrew: The Source of Languages* (Jerusalem: Yerid HaSefarim, 1987), p. 79.

יָנָה, which is the root meaning to *oppress*, to *tread down*, to *trample underfoot*, to *deceive, beat, trick, bamboozle, maltreat, vex, annoy,* or *irritate.* When the form יָ combines with the letter energy intelligence of ק, which is cosmic א, there forms the root יָנָק, which means to *suck, absorb,* to *suckle, breast-feed,* or *nurse.*

> For they shall *suck* of the abundance of the seas, and of treasures hid in the sand.[33]

> If only you were to me like a brother, who was *nursed* at my mother's breasts![34]

> I will make thee an eternal excellency, a joy of many generations. Thou shalt also *suck* the milk of the nations, and shalt *suckle* the breast of kings: and thou shalt know that I the Lord shall save thee.[35]

> Rejoice with Jerusalem, and be glad with her, all you that love her: rejoice for joy with her, all you that did mourn for her: that you may *suck,* and be satisfied with the breast of her consolations: that you may drink deeply, and be delighted with the abundance of her glory. For thus says the Lord, "Behold, I will extend peace to her like a river, and the glory of the nations like a flowing stream: then shalt thou *suck,* thou shalt be carried upon her sides, and be dandled upon her knees."[36]

To make sense of all of this, we must understand that wine is the spiritual essence of the grape and that the essence is more than the physical grape itself. A wine maker is one who creates more than what is initially given. However, to be fully conscious of the greater qualities and essences than those that appear in physical reality, we must be conscious of spiritual reality as well. When we are fully conscious of the physical and spiritual realms in all our situations and in all our actions, our situations and actions naturally bring forth Godliness into

---

33. Deuteronomy 33:19.
34. Song of Songs 8:1.
35. Isaiah 60:15-16.
36. Isaiah 66:10-12.

our existence. We become the means by which the world is able to suckle the Divine goodness. We nurse the world. On the other hand, when we are not conscious of the physical and spiritual realms, our actions become actions that oppress, deceive, maltreat, and irritate. Our actions are actions of עָוֹן, which means *sin, crime, offense, iniquity, trouble, suffering, punishment, evil,* and *wickedness*.

> And if a person sin and commit any of these things which are forbidden to be done by the commandments of the Lord; though he know it not, yet is he guilty, and shall bear his *iniquity*.[37]

> But the person who acts presumptuously, whether he be born in the land, or a stranger, that person dishonours the Lord; and that soul shall be cut off from among his people. Because he has despised the word of the Lord, and has broken his commandment, that soul shall utterly be cut off; his *iniquity* shall be upon him.[38]

> For behold, the Lord comes out of his place to punish the inhabitants of the earth for their *iniquity*.[39]

And our actions become actions of עִיֵן, which means to be *hostile, inimical, antagonistic,* and to *hate*. We engage in עָוֶל, *wrong, injustice,* and *iniquity*. We become עוֹיֵן, *hostile, unfriendly,* and *inimical*. We become עַוָּל, a *wicked one*. This is the concealed meaning of ע.

When the letter energy intelligence of ע combines with the letter energy intelligence of ב, which means *container*, there results the word עָב, which means *density* or *thickness* or means *cloud* and *darkness*.

> And it came to pass in the meanwhile that the sky became darkened with *clouds* and wind, and there was a great rain.[40]

And when this cloud combines with ד, whose energy intelligence is physical existence, there results the word עָבַד, which is the verb to *work, labor, toil, till, cultivate, serve,* or *worship*.

---

37. Leviticus 5:17.
38. Numbers 15:30-31.
39. Isaiah 26:21.
40. 1 Kings 18:45.

And He said to Abraham: "Know surely that thy seed shall
be a stranger in a land that is not theirs, and shall *serve*
them; and they shall afflict them four hundred years; and
also that nation, whom they shall *serve*, will I judge; and
afterwards shall they come out with great substance.[41]

And the Egyptians made the children of Israel *serve* with
rigor: and they made their lives bitter with hard bondage,
in mortar, and in brick, and in all manner of bondage in
the field: all their bondage, wherein they made them *serve*,
was with rigor.[42]

What is this that you have done to me? Did I not *serve*
you for Rachel?[43]

Josiah removed all the detestable idols from all the territory
belonging to the Israelites, and he had all who were present
in Israel *serve* the Lord their God.[44]

There is also formed the word עֶבֶד, which is the noun meaning
servant.

My Lord, if now I have found favor in thy sight, pass not
away, I pray thee, from thy *servant*: let a little water, I
pray you, be fetched and wash your feet, and rest yourselves
under the tree.[45]

When the density עָב combines with the letter energy intelligence
of ר, which means cosmic container, there results the verb עָבַר, which
means to *make pregnant, impregnate, fecundate,* or *conceive* as well as
the alternate meaning of to *become angry*. Also the noun עֻבָּר forms,
which means *embryo* or *fetus*.

When the letter energy intelligence of ע combines with ג, the letter
energy intelligence of nourishment, there results the word עַג, which
means to *circle*. And when this circling is combined with the letter

---

41. Genesis 15:13-14.
42. Exodus 1:13-14.
43. Genesis 29:25.
44. 2 Chronicles 34:33.
45. Genesis 18:3-4.

energy intelligence of ב, there results the verb עָגַב, which means to *make love.*

When the letter energy intelligence of ע combines with the letter energy intelligence of ד, there results the word עַד, which means *eternity.* Eternity is the flow of א projected into and wrapped into physical existence. Also, there forms the word עֵד, which means *witness, evidence,* and *testimony.* Our thoughts, words, and actions constitute our evidence and testimony of just exactly how we have created a dwelling place for Godliness in physical existence.

When the letter energy intelligence of ע combines with the letter energy intelligence of its archetype ז, there forms the word עַז, which means *strong, powerful, mighty, fierce, violent, courageous, sharp, bright, vigorous, intense,* and *energetic.*

> But the people who live there are *powerful,* and the cities are fortified and very large.[46]

There is the word עֹז, which means *strength, power, might, violence, vigor, courage, valor, splendor, glory,* and *praise.*

> The Lord gives *strength* to His people; the Lord blesses His people with peace.[47]

> Lord, by Thy favor Thou hast made my mountain to stand with *strength.*[48]

> That *power* belongs to God.[49]

When the letter energy intelligence of ע combines with ל, the letter energy intelligence of teaching, there forms עַל, which as a prefix means *super* and as a preposition mean *on, upon, concerning,* or *toward* and there forms the word עֹל, which means *yoke, burden,* or *servitude.*

> Tell the Israelites to bring you a red heifer without defect or blemish and that has never been under a *yoke.*[50]

---

46. Numbers 13:28.
47. Psalms 29:11.
48. Psalms 30:8.
49. Psalms 62:12.
50. Numbers 19:2.

With the letter energy intelligence of ע it is our Divine service to
teach full consciousness and when we do so there forms the word עָלַל,
the verb to *attend, do, act, work* and also the verb to *ascend, land,
enter,* or *visit* and the related word עֲלִילוֹת, *deeds.*

> Let all their wickedness come before Thee; And *do* to them
> as Thou hast *done* to me, for all my transgressions.[51]

> Incline not my heart to any evil thing, to practice wicked
> *deeds* with men who work iniquity.[52]

Our actions and the work they accomplish ascend and become more
than what they are on the surface. In that way, they bring Godliness
into existence.

When the word עַל combines with the letter energy intelligence of ם,
there forms the root עלם, which means to *disappear, vanish, be hidden,*
or *concealed.*[53]

> And if the whole congregation of Israel sin through igno-
> rance, and the thing be *hidden* from the eyes of the as-
> sembly, and they have done something against any of the
> commandments of the Lord concerning things which should
> not be done, then they have incurred guilt.[54]

> Thou hast set our iniquities before Thee, our *hidden* sins in
> the light of Thy countenance.[55]

The Godliness brought into existence is often concealed. Indeed עָלַם
is a word meaning *world.* The world is a place in which Godliness is
hidden and it waits to be revealed by a full *insight* and *consciousness.*

When ע itself combines with the letter energy intelligence of ם,
there forms the word עַם, which means *nation, people, folk, community, populace, inhabitants, tribe, kinsman,* or *relative* and there forms
the word עִם, which means *with, together, in the company of, at, by,*

---

51. Lamentations 1:22.
52. Psalms 141:4.
53. *The Bahir,* trans. and comm. Rabbi Aryeh Kaplan (Northvale, NJ: Jason
Aronson, 1995), p. 5.
54. Leviticus 4:13.
55. Psalms 90:8.

near, beside, while, or *during.* From this we see that the revealment of Godliness cannot take place in situations isolated from people. The revealment takes place in family, in community, in nations. It happens by, with, and in the company of people.

When the letter energy intelligence of ע combines with ו there forms the word עַז, *cattle,* and when it combines with ף there forms the root עָף, to *fly.* When ע combines with ץ, there forms the word עֵץ, *tree, wood,* or *log.* When it combines with the letter energy intelligence of ר, there forms the root ער, which is the verb to *awake* and the word עֵר, which means *awake, alert, active, aroused,* or *vigilant.* Our consciousness must be awake, alert, active, and aroused if we are always to maintain a full consciousness of the physical and spiritual. If we do not maintain this full consciousness, our reality will become unfriendly and our enemy. This is because the word עַר has a second meaning of *enemy* or *adversary.* And we will become like cattle being led to the slaughterhouse by an inexplicable and determined cause. We will be like birds trying to fly away from our reality. In such a reality we can have no freedom, for this reality wrapped in the container ב, becomes עֶרֶב, which means a *swarm of beasts.*

When the energy intelligence of ע combines with ת, which is the energy intelligence of cosmic existence and true law, there forms the word עֵת, which means *time, season, term, period, era,* or *epoch.* Time is consciousness of true law in cosmic existence.

To put the revealed and concealed meaning of ע in perspective, consider that it is through consciousness that we see. And what is it that we see through consciousness? We see what has been born in creation. We see what is coming forward and becoming known. We see what was hidden and is now revealed. We see what has risen above and appears in open view. We see that which was hidden and unmanifest inside and has come outside to be manifest. From this point of view, consciousness is not so much the screen of awareness of our external reality, which is the outside. It is the screen of awareness of our internal reality, which is the inside. And this internal reality we create. It is by the letter energy intelligence of ע that we use our insight to make and use every situation (external reality) as a means for higher achievement or purpose. We do this by bringing unity to diversity and establishing harmony among multiplicity.

How is it possible to bring unity to a situation that can be full of conflict and diversity? How is it possible to establish harmony and balance in that which has the appearance of disharmony and multiple imbalances? We can do this by connecting to God: using our intuition and insight to recognize the Godliness in everything. In short, we do it by rising above the illusion of diversity and multiplicity. We do it by manifesting an internal reality of peace, tranquility, balance, and unity. This is our true essence and this essence is at one with what we call our external reality.

In order to be fully conscious of this unity, this oneness, there must be an existential distinction, an axis of unity–diversity. Otherwise, the concept of unity could not arise in consciousness. To enable the consciousness of unity to occur, there must be the concept of disunity or diversity. So diversity exists, but it exists as appearance, as illusion. It does not exist in essence. Nothing has the essence of disunity for all comes from God.

This understanding of inner and outer reality does not imply that, therefore, we need only observe what is in our outer reality and proclaim or understand its unity through and through. For we are part of that reality and the unity that it is calls upon us to act. Our action and work are part of the unity. The external reality does not exist independent of our internal reality. Indeed, it is our internal reality that fecundates and makes love to our external reality. The unity is a unity of the two combined. We can conceive of this unity as the eternal circle, strong, powerful, mighty, full of glory and praise. And the actions we are called upon to do are actions that in one way or another fulfill the unity that is. This totality is what is in our consciousness and is what must in each and every instance rise up, come forward, and become manifest and revealed.

Pey פֵּא: Speech and Freedom

The seventeenth letter of the Hebrew alphabet is פ, spelled פֵּא, and alternately spelled פֵּה. It has the numerical value of 80. It also has a final form ף, which has the numerical value of 800. The form פֵּא is related to the word פֶּה, *mouth, speech, saying, order, command, orifice, opening, entrance, mouthful,* and *extremity* or *border.*

> And the Lord said to him: "Who has made a man's *mouth?* or who makes a man dumb, or deaf, or seeing, or blind? Is it not I the Lord?"[1]

> If there be a prophet among you, I the Lord make myself known to him in a vision, and speak to him in a dream. My servant Moses is not so, for he is the trusted one in all my house. With him I speak *mouth* to *mouth,* manifestly, and not in dark speeches, and the similitude of the Lord does he behold.[2]

Everything that happens, physically, mentally, emotionally, or spiritually can be transformed into action only after passing through the border, through the entranceway into our existence, which metaphysically speaking means being expressed verbally or nonverbally through the mouth.

The word פֶּה is cognate to the word פֹּה, which means *here* or *in this place.*

When the angels talk to Lot they use the word פֹּה.

> And the men said to Lot: "Do you have anyone else *here* – sons-in-law, sons or daughters, or anyone else in the city who belongs to you?[3]

In the incident of the sacrifice of Isaac, Abraham uses the word פֹּה.

---

1. Exodus 4:11.
2. Numbers 12:6-8.
3. Genesis 19:12.

He said to his servants: "Stay *here* with the ass while I and the boy go over there. We will worship and then we will come back to you."[4]

Joseph uses the word פֹה just before he interprets the dream of Pharaoh's cupbearer and baker.

For I was stolen away out of the land of the Hebrews: and *here* also have I done nothing that they should put me into the dungeon.[5]

When the elders of Moab and Midian come to Balaam to give him Balak's message, Balaam use the word פֹה.

And he said to them: "Lodge *here* this night and I will bring you back word, as the Lord shall speak to me."[6]

When the Gadites and the Reubenites want to stay in the cattle country Moses uses the word פֹה.

And Moses said to the children of Gad and to the children of Reuben: "Shall your brethren go to war, and shall you sit *here*?"[7]

And then the Gadites and the Reubenites use the word פֹה.

And they came near to him and said: "We will build sheep-folds *here* for our cattle, and cities for our little ones."[8]

When Moses is recounting to the Israelites the giving of the Ten Commandments, he uses the word פֹה.

The Lord did not make this covenant with our fathers, but with us, even us, who are all of us *here* alive this day.[9]

---

4. Genesis 22:5.
5. Genesis 40:15.
6. Numbers 22:8.
7. Numbers 32:6.
8. Numbers 32:16.
9. Deuteronomy 5:3.

When Moses recounts how the Israelites could no longer stand to hear the voice of God, God tells Moses:

> But as for thee, stand *here* by me and I will speak to thee all the commandments and the statutes, and the judgments, which thou shalt teach them, that they may do them in the land which I gave them to possess it.[10]

In the recounting of the laws and norms, the word פֹה is used.

> You shall not do after all the things that we do *here* this day, every man whatever is right in his own eyes.[11]

Finally, just before the description of what terrible things will happen if any one of the Israelites turns away from God, the word פֹה is used.

> Neither with you only do I make this covenant and this oath: but with him that stands *here* with us this day before the Lord our God, and also with him that is not *here* with us this day.[12]

It is clear from the way פֹה is used in the Pentateuch that here is the place where significant things are about to happen. Here, in this place, the mouth is the entrance or opening to action, which is the fruition of any internal spiritual event.

Now, the essence of a spiritual event can be understood from the gematria of פֹה. פֹה has a value of 85. The word כָּמֹכָה, which means *like you*, also has the gematria of 85.

> Who is *like Thee*, O Lord, among the gods? Who is *like Thee*, glorious in holiness, awesome in praises, doing wonders?[13]

In addition to whatever else it is, the internal spiritual event recognizes and acknowledges, with amazement, the benevolence of the Divine, and that there is nothing that the Divine can be compared with.

The word אֲמַלְטָה has the gematria of 85 and means *let me escape*.

---

10. Deuteronomy 5:28.
11. Deuteronomy 12:8.
12. Deuteronomy 29:14.
13. Exodus 15:11.

Behold now, this town is near enough to run to, and it is a
little one: Oh, *let me escape* to there (is it not a little one?)
and my soul shall live.[14]

What is it that we use our freedom for? We use our freedom to escape
the destruction that is inherent in seeing the world as only material and
limited. And when we see the world in its spiritual aspects as well and
when we act in accordance with these spiritual aspects, then we bring
to fruition the internal spiritual event. We bring into manifestation the
inner spiritual force. This can be seen by spelling out פֵּה הֵא אׇ :פֵּה. The
gematria is 91, the combined gematria of יְ־הֹ־וַ־הֹ and אֲדֹנָי, the names
used to denote that aspect of God that brings existence into being and
is associated with judgment in the kingdom.[15] This is reinforced by
the word אֱלֹהֵיהֶם which has a gematria of 91 and means *their God*.

And Pharaoh's servants said unto him: "How long shall
this one be a snare unto us? Let the men go, that they may
serve the Lord *their God*. Knowest thou not yet that Egypt
is destroyed?"[16]

And they shall know that I am the Lord *their God*, who
brought them forth out of the land of Egypt, that I might
dwell among them. I am the Lord *their God*.[17]

They shall be holy unto their God, and not profane the
name of *their God*; for the fire-offerings of the Lord, the
bread of *their God*, they do offer: therefore, they shall be
holy.[18]

And yet for all that, when they are in the land of their
enemies, I will not reject them, neither will I abhor them,
to destroy them utterly, and to break covenant with them;
for I am the Lord *their God*.[19]

14. Genesis 19:20.
15. Rabbi Matityahu Glazerson, *From Hinduism to Judaism* (Jerusalem: Himelsein
Glazerson Publishers, 1984), p. 92.
16. Exodus 10:7.
17. Exodus 29:46.
18. Leviticus 21:6.
19. Leviticus 26:44.

This is reinforced by the word הָאֱלֹהִים, which also has the gematria of 91 and which means *the God* and is used throughout Genesis.

Having the numerical value of 80, פ is the projection into time and conditioned physical existence of the essence of the letter energy intelligence of ח, which has the numerical value of 8 and means the archetype of life. Also, the numerical value of פ, 80, is the same as the numerical value for מֵם, the spelling of the letter מ. This reminds us that the fruition of any internal event must be the meaning of מ, perfection and completion. This is the revealed meaning of the letter energy intelligence of פ.

The shape of the letter פ is that of a כ with a 180-degree rotated י. The כ symbolizes כְּלִי, which means *container, vessel,* or *tool.* This symbolism is reinforced by the word פַּךְ, which means *flask, bottle, jar,* or *vessel.* The י symbolizes the soul bound in the human body, which is a container or tool for the soul. The spirituality of the י inside the פ means that the mouth is an entrance for manifesting Godliness. Hence, if the mouth is not being used for Divine service, the entranceway should be closed.

The concealed meaning of פ can be understood from the word פְּדוּת, which means *redemption, deliverance, division, distinction,* or *separation.*

> And I will put a division [distinction] between my people and thy people: tomorrow shall this sign be.[20]

The deliverance that the letter energy intelligence פ brings is deliverance from enslavement and violence, a separation from enslavement and violence. Where there is no enslavement and violence, freedom must reign. And where freedom reigns, there is the possibility of causing the future to be as we want it to be. There is the possibility of changing ourselves, or growing, and entering a higher state of consciousness, a higher state of being.

Supportive of this concealed meaning are some of the combinations that ף makes with the other letter energy intelligences. When ף combines with the letter energy intelligence of א, the unbridled pulsating force, there forms the word אַף, which means *nose.*

---

20. Exodus 8:19.

> And the Lord God formed man of the dust of the ground,
> and breathed into his *nostrils* the breath of life; and man
> became a living soul.[21]

It is through the nose that we breathe. Breathing through the nose supplies air at the physical level and prana energy at the metaphysical level. It is by the light energy intelligence of the air that we breathe that we have the energy to exercise our freedom to change ourselves, as well as the energy to exercise our freedom to speak.

When ף combines with the letter energy intelligence of ג, there forms the word גף, which means *wing*[22] or *flight* as well as *hand*, *arm*, *back*, *body*[23], *person*, *handle*, *rim* (of a vessel or extremity). And when ף combines with ע, which is the letter energy intelligence of insight and consciousness, there forms the root עף, which means to *fly*. Freedom means that we use our metaphysical wings to fly. This flying, which is an exercise of freedom and free will, results in physical changes in the kingdom of מַלְכוּת. Many of these changes we bring about because of the resulting actions we take using our hands, arms, back, and body. Other changes we bring about because by causing our vessel to exist at its rim, at its extremity, the challenge created sets up circumstances to further develop, test, and exercise our free will. In this manner we grow. And as we grow our vessel has more and more affinity with the light.

When the letter energy intelligence of ף combines with the letter energy intelligence of ש there forms the root שף, which means to *bruise*, *crush*, *grind* (grain), *rub*, *polish*, or *plaster*. Growing means that there must be constant refinement as we go from level to level. Our vessel must transform. Transformation means that we must bruise old patterns. We must sometimes crush patterns by which we remain in a lower state of consciousness. We must refine our vessel by grinding, rubbing, and polishing.

Exercise of *freedom* is fundamentally involved with *speech*, the channel through which ideas and thoughts are communicated. So it is no surprise that when ף combines with the letter energy intelligence of ד,

---

21. Genesis 2:7.
22. Daniel 7:4,6.
23. Exodus 21:3.

which is the archetype for physical existence, there forms the word דַף, which means *page*, *leaf*, or *plank*. One principal form of communication is the written word on a page of paper. Also, when ף combines with נ, the letter energy intelligence of emergence, there forms the word נָף, which means a *halyard*, a *rope*, or *tackle* for hoisting and lowering sails. It is by our halyard that we put our sails in position so that whatever the external wind currents are, our vessel sails in the direction we will it to travel.

There is much that can be hidden under the wings of freedom. Among them is the word פֶּשַׁע, which means *guilt* or *transgression* and the root פָּשַׁע, which means to *transgress*, *rebel*, *revolt*, and to *neglect*.

> What is my *trespass*? What is my sin, that you have so hotly pursued after me?[24]

> Now please forgive the *trespass* of your brothers and their sins; for they did evil to you. And now please forgive the *trespass* of the servants of the God of your father.[25]

> For all manner of *trespass*, whether it be for ox, for ass, for sheep, for a garment, or for any manner of lost things, of which one can say: This is it, the cause of both parties shall come before the judges; and whom the judges shall condemn, he shall pay double to his neighbor.[26]

> Take heed of Him and obey his voice. Provoke Him not. For He will not pardon your *transgressions*: for My name is in him.[27]

> The Lord passed by him and proclaimed: "The Lord, is a compassionate and gracious God, slow to anger, abounding in loving-kindness and truth; maintaining mercy unto the thousandth generation, forgiving iniquity, and *transgression* and sin.[28]

---

24. Genesis 31:36.
25. Genesis 50:17.
26. Exodus 22:8.
27. Exodus 23:21.
28. Exodus 34:6-7.

And he shall make atonement for the holy place, because of the uncleanness of the children of Israel, and because of their *transgressions* in all their sins.[29]

And Aaron shall lay both his hands upon the head of the live goat, and confess over him all the iniquities of the children of Israel, and all their *transgressions* in all their sins, putting them upon the head of the goat, and shall send him away by the hand of an appointed man into the wilderness.[30]

The Lord is longsuffering and great in love, forgiving iniquity and *transgression*, but by no means clearing the guilty, punishing the iniquity of the fathers upon the children to the third and fourth generation.[31]

In our exercise of *speech* and *freedom*, we must use care when we *do, make, influence, form, create,* or *act,* פָּעַל.

You will bring them in and plant them on the mountain of your inheritance. The place, O Lord, you *made* for your dwelling, the sanctuary, O Lord, your hands established.[32]

It will now be said of Jacob and of Israel: "See what God has *done!*"[33]

And the Lord has not *done* all this.[34]

We must use care when we do to keep from *tottering*, which is the root פָּק, into *transgression*, פֶּשַׁע. We must *turn away*, פָּנָה, speaking about *worthless matters* or *refuse*, which is the word פְּסֹלֶת. And what are worthless matters, matters inappropriate to talk about? Such matters are gossip and rumors. The verb root used in the phrase of spreading a rumor is פָּרַח, which means to *fly*, to *break out*, and to *speak out*. In the Pentateuch, פָּרַח is associated with the breaking out of leprosy.

---

29. Leviticus 16:16.
30. Leviticus 16:21.
31. Numbers 14:18.
32. Exodus 15:17.
33. Numbers 23:23.
34. Deuteronomy 32:27.

The priest shall examine it and if it appears to be more than skin deep and the hair in it has turned white, the priest shall pronounce him unclean. It is the plague of leprosy that has *broken out* in the boil.[35]

The priest shall examine it and if the hair has turned white in the bright spot, and it appears to be more than skin deep, it is leprosy that has *broken out* in the burn.[36]

With the exercise of sufficient care in what we do and say, we create the conditions for פרח, whose other meaning is to *bud, blossom, bloom, flower*, to *sprout, flourish, prosper*, and *thrive*.

The staff belonging to the man I choose will *sprout* and I will rid myself of this constant grumbling against you by the Israelites.[37]

The next day Moses entered the Tent of the Testimony and saw that Aaron's staff, which represented the house of Levi, had not only *sprouted*, but had budded, blossomed and produced almonds.[38]

In the days to come, Jacob will take root, Israel will bud and *blossom* and fill all the world with fruit.[39]

The desert and the parched land will be glad; the wilderness will rejoice and *blossom*. Like the crocus, it will burst into *bloom*; it will rejoice greatly and shout for joy.[40]

All the trees of the field will know that I the Lord bring down the tall tree and make the low tree grow tall. I dry up the green tree and make the dry tree *flourish*.[41]

---

35. Leviticus 13:20.
36. Leviticus 13:25.
37. Numbers 17:5.
38. Numbers 17:8.
39. Isaiah 27:6.
40. Isaiah 35:1-2.
41. Ezekiel 17:24.

> Let us go early to the vineyards to see if the vines have *bud-ded*, if their blossoms have opened, and if the pomegranates are in bloom. There I will give you my love.[42]

The form **פא** combines with the letter energy intelligence of ה, which is the archetype for power of being, and the letter energy intelligence of ר, which is the archetype for cosmic container. With ה, there forms the word פֵאָה, which means *edge, corner, extremity, side, border, facet,* or *region*. It also carries the meaning of *curl of hair* or *lock of hair*.

> Make four gold rings for the table and fasten them to the four *corners*, where the four legs are.[43]

> And when you reap the harvest of thy land, thou shalt not reap to the *edges* of thy field and the gleaning of thy harvest thou shalt not gather.[44]

> Do not cut the hair at the *sides* of your head or clip off the *edges* of your beard.[45]

Also, there forms the word פֵאָה, which means to *blow away, scatter, destroy* and *put an end to*.

> I said I would *scatter* them and erase their memory from mankind.[46]

Freedom is lived at the inner extremity, at the corner, at the knife's edge. And when freedom is so lived, it blows away and scatters all inertia and limitation that tries to hold things static and in place. When freedom is so lived, we reach beyond, break through the limitations of the world, and transcend ourselves. Rabbi Schneerson teaches

---

42. Song of Songs 7:12.
43. Exodus 26:26.
44. Leviticus 19:8.
45. Leviticus 19:27.
46. Deuteronomy 32:26.

when Jacob was promised אֶרֶץ יִשְׂרָאֵל, that promise was connected with וּפָרַצְתָּ[47] breaking forth – going beyond the barriers of reason and logic. Even though the world in which we live was structured by God to be limited and defined, the purpose of that limitation was so that a Jew will reach the service of וּפָרַצְתָּ and break through the boundaries and limitations of the world.[48]

Thus it is no surprise when פָא combines with ר, forming the root פָאר, which means to *adorn, beautify, decorate, ornament, embellish, praise, glorify,* or *crown* and פְּאֵר, which means *glory, luxury,* or *magnificence* as well as the alternate meaning *headdress.*

Surely thou will summon nations thou knowest not, and nations that do not know thee will run to thee, because of the Lord your God, the Holy One of Israel, for He has *glorified* thee.[49]

The glory of Lebanon shall come to thee, the cypress, the maple, and the box tree, together, to *beautify* the place of my sanctuary; and I will make the place of my feet glorious.[50]

Blessed be the Lord God of our fathers, which has put such a thing as this in the king's heart, to *beautify* the house of the Lord which is in Jerusalem.[51]

The thoughts in the mind are at the extremity of the physical realm. They reach the physical realm in communication through the mouth. The spoken thoughts that emanate from the mouth have the power to scatter and destroy obsolete structure while at the same time to

---

47. Genesis 28:14. וּפָרַצְתָּ is from the root פרץ, which means to *break, break through, break out, erupt, demolish, tear down, destroy, make a breach, crack,* to *scatter,* to *rush upon,* to *burst,* to *spread,* to *increase,* or to *overflow.*
48. Rabbi Menachem Schneerson, *Sichos in English,* vol. 8 (Brooklyn, NY: Sichos in English, 1981), pp. 141-142.
49. Isaiah 55:5.
50. Isaiah 60:13.
51. Ezra 7:27.

beautify, glorify, and crown the magnificence of physical existence by breaking through all self-imposed limitation. The choice is ours to exercise that freedom and grow or to not exercise it and to waste away in lifeless form and structure. Let us choose to glorify and crown.

צֶדִי

Tzadi צ: Righteousness and Humility

The eighteenth letter of the Hebrew alphabet is צ, spelled צָדִי. It has the numerical value of 90. It has a final form ץ, which has a numerical value of 900. One word related to צָדִי is צְדִי, which means *lateral* or *side*.

> The tent curtain will be a cubit longer on both *sides*; what is left will hang over the sides of the tabernacle so as to cover it.[1]

Within צְדִי is the root צד, which means to *capture*. What צ captures is ג, the letter energy intelligence of emergence, for the shape of the letter צ is that of a humble ג bowed down in humility and carrying on its back the creative force of the י, whose energy intelligence is that of the unbridled pulsating force of א projected into conditioned existence of time, space and causality.[2] What is it that emerges through צ? We just need to see how צ relates to ק to get the answer. When ק, the cosmic unbridled pulsating force of א, is captured, the word צַדִיק forms. צַדִיק is an alternate form of צְדִי and carries the meaning of one who is *right, righteous, just, innocent, honest, upright, pious,* or *correct*.

> Noah was a *just* man and perfect in his generation, and Noah walked with God.[3]

> And the Lord said to Noah: "Come thou and all thy house into the ark. For thee have I seen *righteous* before me in this generation.[4]

> And Abraham drew near and said: "Wilt thou also destroy the *righteous* with the wicked?"[5]

---

1. Exodus 26:13.
2. Rabbi Michael Munk, *The Wisdom in the Hebrew Alphabet* (Brooklyn, NY: Mesorah Publications, 1988), p. 192.
3. Genesis 6:9.
4. Genesis 7:1.
5. Genesis 18:23.

Far be it from Thee to do after this manner, to slay the *righteous* with the wicked: and that the righteous shall be as the wicked, far be it from Thee.[6]

But Avimelech had not come near her. And he said to the Lord: "Wilt Thou slay also a *righteous* nation?"[7]

He is the Rock, His work is perfect. For all His ways are justice. A God of truth and without iniquity, *just* and right is He.[8]

There is the related root צדק, which is the verb to be *right, correct, just, righteous,* and *innocent.* The corresponding noun is צֶדֶק, which means *justice, rightness, righteous, righteousness,* and *just* or *true.*

Just balances, *just* weights, a *just* efa, and a *just* hin shall you have: I am the Lord your God, who brought you out of the land of Egypt.[9]

And I charged your judges at that time, saying: "Hear the causes between your brethren, and judge *righteously* between every man and his brother, and the stranger that is with him."[10]

Judges and officers shalt thou appoint within all thy gates, which the Lord thy God gives thee for thy tribes: and they shall judge the people with *righteous* judgment.[11]

Follow *justice* and *justice* alone so that you may live and possess the land the Lord your God is giving you.[12]

They will summon the people to the mountains and there they will offer sacrifices of *righteousness*; for they shall suck of the abundance of the seas, and of treasures hid in the sand.[13]

---

6. Genesis 18:25.
7. Genesis 20:4.
8. Deuteronomy 32:4.
9. Leviticus 19:36.
10. Deuteronomy 1:16.
11. Deuteronomy 16:18.
12. Deuteronomy 16:20.
13. Deuteronomy 33:19.

The gematria of צָדִי is 104. Also with the gematria of 104 is the word וַיִּפַּח, *breathed*. It is the third person masculine singular imperfect form of the root נפח, meaning to breathe.

> Then the Lord God formed the man from the dust of the ground and *breathed* into his nostrils the breath of life; and the man became a living soul.[14]

The word לְלַמֵּד is the infinitive form of the root למד, meaning to *teach*. It has the gematria of 104. Moses uses it in speaking to the Israelites.

> And the Lord commanded me at that time to *teach* you statutes and ordinances, that ye might do them in the land whither ye go over to possess it.[15]

> Now this is the commandment, the statutes, and the ordinances, which the Lord your God commanded to *teach* you, that ye may do [them] in the land whither ye go over to possess it. That thou be in awe of the Lord thy God, to keep all His statutes and His commandments, which I command thee; thou, and thy son and thy son's son, all the days of thy life. And that thy days may be prolonged. Hear therefore, Israel, and observe to do that it may be well with thee, and that you may increase mightily, as the Lord, the God of thy fathers, have promised unto thee – a land flowing with milk and honey.[16]

So from here we learn that on one level God's breathing is parallel to the teaching of the commandments. On another level we learn that God's breathing is parallel to the observing and the doing of the commandments. And the one who thinks, speaks, and does in accordance with the commandments is one who is righteous.

The full gematria of צָדִי can be determined by spelling out צָדִי דָלֶת יוֹד. The full gematria is 558. The word וּמִצְוֹתָיו, *and his commandments*,

---

14. Genesis 2:7.
15. Deuteronomy 4:14.
16. Deuteronomy 6:1-3.

also has the gematria of 558. It is remarkable how the full gematria of צַדִּי reinforces the gematria of צַדִּ.

> Therefore, thou shalt love the Lord thy God, and keep His charge, and His statutes and His ordinances, *and His commandments* always.[17]

> This day the Lord thy God commandeth thee to do these statutes and ordinances; thou shalt therefore observe and do them with all thy heart, and with all thy soul. Thou has set apart the Lord this day to be thy God, and that thou wouldest walk in His ways, and keep His statutes, *and His commandments*, and His ordinances, and hearken unto His voice.[18]

When the power of being of ה is breathed into a side צַדִּי path instead of the main path, there forms the word צְדִיָּה, which means *evil design, wicked intent, malice*, or *malicious intent*.

> But if without hostility, someone suddenly shoves another or throws something at him without *malicious intent*, or without seeing him drops a stone on him that could kill him, and he dies, then since he was not his enemy and he did not intend to harm him, the assembly must judge between him and the avenger of blood according to these regulations.[19]

From this we learn that we must stay on the main path. To stay on the main path is to will one thing; anything else is doublemindedness.

The numerical value of צ is 90. This means that it is the projection into conditional existence of time, space, and causality of the energy intelligence of ט, which has the numerical value of 9. And the energy intelligence of ט is goodness and affirmation. Goodness and affirmation projected into conditioned existence are *righteousness* and *humility*.

How is it that affirmation projects into humility? To affirm and bless all requires that there be space in our heart for God rather than

---

17. Deuteronomy 11:1.
18. Deuteronomy 26:16-17.
19. Numbers 35:22-24.

א

a space for an ego to grow and become an inflated ego. If all the space is for God and there is no space for the inflated ego, then what must result is a humble person.

Likewise, in order for there to be the space and possibility for us to make space for God in our hearts, God, by a process of self-withdrawal, restriction, confining, or contraction, a צִמְצוּם, makes a place for us to grow and exercise our free will.[20] It is one of the paradoxical mysteries that we can become aware of the presence of God only when the Holy One restricts His presence to make a place for us to make a place for Him. The concealed meaning of אֲ can be determined from דִי. The word דִי means *adequacy, sufficiency, plenty,* or *enough.*

And if his means are not *sufficient* for a lamb, then he shall bring for his trespass, which he has committed, two turtledoves, or two young pigeons, to the Lord; one for a sin offering, and the other for a burnt offering.[21]

And if her means are not *sufficient* for a lamb, then she shall take two turtledoves, or two young pigeons: the one for a burnt offering, and the other for a sin offering; and the priest shall make atonement for her and she shall be clean.[22]

But if his means are not *sufficient* to regain it, then that which is sold shall remain in the hand of him who has bought it until the year of the jubilee: and in the jubilee it shall go out, and he shall return to his possession.[23]

If there be among you a poor man, one of thy brethren within any of thy gates in thy land which the Lord thy God gives thee, thou shalt not harden thy heart, nor shut thy hand from thy poor brother; but thou shalt open thy hand wide to him and shalt surely lend him *sufficient* for his need, in that which he lacks.[24]

20. Rabbi Yehuda Ashlag, *Kabbalah: A Study of the Ten Luminous Emanations* (Jerusalem: Research Centre of Kabbalah, 1978), p. 67.
21. Leviticus 5:7.
22. Leviticus 12:8.
23. Leviticus 25:28.
24. Deuteronomy 15:7-8.

Since צַדִּיק is the alternate to צֶדֶק, the concealed meaning can also be determined from דיק. The word דֵּיק means *bulwark* or *defense wall* and the word דִּיֵק means to *be exact* and *be accurate*. From this we can conclude that being truly righteous and humble is sufficient for spiritual growth and constitutes an adequate defense against the inflated ego. Indeed, being truly righteous and humble is the foundation of the world.

When the letter energy intelligence of צ combines with the pulsating unbridled force of the letter energy intelligence of א, there forms the exclamation צֵא, *go out* or *get out!*

> *Go out* of the ark, thou, and thy wife, and thy sons, and thy sons' wives with thee.[25]

> I am the God of Bet-el where thou didst anoint a pillar, and where thou didst vow a vow to me: now arise, *get out* of this land, and return to the land of thy birth.[26]

> And all these thy servants shall come down to me, and bow down themselves to me, saying: "*Go out*, thee, and all the people that follow thee." And after that I will go out. And he went out from Pharaoh in great anger.[27]

When it combines with the letter energy intelligence of ב, the archetype of container, there forms the word צַב, which has the meanings of *tortoise, turtle,* or *covered wagon.*

> And they brought their offering before the Lord, six *covered wagons*, and twelve oxen: a wagon for every two of the princes, and for each one an ox.[28]

When it combines with ו, the letter energy intelligence of connection and unification, there forms the word צַו, which means *command* or *order* and in biblical usage means *statute, law,* or *precept.*

---

25. Genesis 8:16.
26. Genesis 31:13.
27. Exodus 11:8.
28. Numbers 7:3.

And the Lord spoke to Moses saying: "*Command* Aaron and his sons, saying: 'This is the Torah of the burnt offering.' "[29]

And the Lord spoke to Moses saying: "*Command* the children of Israel that they bring to thee pure oil of pressed olives for the light so that the lamps may be kept burning continually."[30]

And the Lord spoke to Moses saying: "*Command* the Israelites to send away from the camp anyone who has leprosy or a discharge of any kind, or who is ceremonially unclean because of a dead body."[31]

The Lord said to Moses saying: "Give this *command* to the Israelites and say to them: 'See that you present to me at the appointed time the food for my offerings made by fire, as an aroma pleasing to me.' "[32]

The Lord said to Moses saying: "*Command* the Israelites and say to them: 'When you enter Canaan, the land that will be allotted to you as an inheritance will have these boundaries:' "[33]

Command the Israelites to give the Levites towns to live in from the inheritance the Israelites will possess. And give them pasturelands around the towns.[34]

Command the people saying: "You are about to pass through the territory of your brothers the descendants of Esau, who live in Seir. They will be afraid of you, but be very careful."[35]

When it combines with the ה, the letter energy intelligence of life, there forms the word צח, which means *pure, fresh, clear, bright, sunlit, radiant,* or *dazzling white.*

---

29. Leviticus 6:1-2.
30. Leviticus 24:1-2.
31. Numbers 5:1-2.
32. Numbers 28:1-2.
33. Numbers 34:1-2.
34. Numbers 35:2.
35. Deuteronomy 2:4.

My lover is *radiant* and ruddy, outstanding among ten thousand.[36]

For so the Lord said to me: "I will take my rest, and I will look on in my dwelling place, like the *clear* heat in sunlight."[37]

When it combines with ף, the final form of the letter פ, which is the letter energy intelligence of speech and freedom, there forms the verb צָף, to *float*. When the letter energy intelligence of צ combines with its own final form ץ, there forms the root ץצ, to *blossom*.

From these combinations we can conclude that it is the command of God as it is the command of our true will that we be righteous and humble. For we are commanded to go out, get out. To go out from where? To go out from our shells and to do צְדָקָה, deeds of giving and charity and *righteousness*. We make ourselves less; we make others more. This makes us more. We give and our very giving completes the circuit and becomes our receiving. Thereby we become caretakers of the entire world, the internal world and the external world. But this going out to do deeds of giving and charity does not mean doing it in a way that calls attention to the doer. These deeds must be done from the covered wagon. They must be done with privacy and not with public acclaim. The deeds of going out and doing צְדָקָה are pure bright dazzling white actions. They float us on the infinitely deep water of love. They bind and form us to its depths. And we blossom.

The energy intelligence of צ is the kind that fosters community cohesiveness and manifests most easily in community. We find that צבא is the root to *assemble*, *congregate*, *gather together*, *wage war*, *take the field*, or *serve* (in the temple).

And he made the laver of brass, and its pedestal of brass, of the mirrors of the women *assembling*, who *assembled* at the door of the Tent of Meeting.[38]

And the word צִבּוּר means *community*, צִבּוּרִי means *communal, public,* or *congregational*, צֶוֶת means *team* or *crew*, צָרוּר means *packed, tied,*

---

36. Song of Songs 5:10.
37. Isaiah 18:4.
38. Exodus 38:8.

wrapped, bound together, or *preserved,* and צרר is the root to *pack, tie, wrap,* or *bind.* By aligning our consciousness with the letter energy intelligence of צ we become a צִנּוֹר, a *channel, pipe,* or *conduit* by which our activities below become a *coupling, pairing, matching,* or *linking,* צָמוּד, for what we are called upon to do from above. And the white lotus, צָאֵל צָחוֹר, blossoms in צְחֹק, *laughter,* in צַחוּת, *purity, freshness,* and *cleanness* and in צְמִיתוּת, *permanence, perpetuality,* and *perpetuity.*

קוֹף

Qoph ק: Growth and Holiness

The nineteenth letter of the Hebrew alphabet is ק, spelled קוֹף. The numerical value of ק is 100 and its energy intelligence is that of *growth* and *holiness*. Growth and holiness are related to the pulsating unbridled force of the letter א, whose numerical value is 1, thrust into cosmic existence. And it is related to the energy intelligence of spirituality, י, whose numerical value is 10.

The word קוֹף means *monkey* or *ape*.

> For the king had at sea a ship of Tarshish with a ship of Hiram: once in three years the ship of Tarshish came, bringing gold, and silver, ivory, and *apes*, and peacocks. So king Solomon exceeded all the kings of the earth for riches and for wisdom. And all the earth sought of Solomon, to hear his wisdom, which God had put in his heart.[1]

> For the king's ships went to Tarshish with the servants of Huram: once every three years came the ships of Tarshish bringing gold, and silver, ivory, and *apes*, and peacocks. And king Solomon surpassed all the kings of the earth in riches and wisdom. And all the kings of the earth sought the presence of Solomon, to hear his wisdom, that God had put in his heart.[2]

When man does not elevate himself beyond the ordinary, when man does not act in a way to create sacredness, when man does not endow his situation with holiness, man is no more than an ape. However, the verses tell us more. For by association, from קוֹף, *growth* and *holiness*, come riches and wisdom. We can also see this from its gematria. The word קוֹף has a numerical value of 186. One word in the Pentateuch that has the value of 186 is הֲנִמְצָא. It is the interrogative Kal imperfect of the root מצא and means *can we find*.

> And Pharaoh said unto his servants: "*Can we find* such a one as this, a man in whom is the spirit of God?[3]

---

1. 1 Kings 10:22-24.
2. 2 Chronicles 9:21-23.
3. Genesis 41:38.

269

So the wise person is the one in whom is the spirit of God.

The word הַנִּמְצָא is also the Niphal participle of the root מצא preceded with a definite article and means *that was found.*

> And Joseph gathered up all the money *that was found* in the land of Egypt, and in the land of Canaan, for the corn which they bought; and Joseph brought the money into the house of Pharaoh.[4]

> And it shall be, if it make thee answer of peace, and open unto thee, then it shall be, that all the people *that are found* therein shall become for you a body of forced laborers and shall serve you.[5]

A third word in the Pentateuch having the gematria of 186 is וַנֵּפֶן, which means *and then we turned.* It is the Kal consecutive imperfect first person plural of the root פנה, which means to *turn.*

> *Then we turned*, and went up the way to Bashan; and Og, the king of Bashan came out against us, he and all his people, unto battle at Edrei. And the Lord said unto me: "Fear him not; for into thy hand I have delivered him, and all his people, and his land; and thou shalt do unto him as thou didst unto Sihon king of the Amorites, who dwelt at Heshbon."[6]

So the rich person is one who has money, servants, and land. But the rich person has yet more, for the word כְּצַלְמוֹ, which means *after his image*, also has the gematria of 186.

> And Adam lived a hundred and thirty years and begot a son in his own likeness, *after his image*; and called his name Seth.[7]

---

4. Genesis 47:14.
5. Deuteronomy 20:11.
6. Deuteronomy 3:1-2.
7. Genesis 5:3.

Now Adam, whose name indicates wholeness and completeness,[8] was created in the image of God and Seth was created in the likeness, after the image, of Adam. This means that Seth was the treasured essence.[9] He was more righteous than Cain and Abel.[10] Seth is associated with the word שֵׁת, which means *basis* or *foundation*.[11] The Ramban explains that the world was founded from Seth.[12] Seth, after the image of Adam, can also be taken to mean permanence or endurance, for Adam perceived that the descendants of Seth would endure in this world.[13] So from this we learn that the energy intelligence of ק, *growth* and *holiness*, is not only associated with richness, wealth, and land, but also with a founding endurance.

Both the word קֹלֵנוּ, meaning *our voice*, and the word עָנְיֵנוּ, meaning *our affliction*, have the gematria of 186.

> And we cried unto the Lord, the God of our fathers, and the Lord heard *our voice*, and saw *our affliction*, and our toil, and our oppression. And the Lord brought us forth out of Egypt with a mighty hand, and with an outstretched arm and with great terribleness, and with signs, and with wonders.[14]

This tells us that there is another dimension to *growth* and *holiness*. It is the dimension of crying out. For we each have times and situations in which we may be stagnant and lose the sense of holiness. And in these times and situations we must cry out unto the Lord, the God of our fathers, and the Lord will hear our voice and see our affliction and our toil and will bring us forth out of our restriction with a mighty

---

8. *The Zohar*, vol. 5, trans. Harry Sperling, Maurice Simon, and Paul Levertoff (London: Soncino Press, 1978), p. 15.

9. Rabbi Meir Leibush Malbim, *Malbim*, vol. 1, trans. Zvi Faier (Israel: M.P. Press and Hillel Press, 1982), p. 326.

10. Ovadiah Sforno, *Sforno Commentary on the Torah*, trans. Raphael Pelcovitz (Brooklyn, NY: Mesorah Publications, 1987), p. 39.

11. Psalms 11:3.

12. Rabbi Moshe ben Nachman, *Ramban Commentary on the Torah, Genesis*, trans. Charles Chavel (New York: Shilo Publishing House, 1971), p. 98.

13. *Bereishis*, vol. 1, trans. and comm. Meir Zlotowitz (New York: Mesorah Publications, 1977), p. 168.

14. Deuteronomy 26:7-8.

hand and with an outstretched arm. And to where will God bring us forth? God will bring us to the *place*, מָקוֹם, of the altar.

> And he went on his journeys from the South even to Bet-el, unto the place where his tent had been in the beginning, between Bet-el and Ai; unto the *place* of the altar which he had made there at the first; and Abram called there on the name of the Lord.[15]

When we spell out the letters in קוֹף there results קוֹף וָו פֵּא and this has a gematria of 278. The word וַיְבָרֶךְ, which means *and blessed them*, has the gematria of 278.

> *And he blessed them* that day, saying: "By thee shall Israel bless saying, God make thee as Effraim and as Menasseh; and he set Effraim before Menasseh."[16]

> And Aaron lifted up his hand towards the people, *and blessed them*, and came down from offering the sin offering and the burnt offering, and the peace offerings.[17]

So from this we learn that by engaging in the process of growth and being holy we will be blessed.

קוֹף is cognate to the word קוּף, which means *eye of a needle* or the *hole in the ax blade* for the ax handle. The eye of a needle is a small hole through which the thread is run so that the needle and thread may be used to sew a design on a fabric, or mend a cloth, or sew together a garment. The hole in the ax head bottom is the hole in which the handle of the ax is situated. When so placed, the handle gives leverage to the ax head so that the ax can become an effective tool for chopping or hewing wood or timber. From this we can conclude that when the hole is small as in the eye of a needle, it permits the mending of something old and the creation of something new. When the hole is larger as in the bottom of the ax head or blade, it permits the destruction of what nature produces. Small and limited, the hole

---

15. Genesis 13:3-4.
16. Genesis 48:20.
17. Leviticus 9:22.

is an aid to creation. Large, it is an aid to destruction, a destruction that might later make the place for, or create the goods for, a creation.

The ק is the only one of the twenty-two Hebrew letters (not including the final forms) that has a part, its leg, that goes below the line. And it is the leg of the ק that bores the smaller or larger hole, the smaller hole to construct and the larger hole to destruct. No matter whether small or large, something is thrown out; the Hebrew root being קיא, something is thrown through the hole.[18] And what is thrown through the hole relates to the descent we make into physical reality as we slide down the leg of the ק. We can throw out of physical reality the sparks of Godliness we reveal in our descent or we can throw out clouds of darkness by our separation from Godliness.

Growth is cyclic. The seasons winter, spring, summer, and fall constitute the cyclic growth in nature. Winter is a time of hibernation and death. The rejuvenation in winter is what lays the ground for the sprouting aliveness and new beginnings of spring and the flowers of summer. It is therefore no surprise to find קוֹף involved in a word like הַקָּפָה which means *ringing, circling, encirclement, circuit, going round and round* as well as in words like הִקִּיף to *encircle* or *surround*, הַקֵּף to *surround*, and הֶקֵּף *circumference, outline, perimeter, periphery, surrounding,* or *orbit.* We exist surrounded by the void, which is the hole made by the leg of the ק. For it is only in the void that growth can take place.

The shape of the letter ק is combined of the two letters כ and ו, whose combined numerical value is 26, the gematria of the ineffable name of God, יְ-הֹ-וָ-ה.[19]

The concealed aspect וֹף has a value of 86, the gematria of the holy name of God, אֱלֹהִים. The concealed meaning of ק can be inferred from וֹף, which by itself does not constitute a Hebrew word. Therefore, we must examine how וֹף combines with the other letters. When ג, the letter energy intelligence of nurturance, combines with וֹף there results the word גוּף, which means *body, self, substance, essence, person, being, element,* or *matter.* When we give the void or mystery sustenance, when

---

18. The root קיא in everyday conversation means vomit.
19. Rabbi Michael Munk, *The Wisdom in the Hebrew Alphabet* (Brooklyn, NY: Mesorah Publications, 1988), p. 195.

we endow the mystery with meaning, there arises essence, substance, being.

When ח, the letter energy intelligence of life, combines with וף, there results the word חוף, which means *coast, shore, bank,* or *beach.* The coast is at the interface between the land and the sea.

> Zebulun shall dwell at the *shore* of the sea, and he shall be a *shore* for ships; And his flank shall be upon Zidon.[20]

> You have dwelt long enough in this mountain: turn, and take your journey, and go to the mountain of the Emori, and to all the places near it in the plain, in the hills, and in the lowland, and in the Negev, and by the *sea side,* to the land of the Kena'ani, and the Levanon, as far as the great river, the river Perat.[21]

There is also the word חוף, which is the root to *rub* and the word פָ חוֹ, which means *covering, overlapping,* or *congruent.* Our aliveness is a covering of the void. All the rubbing action takes place at the interface that is the coast line, shore, or beach between the aliveness and the void. This action is *involuted,* לִפּוּף. It is rolled inward from the edge. It is turned inward at the margin. It *waves, moves up and down,* and *oscillates,* which is one of the meanings of the word נוּף.

> And thou shalt put all in the hands of Aaron and in the hands of his sons; and shalt *wave* them for a wave offering before the Lord.[22]

> But Na'aman was angry, and went away, and said, Behold, I thought, He will surely come out to me, and stand, and call on the name of the Lord his God, and *wave* his hand over the place, and so heal the infected person.[23]

> In that day shall Egypt be like women; and it shall be afraid and fear because of the *shaking* of the hand of the Lord of hosts, which He *shakes* over it.[24]

---

20. Genesis 49:13.
21. Deuteronomy 1:7.
22. Exodus 29:24.
23. 2 Kings 5:11.
24. Isaiah 19:16.

When thou comest into the standing corn of thy neighbor, then thou mayst pluck the ears with thy hand; but thou shalt not move a sickle to thy neighbor's standing corn.[25]

And there shalt thou build an altar to the Lord thy God, an altar of stones: thou shalt not *lift* up any iron tool upon them.[26]

The earth shook, the heavens also dropped at the presence of God; even Sinai itself was moved at the presence of God, the God of Israel. Thou, O God, didst *shake* out a plentiful rain, whereby thou didst strengthen thy inheritance, when it languished.[27]

The action itself comes to an *end, vanishes,* and is *consumed,* סוף.

How they are brought into desolation in a moment! They are utterly *consumed* with terror.[28]

I will surely *consume* them, says the Lord: there shall be no grapes on the vine, nor figs on the fig tree, and the leaf shall fade; the things I have given them shall pass away from them.[29]

Indeed, it is the *end,* the *last extremity,* the *final conclusion,* that is the meaning of the word סוף.

He has made everything beautiful in his time; also he has set the mystery of the world in their heart, so that no man can find out the work which God has made from the beginning to the *end.*[30]

It is better to go to the house of mourning, than to go to the house of feasting: for that is the *end* of all men; and the living will lay it to his heart.[31]

---

25. Deuteronomy 23:26.
26. Deuteronomy 27:5.
27. Psalms 68:9-10.
28. Psalms 73:19.
29. Jeremiah 8:13.
30. Ecclesiastes 3:11.
31. Ecclesiastes 7:2.

The *end* of the matter, when all is said and done: Fear God and keep his commandments: for that is the whole duty of man.[32]

The tree grew, and was strong, and its top reached to the sky, and it was visible to the *end* of all the earth.[33]

It is thou, O King, that art grown and become strong; for thy greatness is grown, and reaches to heaven, and thy dominion to the *end* of the earth.[34]

That in every dominion of my kingdom men tremble and fear before the God of Daniel: for he is the living God, and steadfast forever, and his kingdom is one which shall not be destroyed, and his dominion shall be even to the *end*.[35]

It *grazes, polishes, smears over*, and *covers*, שׁוּף, the void.

If I say: "Surely the darkness shall *cover* me; even the night shall be light about me."[36]

And it is the *spiritual honeydew, nectar*, or *honeycomb*, which is one of the meanings of צוּף.

The fear of the Lord is clean, enduring forever: the judgments of the Lord are true and are righteous altogether. More to be desired are they than gold, even much fine gold: sweeter also than honey and the *honeycomb*.[37]

Pleasant words are like a *honeycomb*: sweet to the soul, and healing to the bones.[38]

There are many interesting words associated with ק. The root קדשׁ in the Kal form means to *be holy* or to *be hallowed*. Being holy means to separate from the ordinary and treat with special care.

---

32. Ecclesiastes 12:13.
33. Daniel 4:8.
34. Daniel 4:19.
35. Daniel 6:27.
36. Psalms 139:11.
37. Psalms 19:10.
38. Proverbs 16:24.

And thou shalt take of the blood that is upon the altar, and of the anointing oil, and sprinkle it upon Aaron, and upon his garments, and upon his sons, and upon the garments of his sons with him: and he shall *be hallowed*, and his garments, and his sons, and his sons' garments with him.[39]

The Niphal form means *be sanctified* or *be acknowledged as holy*.

Do not profane my holy name. I must *be acknowledged as holy* by the Israelites. I am the Lord, who makes you holy and who brought you out of Egypt to be your God. I am the Lord.[40]

The Piel form means to *put in a state of holiness, sanctify, consecrate,* or to *set apart as holy*.

And God blessed the seventh day, and *sanctified* it: because in it he rested from all his work which God had created and performed.[41]

And the Lord said to Moses: "Go to the people and *consecrate* them today and tomorrow. Have them wash their clothes."[42]

And I will *sanctify* the Tent of Meeting and the altar. Also, I will *sanctify* both Aaron and his sons to minister to me in the Priest's office.[43]

Moses said to the Lord: "The people cannot come up Mount Sinai, because you yourself warned us: 'Put limits around the mountain and *set it apart as holy.*'"[44]

The Pual form means to *be made holy, be made consecrated,* or *be dedicated*.

---

39. Exodus 29:21.
40. Leviticus 22:32-33.
41. Genesis 2:3.
42. Exodus 19:10.
43. Exodus 29:44.
44. Exodus 19:23.

The men of Israel and Judah who lived in the towns of
Judah also brought a tithe of their herds and flocks and a
tithe of the holy things *being dedicated* to the Lord their
God, and they piled them in heaps.[45]

The Hiphil form means to *hallow* or to *sanctify*.

Because all the firstborn are mine. When I struck down all
the firstborn in Egypt, I *hallowed* to me all the firstborn in
Israel, both man and beast. Mine shall they be: I am the
Lord.[46]

But the Lord said to Moses and Aaron: "Because you did
not trust in me enough to honor me as holy in the sight of
the Israelites, therefore, you shall not bring this community
into the land I have given them."[47]

The Hitpael form means to put oneself in a state of holiness, to
consecrate oneself.

Even the priests who come near to the Lord must *sanctify
themselves*, lest the Lord break forth upon them.[48]

I am the Lord your God; *consecrate yourselves* and be holy,
because I am holy.[49]

Tell the people: "*Consecrate yourselves* in preparation for
tomorrow when you shall eat meat. For you have wept in
the ears of the Lord saying: 'Who shall give us meat to eat?
We were better off in Egypt!' Therefore, the Lord will give
you meat and you shall eat."[50]

The word קָדוֹשׁ is the adjective *holy, sacred, hallowed, consecrated,*
or *sacrosanct.*

---

45. 2 Chronicles 31:6.
46. Numbers 3:13.
47. Numbers 20:12.
48. Exodus 19:22.
49. Leviticus 11:44.
50. Numbers 11:18.

I am the Lord your God; consecrate yourselves and be *holy*, because I am *holy*. Neither shall you defile yourselves with any manner of creeping thing that creeps on the earth. For I am the Lord that brings you up out of the land of Egypt to be your God: you shall therefore be *holy* for I am *holy*.[51]

And the Lord spoke to Moses saying: "Speak to all the congregation of the children of Israel and say to them: 'You shall be *holy* for I the Lord your God am *holy*.'"[52]

The Lord shall establish you a *holy* people to Himself, as He has sworn to you, if you shall keep the commandments of the Lord your God and walk in his ways.[53]

The word קְבָעַת means *cup, chalice,* or *goblet*. The cup is for receiving. The root to *receive, accept,* or *be affected with* is קבל and the word *kabbalah*, קַבָּלָה means *receiving, reception,* or *acceptance*.

Hear counsel and *receive* instruction, that thou mayst be wise in thy latter end.[54]

From this we learn that the holy and sacred in life are to be received.

The word קַוָּי means *compensator* or *equalizer*. The word קוֹרֵן means *beaming, shining, radiant*. The word קוֹשֵׁר means *rebel, insurgent, mutineer, conspirator,* or *plotter*; קֶטֶב means *destruction, defeat,* or *plague*; and קָטַל is the verb to *kill* or *slay*. In reference to the hole made by the leg of the ק, we find that the Hebrew root קטן is the verb to *be small,* or *be insignificant*; קָטֵן is the adjective meaning *growing smaller, dwindling, diminishing,* or *contracting*; קֹמֶץ means *handful, a small quantity, a scrap, a small number*; קְמִיצָה means *pinch, small quantity,* or a *grain*; and קַמְצָן means *miser* and *stingy*. The word קָלוּשׁ means *thin, sparse, rare, scanty,* or *meager*. All this tells us that when the hole made by the leg of the ק is small the effect of the destruction is small and it can be understood as a compensation or equalization.

---

51. Leviticus 11:44-45.
52. Leviticus 19:2.
53. Deuteronomy 28:9.
54. Proverbs 19:20.

The word קִיּוּם means *existence, approval, confirmation,* and *affirmation;* קִיֵּם means to *fulfill, affirm, confirm, establish, maintain, preserve, sustain;* קֻיַּם means to *be fulfilled,* to *be confirmed,* or to *be maintained.* The word קַיָּם means *existing, subsisting, alive, in force, effective, valid, enduring, durable, abiding,* and קִיָּם means *existence, endurance* or *everlastingness.* From this we learn that by the hole bored by the leg of the ק, we sustain the void and it in turn provides an everlasting place for our existence and fulfillment.

The word קֵץ means *end,* קֶצֶב means *rhythm, tempo, cadence, rate, speed, meter, measure, form,* and *pattern* as well as *end* or *extremity.* קְצָה means *end, extremity, border, edge, outskirts,* and קָצֶה means *end, extremity,* or *border.* The void created by the hole bored by the leg of the ק has a rhythm and tempo that is at the outer end of all things. Nothing beyond it can be understood or even thought about. Nothing beyond it can be questioned.

In the extremity, in the inexplicable end of the void, is mystery and magic.[55] We learn this because the word קָסוּם means *bewitched, charmed, entranced, enchanted, fascinated,* and *spellbound;* קוֹסֵם means *bewitching, charming, fascinating.* The root קָסַם means to *charm, captivate, fascinate, bewitch, enchant, conjure up,* to *divine,* and to *cast a spell.* The word קֶסֶם means *charm, enchantment, magic, divination, spell,* or *oracle* and the word קֹסֵם means *magician* or *sorcerer.* To become a magician, we must not just exist in the void, we must consciously enter it, affirm it, become one with it, and finally descend the leg of the ק to form it, in accordance with God's will, as we desire it to be.

---

55. This is not the magic of the sorcerer who acts separate from God. Rather, it is the magic of the child who is spellbound by the magnificence and beauty of the world that God creates.

רֵישׁ

Resh ר: The Cosmic Container

The twentieth letter of the Hebrew alphabet is the letter ר, spelled רֵישׁ. It means both *poverty* and *head* or *principal*. It has the numerical value of 200, and its energy intelligence is *cosmic container*. The other letter energy intelligences having to do with container are ב, which has the numerical value of 2 and the energy intelligence of container or vessel archetype, and כ, which has the numerical value of 20 and the energy intelligence of container projected into physical existence.

The cosmic container is a container of contexts. At the cosmic level, every action, every expressed statement, every thought has simultaneous multiple valid contexts. Each context provides for the possibility of our inner movement, a movement that chooses a context by which we interpret any situation. And whatever the dimension one wants to measure this on, these simultaneously valid multiple contexts permit interpretations that can range from one extreme to another. The inner movement permitted by the cosmic container is our freedom, our freedom to give our situations a context and by this means an interpretation. From the letter energy intelligence of ר, we learn that each situation as we experience it does not have its context in it. The situation does not contain its limitation. Rather, its context comes from within us. It is internally generated, something we each do as an exercise of our free will.

The word רֵישׁ does not occur in the Pentateuch. We do find in the Pentateuch a permutation of its letters in the word שָׂרֵי. This is the plural constructive form of the noun שַׂר, which means *official, master, head, chief, commander, ruler, leader,* or *prince*. And of course, Sarai, the name of Abraham's wife before the letter ה was added changing it to Sarah, is spelled with the same letters: שָׂרַי.

When Abraham goes down to Egypt to sojourn there because of the severe famine in the land where he dwelled, the Egyptians see how beautiful Sarai is and they bring her to Pharaoh.

> And when Pharaoh's *officials* saw her, they praised her to Pharaoh and she was taken into his palace.[1]

---

1. Genesis 12:17.

When Pharaoh hears that Joseph's brothers have come to Egypt, he invites the entire family in, giving them the best of the land.

> The land of Egypt is open before you; settle your father and your brothers in the best part of the land; let them stay in the region of Goshen. And if you know any capable men among them, put them *in charge of* [make them *rulers* over] my livestock.[2]

When a new king arises over Egypt and no longer recognizes Joseph, the new king schemes to make the Israelites slaves.

> Therefore they did set over them *taskmasters* to afflict them with their burdens. And they built for Pharaoh treasure cities, namely Pithom and Raamses.[3]

When Jethro, Moses' father-in-law, brings Moses' sons and wife to him in the wilderness and sees how Moses sits as magistrate among the people from morning until evening, he advises Moses the following:

> You shall also seek out from among all the people capable men who fear God, trustworthy men who spurn ill-gotten gains; and set these over them as *chiefs* of thousands, *chiefs* of hundreds, *chiefs* of fifties, and chiefs of tens.[4]

From these verses we learn a lesson about contexts. As Sarai was brought to the palace of Pharaoh, each situational context brings us to the palace of the Egyptians, the palace of limitations. And why is מִצְרַיִם, Egypt, the land of limitation? Because מִצְרַיִם is from the root מצר, which means to *bound*, *border*, *fix boundaries*, or *limit*. And once in the land of the Egyptians as Joseph's family was, we are offered the best of the land. This means that we are offered the best of illusions: the illusion that we are subject to the land of limitation. And once we buy into being subject to limitation, just as the Israelites were enslaved by the Egyptians, we too become enslaved by limitation. We become

---

2. Genesis 47:6.
3. Exodus 1:11.
4. Exodus 18:21.

so enslaved to the illusion that we do not even become aware that we have fallen into the illusion. We engage in activities of building empty cities, vain structures, that which has appearance but no essence. We choose context whose purpose is for the sake of protecting us, but that in reality separates us and limits our ascent. And when our ascent is limited, we descend. We can descend to the forty-ninth level, and we are רָי"שׁ, in *poverty*. We are *poor*.

> He who tills his land shall have plenty of bread, but he who follows after vain persons shall have *poverty* enough.[5]

But in our darkest moment, the sun shines. For there are always trustworthy and righteous people, chiefs and masters, who with God's help can make us aware that we have fallen into the illusion and help lead us to freedom. But if we do not listen to them?

> *Poverty* and shame come to him who refuses instruction: but he who heeds reproof shall be honored.[6]

So bathed in the sunshine, in the holy instruction of Torah, we can leave enslavement and enter freedom. We can go beyond whatever limitation the appearance of our situation seems to have.

Because the context of a situation is not connected to the situation, the light that is always present is concealed. What light we each can reveal comes about by choosing a context for each situation and responding to the situation by thoughts, words, and actions in accordance with the interpretation of the situation in the chosen context. It is this way that we each have complete responsibility for the motivation behind whatever we do.

How do we know that there is light that is always present? We know that because the gematria of רָי"שׁ is 510 and this is the gematria of the word תּוּקַד, which means *shall be kept burning* and occurs exactly three times in the Pentateuch. Rabbi Schneerson teaches that

> three is associated with the concept of חֲזָקָה, a threefold sequence associated with strength and permanence.[7]

---

5. Proverbs 28:19.

6. Proverbs 13:18.

7. Rabbi Menachem Schneerson, *Sichos in English*, vol. 48 (Brooklyn, NY: Sichos in English, 1991), p. 81.

Each of the three occurrences of תּוּקַד is in reference to the fire that shall ever be burning on the altar in the temple.

> This is the Torah of the burnt offering: It is the burnt offering which shall be burning upon the altar all night until the morning, and the fire of the altar *shall be kept burning* in it.[8]

> And the fire upon the altar *shall be kept burning* in it; it shall not be put out.[9]

> The fire *shall ever be burning* upon the altar; it shall never go out.[10]

The full gematria of רֵישׁ is רֵישׁ יוֹד שִׁין, 890. The word תְּמִימֹת, which means *complete* or *full*, has the gematria of 890. It is used in the passage telling us about the counting of the omer.

> From the day after the sabbath, the day that you bring the sheaf of wave offering, you shall keep count until seven *complete* weeks have elapsed: you shall count fifty days, until the day after the seventh week; then you shall bring an offering of new grain to the Lord.[11]

There is a count of seven weeks, one week for each Sephirah חֶסֶד, גְּבוּרָה, תִּפְאֶרֶת, נֶצַח, הוֹד, יְסוֹד, and מַלְכוּת. Within each week there are seven days and these days are for the seven Sephirot within each Sephirah. The purpose of the counting of the omer is for the refinement of our animal soul.[12] The contemplation associated with the counting is for the purpose of sifting out all evil, purifying the emotional traits of our animal soul. And by purifying our emotional traits, we purify and elevate that portion of the world connected to our soul. And it is begun just after the Sabbath because

---

8. Leviticus 6:2.
9. Leviticus 6:5.
10. Leviticus 6:6.
11. Leviticus 23:15.
12. Rabbi Menachem Schneerson, *Likkutei Sichot*, vol. 3 (Brooklyn, NY: Kehot Publication Society, 1987), p. 169.

the aspect of "the morrow after the Shabbat" transcends the Shabbat itself; it is "a light transcending . . . the order of the creative process."[13]

Rabbi Schneerson teaches that by counting the omer,

> the entire world is brought to a state of perfection and completeness. The expression, "world," includes all levels of the creation, including the highest emanations and types of existence. By completing our count, we bring completion to these heavenly realms.[14]

The Zohar tells us:

> They were to count "for themselves," so as to be purified with supernal holy waters, and then to be attached to the King and to receive the Torah.[15]

We read in *Midrash Rabbah*:

> Rabbi Hiyya taught: Seven weeks shall there be complete. When are they regarded as "complete"? When Israel do the will of the Omnipresent.[16]

So we see that it is the will of the Omnipresent that we refine our emotional traits. And how do we do this? We do it by being in situations and choosing a context. For the context we choose reveals to our consciousness the level on which our emotions are operating. And once we consciously understand what our emotional level is, we can do something about it. We can change and grow, purifying and elevating our emotions step by step. By this means, we make ourselves "shine."[17]

Thus the *cosmic container* makes it possible for us to participate in a creative process, ascending to ever higher levels of purity, and

---

13. Ibid., p. 174.
14. Rabbi Schneerson, *Sichos in English*, vol. 17, p. 104.
15. *The Zohar*, vol. 5, p. 122.
16. *Midrash Rabbah*, vol. 4, *Leviticus* (28:3), trans. J. Israelstam and J. Slotki (London: Soncino Press, 1983), p. 361.
17. Rabbi Schneerson, *Sichos in English*, vol. 17, p. 105.

establish an affinity with the Creator. For to be like the Creator means that we must have a choice to create as we will. The primal creation is the ever present light, the desire to share. We cannot create light. But the cosmic container has the space by which the ever present light is individually concealed to each of us. By choosing a context by which a situation can be interpreted, we can individually reveal the light. This context is on its own level a vessel and the interpretation we give is on its own level a light. This is the revealed meaning of the letter energy intelligence ר.

The concealed meaning of the letter ר can be learned from the word יֵשׁ, which means *there is, there are* and also *existence, substance, being, reality, possessions,* or *assets*. After Isaac blesses Jacob, Jacob leaves Beersheba and sets out for Haran. There he has a dream in which God speaks to him.

> Jacob awoke from his sleep and said: "Surely *there is* the Lord in this place, and I did not know it!"[18]

After Jacob and his family leave Laban, Jacob sends three successive groups of his servants with gifts to his brother Esau. When Jacob and Esau meet, Esau asks him why he sent such gifts. Jacob replies that it is to win favor in his sight. Then Esau replies:

> *There is* for me enough. My brother, let what you have remain yours.[19]

After Joseph is sold as a slave and taken to Egypt, Potiphar puts him in charge of his household.

> And from the time that the Egyptian put him in charge of his household and of all his *possessions*, the Lord blessed his house for Joseph's sake, so that the blessing of the Lord was upon everything that he *owned*, in the house and in the field.[20]

Finally, we read in Proverbs:

---

18. Genesis 28:16.
19. Genesis 33:9.
20. Genesis 39:5.

That I may cause those who love me to inherit *substance*;
and I will fill their treasures.[21]

Here we learn that the place of God is in our daily situations. And
we do not know it! So to the gift of Jacob, the holy sparks concealed
within the situation, we say as Esau said to Jacob: we have enough.
But if we choose the context in which to interpret the situation in the
highest possible manner, then we will reveal the holy sparks and the
blessing of the Lord will be upon everything that we possess and we
will inherit substance.

Rabbi Yehudah Leib Eiger of Lublin teaches that

> a person who lives a hallowed life is superior to the animal
> in that he is capable of finding the spark of holiness that is
> contained within everything physical. It is this divine spark
> that imparts life to every physical being. Finding a spark
> of holiness in even the lowliest corporeal act constitutes the
> essence of serving God.[22]

Rabbi Eiger tells us that it is our myriad illusions that hinder us from
finding these sparks.

So there is reality and there is illusion. Reality means the inner
reality. The question is: does the inner movement of our being arise
from a desire to receive for our self alone or the desire to receive for
the sake of sharing? This is the only question of the inner reality. This
is the only substance. The choices we make constitute our only real
possessions, our only real assets.

Illusion means outer reality. Outer reality has to do with physical
existence. When our attention is focused on the things of physical
existence, on the things of physical substance, on materiality and the
choices of materiality, we participate in the illusion. For whatever these
choices are, whatever our decisions are, whatever we choose to build or
tear down, however we choose to rearrange this physical reality, these
results will undergo change forced by ourselves, other individuals, or

---

21. Proverbs 8:21.
22. Avraham   Yaakov   Finkel,   *The Great Chasidic Masters*   (Northvale, NJ:
Jason Aronson, 1992), p. 175.

the natural processes of growth and decay of physical reality. These results are not what we can take with us. They are not our possessions. For them, we are only a temporary caretaker. They are the contents of the illusion.

It is very easy to be so engrossed by this physical reality, so involved in the illusion, that we forget what real reality is for us. We forget the purpose of reality and the purpose of illusion. We forget about what our free choice is really about. We get involved with careers, houses, furniture, cars, and money, forgetting that these are only containers, only vessels for the individual greater or lesser revealment of the light according to the desire we manifest to receive for ourself alone or to receive for the sake of sharing. Indeed, it can be no other way. For the manifestation of the desire to receive can be only through the vessel of physical reality. It can be only through the creative process. It can only be by breaking through the limitation of the illusion that the revealment takes place. This is the concealed meaning of ר.

The letter ר is related to the word רֹאשׁ, which means *head*. One permutation of the letters of רֹאשׁ is אֶשֶׁר, which is the noun meaning *happiness*. Another word beginning with the letter ר is רָצוֹן which means *will, wish, desire*, or *volition*. One permutation of the letters of רָצוֹן is צִנּוֹר, which means *pipe* or *channel*. Putting this all together, we learn that when we use our head, רֹאשׁ, to have the will, רָצוֹן, to live in happiness, אֶשֶׁר, in all our circumstances, because we know that each circumstance, no matter how difficult, is a blessing from God, we create a channel connecting the upper world to the lower world, through the *cosmic container*, which opens the gates of heaven and showers the lower world with the light of God. And this is the meaning of the first line of the afternoon prayer beginning with אַשְׁרֵי, *happy*.

אַשְׁרֵי יוֹשְׁבֵי בֵיתֶךְ

Happy are those who dwell in Your House.[23]

The revealment of the light can be to a greater or lesser extent. The degree of revealment is the degree to which the context we choose is one of a desire to share. As we are ourselves a vessel and as the property of

---

23. *Siddur Tehillat Hashem* (Brooklyn, NY: Merkos L'Inyonei Chinuch, 1979), p. 96.

a vessel is to be filled, to receive, we can establish an affinity to the light by choosing to receive for the sake of sharing. But as the choice must be a free choice, there must be the possibility of choosing to receive for oneself alone. So the extremes of the interpretations that can be given to each situation, to each thought, to each expressed word, and to each action are in effect the extremes of manifesting the desire to receive for oneself alone and the desire to receive for the sake of sharing. Paradoxically, the *cosmic container* conceals the ever present light and by concealing makes possible its individual revealment.

We can learn about the manifestation of the extremes of the desire to receive for oneself alone and the desire to receive for the sake of sharing by examining some of the ר-words that have multiple and contradictory meanings. For this multiplicity is the multiplicity that parallels the multiple possible contexts we can choose in interpreting the meaning of each situation we encounter. Rabbi Glazerson teaches us about the underlying significance of the same word having two different or opposite meanings. He says that

> the underlying significance of this phenomenon is that we creatures of flesh and blood are limited in our perceptions. We cannot fathom the profundities of the ways by which the Holy One, Blessed is He, conducts His world. As a result, certain events appear to us as destructive disasters, when in truth their purpose is to rectify and perfect the world.[24]

Rabbi Glazerson goes on to say that if we are strong in our faith we will find those situations that have the appearance of destructiveness to be ones that illuminate the ways of God. And if our faith is weak then these same events will only increase our doubts and further weaken our faith.

So the way to understand situations that appear to be destructive is to see that the destructive aspect is relative to our desire to receive for ourselves alone. Here ourselves means us and possibly those who are nearest us. But when we take a more global view, we find that

---

24. Rabbi Matityahu Glazerson, *Letters of Fire*, trans. S. Fuchs (Jerusalem: Feldheim, 1991), p. 141.

the situation having the destructive appearance actually affords us the opportunity to do in order to share.

We have already mentioned that the letter ר, spelled רֵישׁ, means both *poverty* and *head* or *principal*. The word רָשׁ means *poor* or *beggar*. Thus the energy intelligence of ר spans both the high and the low. The word רַב has the meaning of *rabbi, teacher, minister, officer,* and *master*. Also it means *archer*, and it means *enough*. In addition, it means *numerous, many, great,* and *much*. As a prefix, it has the meaning of *poly* or *multi*. The root רב is the verb to *quarrel* and the word רֹב means *most, majority, multitude, abundance, plenty,* or *plethora*.

The root רמם means to be *infested with maggots* or to be *infested with worms* as well as meaning to *rise* and *be exalted*. The word רַע means *bad, inferior, worthless, dangerous, malignant, evil, wicked, unkind, noxious, displeasing, repugnant* and *slim*. The word רָע means *evil, wickedness, harm, injury, trouble, calamity, misfortune, woe,* and *wrong*. The word רֹעַ means *malice, wickedness, badness,* and *vice*. However, the word רֵעַ means *friend, comrade, fellow companion, neighbor, amicable* as well as *thought, idea,* or *meaning*. When we choose to receive for ourself alone, we engage in an act of deceit and betrayal. This is the bad and the inferior. When we choose to receive for the sake of sharing, we establish a close affinity to the Creator. We establish ourselves on a high ground. This is the friend.

The root רעע means to be *bad, worse,* to *feel distress* and it also means to *break, crush,* or *shatter*. The word רָשׁוּת means *authority* and it also means *poverty*. The root רתק means to *join, bind, hold,* to *knock,* and to *moor* as well as to be *disconnected* or *unchained*. The root רכס means to *fasten, bind, button, tie up,* or *clasp* while it also means to *trample, stamp,* or *tread*. The root רמה means to *throw, cast, hurl,* or *shoot,* while רמה is also the root meaning to *deceive, cheat, bamboozle, swindle, beguile,* or *betray* and רָמָה means *height* or *high place*.

Each context we choose for a situation creates a vessel that has within it the script by which our chosen role is played out. That role can range anywhere from trampling and disconnecting by choosing to receive for ourself alone or binding and connecting by choosing to receive for the sake of sharing. Let us learn to choose to receive for the sake of sharing.

Shin שׁ: Cosmic Nourishment

The twenty-first letter of the Hebrew alphabet, שׁ, has two forms, Shin שׁ and Sin שׂ, that are spelled שִׁין and שִׂיןrespectively. The spelling שִׁין is similar to the spelling of the word שַׁיִן, which means *urine*. Without the yod, the spelling שִׁין becomes שֵׁן, which means *tooth*, *claw*, or *jaw*. With the chewing of the teeth the breakdown and digestion of the food we eat begins. This food when digested and metabolized is the energy source enabling us to think, speak, and do. The waste products of the metabolization process are released by breathing, שְׁאִיפָה, and in urine, שַׁיִן. This tells us that שׁ represents the totality of an overall process, one that is שָׁלֵם, *whole*, *entire*, *intact*, *complete*, *integral*, *full*, and *perfect*, by which we have the energy to do.

Such an overall process is one that we must repeat again and again. Thus it should be no surprise that שָׁנָה is the root meaning to *repeat*, *do over again*, *reiterate*, or *revise*. This is reinforced by the root שָׁב, which means to *return*, *come back*, *be transformed*, *repeat*, *do again*, or *go back*. And what we repeat again and again becomes learned and inculcated within us. Interestingly enough, שָׁנָה is the root of the verb meaning to *study*, *learn*, *teach*, or *inculcate*. But this is not all, for when we learn and then do based on what we have learned, we cause change in ourselves and our surroundings. The root שָׁנָה also has the meaning to *change*, to *be changed*, *be different*, or *become different*. The word for change or modification is שִׁנּוּי. Since changes can take place only in a world having time, we should not be surprised to find that the Hebrew word for *year* is שָׁנָה and *second* (in the sense of 1/60th of a minute) is שְׁנִיָה.

The gematria of שִׁין is 360. This is the gematria of the word הַשָּׁנָה, which means *the year*.

> The land into which you go to possess, is a land of hills and valleys, and drinks water of the rain of heaven: a land which the Lord thy God cares for: the eyes of the Lord thy God are always upon it, from the beginning of *the year* to the year-end.[1]

---

1. Deuteronomy 11:12.

The land we go to possess is a state of consciousness complete and full of Godliness. This is the land that God cares for. This is the land that the eyes of God are always upon throughout the year.

The gematria of the word שְׁמֶךָ and its direct object form שִׁמְךָ, meaning *your name*, is also 360.

> Now the Lord said to Abram: "Get thee out of thy country, and from thy kindred, and from thy father's house, to the land that I will show thee. And I will make of thee a great nation, and I will bless thee, and make *thy name* great, and thou shalt be a blessing, and I will bless them that bless thee and I will curse them that curse thee."[2]

> Neither shall *thy name* any more be called Abram, but *thy name* shall be Abraham: for a father of many nations have I made thee.[3]

Here we learn that, however completely full our consciousness was of Godliness yesterday, today is a new day. Today we are to reach a new land. And so we are commanded to go out of our country. Leave the land of God consciousness we had yesterday and go to the land of God consciousness that God shows us today. And when we go we will become a great nation. God will bless us and make our name great and we will be a blessing. And our name will acquire the addition of a ה, the ה of הוה, the root meaning to *be*.

> And he said to him: "What is *thy name*?" And he said, "Jacob." And he said: "*Thy name* shall be called no more Jacob, but Israel. For thou hast contended with God and with men, and hast prevailed."[4]

> And God said to him: "*Thy name* is Jacob. *Thy name* shall not be called anymore Jacob, but Israel shall be *thy name*." And he called his name Israel. And God said to him: "I am God Almighty: be fruitful and multiply; a nation and

---

2. Genesis 12:1-3.
3. Genesis 17:5.
4. Genesis 32:28-29.

שׁ

a company of nations shall be of thee and kings shall come
out of thy loins."[5]

Moving into a higher level of God consciousness is not easy. We
will meet with resistance. This resistance is inside of us. And we will
struggle with it. Little by little we will tame it. When this resistance
has been transformed to love God, then our name shall also become
Israel, for we will have contended and struggled with God and men.
And we will have prevailed in revealing the light and bringing forth
Godliness when it appeared that there was only darkness.

The gematria of the word וַיְשַׁלְּחוּ is also 360. It is the third person
plural Piel imperfect, with the conjunctive prefix, of the root שׁלח,
which means to *send*. The Egyptian King used it in sending Abram
out of Egypt.

And Pharaoh commanded his men concerning him: and
they *sent* him away, and his wife, and all that he had. And
Abram went up out of Egypt, he and his wife, and all that
he had, and Lot with him, into the Negev.[6]

The meaning of this in the context of the energy intelligence of
שׁ is that our movement into a higher level of God consciousness is
a movement away from limitation. In essence, each successive higher
level of God consciousness we live in sends away more and more of our
limitations.

The gematria of the word יָשָׁן, which means *old*, is also 360.

And you shall eat *old* store, and remove the *old* because of
the new.[7]

The plain meaning of this verse is that the old grain, which tastes
very good, will be eaten. But we will not have the chance to even
eat it all up, for the new grain will be so abundant that the old grain
will have to be removed from the storehouses to make room for the
new. From the perspective of the energy intelligence of שׁ, it means

---

5. Genesis 35:10.
6. Genesis 12:20.
7. Leviticus 26:10.

that entering the land of a higher level of God consciousness produces very abundant grain, so abundant and so meaningful that it will supplant the nourishment we have saved up from our lower level of God consciousness.

The full gematria of שׁ is שִׁין יוֹד נוּן, which totals 486. The word וּבְמְחֹלֹת, *and with dancing*, also has the gematria of 486. After Pharaoh and his chariots were drowned in the Red Sea, Moses sings a song of triumph. Then Miriam and the women dance.

> And Miriam the prophetess, the sister of Aaron, took a timbrel in her hand. And all the women went out after her with timbrels and with dancing.[8]

Until the Israelites took the plunge into the Red Sea, the situation looked very dark and grim to them. But when their faith prevailed and they plunged into the Red Sea, the sea parted and they were able to cross. Miracles happen after we take the plunge. And when the miracles happen we dance the eternal dance.

שׁ has the numerical value of 300. Thus שׁ has a close relationship to ג, whose numerical value is 3. This is reinforced by the shape of שׁ, which has three columns. שׁ also has a close relationship to ל, whose numerical value is 30. To understand these relationships consider that ג is the archetype of nourishment. ל is the archetype of nourishment projected into physical existence. Its meaning is teaching and purpose. שׁ is the projection of the archetype ג into the cosmos and so has the meaning of *cosmic nourishment*. This is its revealed meaning: it is what we do again and again, it is the changes that we cause, the teaching that we do, the learning that we do, which serves as nourishment for the cosmos. And when we do what we do with wisdom, we use our brain, מֹחַ, to bind ourselves with the שׁ, thereby creating the root שׂמח,[9] which means to *rejoice, be glad,* or *be happy.*[10] Scripture says:

> Because the Lord thy God shall bless thee in all thy produce, and in all the work of thy hands, and thou shalt be

---

8. Exodus 15:20.

9. Deuteronomy 16:15, 33:18.

10. Rabbi Matityahu Glazerson, *From Hinduism to Judaism* (Jerusalem: Himelsein Publishers, 1984), p. 27.

altogether joyful [שָׂמֵחַ].[11]

This is reinforced by the word שָׂשׂ,[12] which means *rejoice* and the word שָׂשׂוֹן, which means *joy*. There are a few places in Scripture where שָׂשׂוֹן and שִׂמְחָה occur together.[13]

The form of the letter שׁ is that of a base with three arms extending upward. Each of these arms corresponds to a different aspect of our intellectual thought process. These are the conceptual, the emotional, and the practical.[14] The right arm of the שׁ is a י. Thus from the right side flows wisdom.[15] The left arm of the שׁ is a ז. Thus from the left side flow weapons and movement. And the central arm of the שׁ is a ו. So from the central arm there is a connection. All three arms connect to the base of the שׁ. This teaches us that as *cosmic nourishment*, שׁ harmonizes and balances the spiritual energy intelligences of its three arms.[16] This is the revealed meaning of שׁ.

The concealed meaning of שִׁין can be discerned from words of the form יִן or words beginning with ינ. יַיִן is the word for *wine*. The root of the verb to *oppress*, *tread down*, or *trample* underfoot is ינה and the root of the verb to *suck* or *absorb* is ינק. The word יְנִיק means *child* or *young* and the word יְנִיקָה means *sucking, suction, absorption*, or *young twig*. Our sustenance, which is what we *absorb*, is held in the physical reality we are given. In and of itself, this physical reality is empty. At a higher level it is in fact a nonentity, nothingness, אִין. We must think of physical reality as a vessel to hold sustenance, to hold essence. But when we think that physical reality is the essence instead of being the medium in which the essence is expressed, we will *deceive, cheat, trick*, and *oppress* (ינה) ourselves.

When we are conscious of physical reality as a holder of essence, we open ourselves to absorb and receive the essence. We become like a

---

11. Deuteronomy, 16:15.

12. Psalms, 119:162.

13. Isaiah 22:13, 35:10, 51:3, 51:11, Jeremiah, 7:34, 15:16, 16:9, 25:10, 33:11, Psalms 51:10, Zechariah 8:19, Esther 8:16, 8:17.

14. Rabbi Nachman, *Likutey Moharan*, vol. 3, trans. Moshe Mykoff, commentator Chaim Kramer (Jerusalem: Breslov Research Institute, 1990), p. 68.

15. This is because on the tree of life the letter י is associated with the Sephirah Wisdom.

16. Rabbi Glazerson, *From Hinduism to Judaism*, p. 83.

winemaker who can extract the wine, יַיִן, which is the essence, from the grape. We become like a baby *sucking* (יָנַה) milk from the mother's breast. And we are able to maintain a young and childlike attitude toward the wonders we find in the magic of essence. This leads us to the concealed meaning of שׁ: true *nourishment* and sustenance is inner nourishment and inner sustenance. True nourishment and sustenance are in what we discover and intuit the physical form expressing.

There are a variety of words that further explain the particulars of the meaning of שׁ. The word *second* (ordinal two) is שֵׁנִי. Like שָׂעִיר, שֵׁנִי has the gematria of 360. The second Sephirah is חָכְמָה, *wisdom*. The second Sephirah of the emotions is גְּבוּרָה, *strength*. The word שִׁנֵּי is the constructive plural for *teeth* and the word שִׁנַּי means *my teeth*. Teeth are then related to wisdom and strength[17]

> Thou hast broken the *teeth* of the wicked.[18]

> For a nation is come up upon my land, mighty, and without number, whose teeth are the *teeth* of a lion, and he has the fangs of a lioness.[19]

> My bone cleaves to my skin and to my flesh, and I am escaped with the skin of *my teeth*.[20]

> He has also broken *my teeth* with gravel stones, he has pressed me down into the ashes.[21]

Also, from the word שֵׁנִי, *second*, we learn that we are second. The *Almighty* God, שַׁדַּי, is first. And what does שַׁדַּי mean? The word דַּי means the *requisite, necessary supply, sufficiency,* or *plenty*. As an adverb it means *enough*. Therefore, שַׁדַּי means: that there is enough or who is enough.[22] God has enough. God is enough. The Divinity of God possesses enough sufficiency for every creature.[23]

---

17. Rabbi Matityahu Glazerson, *Hebrew: The Source of Languages*, trans. J. Weil (Jerusalem: Yerid HaSefarim, 1988), p. 27.
18. Psalms 3:8.
19. Joel 1:6.
20. Job 19:20.
21. Lamentations 3:16.
22. *The Babylonian Talmud, Seder Moed*, vol. 4, *Hagigah* (12a), trans. I. Abrahams (London: Soncino Press, 1938), p. 65.
23. Rashi, Genesis 17:1.

Thou openest Thy hand and satisfyeth the desires of every living thing.[24]

No matter how far we may have placed ourselves from God, when we return, there is enough Godliness for God to forgive us so that we are able to find God again. There is enough Godliness to satisfy the needs of all creation.[25] Related to this, the word שַׁד means a *mother's breast milk* and שַׁד or שֵׁד means *breast, teat, tit, nipple, bosom, protuberance* as well as *affluence* and *source of blessing*. The suffiency of God for us is analogous to the mother's breast milk for her infant child.

If we reverse the order of God first and us second, we will become שָׁחוּץ, *arrogant, haughty, conceited,* and *supercilious*. We will become full of שַׁחַץ, *pride*. We will become שָׁחַץ, *boastful* and *proud*. And then the *Divine Presence*, שְׁכִינָה, the essence, will no longer be near us. Instead of *aspiring, yearning,* and *striving*, which at the higher level is breathing, all of which is expressed by the root שׁאַף, we will *crush, trample, tread upon,* and *oppress*, all of which is expressed by the same root שׁאַף. We will *err, blunder, make mistakes, lose our way,* and *go astray*, the root for which is שָׁגָה. We will *spoil, hurt, waste, ruin, destroy,* and *corrupt*, the root for which is שָׁחַת. We will *lie, betray, deceive, act falsely* and *swindle*, the root for which is שֶׁקֶר.

With Godliness first, we will be satisfied and content. We will feel we have abundance and have received enough, the root for which is שָׂבַע. From this we learn the inner meaning of the number seven, שֶׁבַע: satisfied and content, complete, for שַׁבָּת is the word for Sabbath, the day of rest when all had been completed, the seventh day. שַׁבָּת can be understood as the daughter, בַּת of שׁ. Rabbi Glazerson tells us that daughter here means Israel for שַׁבָּת is the time when Israel is wed to the שׁ, the שׁ standing for שֶׁרֶשׁ, which means *root*, the root or universal existence.[26] The root of universal existence is *cosmic nourishment*.

The gematria of שַׁבָּת is 702. Now 702 is 27 times 26. There are 22 Hebrew letters plus 5 final forms, which make a total of 27 distinct forms. The Tetragrammaton יְהֹוָה has the gematria of 26. From this we learn that in creating this world, God continuously projects

---

24. Psalms 145:16.
25. Rabbi Nachman, *Likutey Moharan*, vol. 3, p. 56.
26. Rabbi Glazerson, *From Hinduism to Judaism*, p. 23.

Himself (26) through each of the 27 letters. So שַׁבָּת (702) is God's name as it manifests in this created world.[27]

A reordering of the letters of the word for *second*, שֵׁנִי, produces the Hebrew word for *womanly* or *feminine*, נָשִׁי. To that which is above us we must be feminine. Only to that which is below us can we be masculine and manifest the *ruler*, the *governor*, the *master*, שַׁלִּיט.

The letter energy intelligence שׁ is associated with the words שְׁמוֹ, *his name* and שָׁם, *there*.

> And Moses said to God:
>
>> Behold, when I come to the children of Israel, and shall say to them
>>
>>> The God of your fathers has sent me to you.
>>
>> And they shall say to me.
>>
>>> What is *His Name*?
>>
>> What shall I say to them?
>
> And God said to Moses:
>
>> I shall ever be what I now am. אֶהְיֶה אֲשֶׁר אֶהְיֶה.[28]

So from this we learn that *His Name* is associated with *I shall ever be what I now am.*

And with the combination שְׁמוֹ שָׁם, *His Name there*, the Pentatuech tells us:

> To the place that the Lord your God shall choose out of all your tribes to put *His Name there*, even unto His habitation shall ye seek and there shalt thou come.[29]
>
> But when you traverse the Jordan, and dwell in the land which the Lord your God giveth to you to inherit, and when

---

27. Pinchas Peli, *The Jewish Sabbath* (New York: Schocken Books, 1988), p. 149; here Peli is quoting an idea from the book *B'nai Issachar*, by Rabbi Zvi Elimelech.
28. Exodus 3:14.
29. Deuteronomy 12:5.

He giveth you rest from all your enemies round about, so that ye dwell in safety; then there shall be a place which the Lord your God shall choose to cause *His Name* to dwell *there*.[30]

And thou shalt eat before the Lord thy God, in the place which he shall choose to cause *His Name* to dwell *there*.[31]

And thou shalt rejoice before the Lord thy God, thou, and thy son, and thy daughter, and thy manservant, and thy maidservant, and the Levite who is within thy gates, and the stranger, and the fatherless, and the widow that are among you, in the place which the Lord thy God shall choose to cause *His Name* to dwell *there*.[32]

This teaches that *His Name, I shall ever be what I now am*, means that we shall seek and come to His habitation, that there we will dwell in safety, that there we will eat and be nourished, with cosmic nourishment, and there we will rejoice.

And it shall be, when thou art come in unto the land which the Lord thy God giveth thee for an inheritance, and dost possess it and dost dwell therein: that thou shalt take of the first of all the fruit of the earth, which thou shalt bring in from thy land that the Lord thy God giveth thee; and thou shalt put it in a basket, and shalt go to the place which the Lord thy God shall choose to cause *His Name* to dwell *there*.[33]

Rabbi Schneerson explains that on this verse the Baal Shem Tov teaches that

this means that wherever a Jew finds himself he must realize that his purpose is to reveal Godliness there and make it a dwelling place for His Name. So God wants a revelation of

---

30. Deuteronomy 12:11.
31. Deuteronomy 14:23.
32. Deuteronomy 16:11.
33. Deuteronomy 26:1-2.

Godliness in the whole world: in every country, every city, every neighborhood and every home.[34]

What is the place of the revelation of Godliness? The place is His habitation? His habitation is in the land that the Lord our God has given us. We will be in the land when we take the first of the fruit of the earth, that which we have helped produce in the physical realm for the purpose of its spiritual elevation, and put it in a basket and return it to God. And when we do, the Lord our God shall choose to cause *His Name* to dwell *there*, that is, to dwell in us.

The letter energy intelligence שׁ has a dimension that relates to fire and flame. The biggest fire is the *sun*, שֶׁמֶשׁ. The word שָׁבִיב means *small flame*, *spark*, or *ray of light*. The verb root שׁלהב means to *inflame, kindle, fan, arouse, excite, set ablaze, set alight, fire*, or *ignite*. The related word שַׁלְהֶבֶת means *flame* or *blaze*. שׂרף is the root of the verb to *burn* or *destroy by fire*. שְׂרֵפָה means *fire conflagration*, or *burning*. When שׁ is preceded by א there results the word אֵשׁ, which means *fire*. When א is preceded by שׁ with a ׳ in between the word שִׂיא results. שִׂיא has the meaning of *height, summit, climax, peak, crest, acme, pinnacle, culminating part*, and *maximum*.

What is the nature of the flame of fire? The flame of fire reaches upward toward the *summit*, שִׂיא, its source. It tries, but is unable to escape from that which it burns. And that which it burns, it changes and destroys. The fire by destroying produces heat and light, both of which are useful forms of energy when properly *governed* and *controlled*, שָׁלַט. In a spiritual sense, it is by the energy intelligence of the fire of שׁ that we either burn and explode our own vices on others or we burn away, destroy, and reduce our vices to nothing.

When the fire energy intelligence of שׁ is improperly used, we destructively expode and inflict our vices on others. The result is fiery action: from the root שׁבר of the verb meaning to *break, shatter to pieces, tear, kill, ruin, destroy, demolish*, and *wreck*; from the root שׁחת of the verb meaning to *spoil, hurt, waste, ruin, destroy, sin, act basely* or *corruptly*; from the root שׂטן of the verb meaning to *hate, denounce, condemn, speak against*, to *act the adversary*; from the root שׂםה of

---

34. Rabbi Menachem Schneerson, *Sichos in English*, vol. 23, (Brooklyn, NY: Sichos in English, 1985), p. 223.

the verb meaning to *plunder, rob, loot, spoil, pillage, sack, despoil*; from the root שׁסף of the verb meaning to *become angry, to cut, to slash*; and from the root שׁדד of the verb meaning to *rob, pillage, plunder, despoil, destroy, ravage, devastate, ruin, lay waste, oppress, overpower,* and *be violent.* These actions, which are actions manifesting a separation and disconnection to Godliness, destroy us. We become שׁוֹמֵם, *empty, desolate, lonely,* and *depressed.*

But when this fire energy intelligence of שׁ is used with *intelligence, understanding,* and *reason,* שֵׂכֶל, we burn away our vices. This brings us closer to Godliness, our source, which becomes *joined* or *connected,* שָׁלוּב, to us. We become a *dwelling,* a *lodging,* שֶׁכֶן, for Godliness. The result is שָׁלֵו, a *calm, quiet, tranquil, carefree,* and *secure state,* שָׁלוֹם, *peace* and *well-being,* שָׂמֵחַ, a *glad, happy, joyful, cheerful* state. Our lives manifest שֶׁפֶר, *grace, beauty,* and *loveliness.* We *serve, attend, minister,* and *play our role,* the verb root being שׁמשׁ, the same letters as שֶׁמֶשׁ, the *sun.* In effect we have taken the מַיִם, the earthly water, and purified it with fire, אֵשׁ. This frees the שׁ of אֵשׁ to combine with מַיִ, creating a *heaven,* שָׁמַיִם, on earth in which the Godly unbridled force of א is revealed.

Tav ת : True Law

The twenty-second letter of the Hebrew alphabet is ת. The letter ת has the numerical value of 400. The energy intelligence of ת is the archetype of physical existence projected into cosmic manifestation. As such it is related to ד, which has the value of 4 and whose energy intelligence is the archetype of physical existence. It is related to מ, which has the value of 40, and whose energy intelligence is perfection and completion.

To understand what this means, consider the spelling of the letter ת. It is spelled תו. The word תו[1] has the meaning *mark, sign, line, feature, musical note,* or *label.*

> And the Lord said to him: "Go through the midst of the city, through the midst of Jerusalem, and set a *mark* upon the foreheads of the people who are sighing and crying over all the abominations that are done in her midst." And to the others he said in my hearing: "Go after him through the city, and strike: let not your eye spare, neither have pity. Slay utterly: the old men and the young men, both maid and little children, and women. But come not near any person upon whom is the *mark*. And begin at my sanctuary."[2]

The Aramaic word תו means *again, further, more.* Now a sign is that by which something is made known. In theology, a sign means that which can be externally recognized and which represents or signifies something internal. A sign, in other words, is a distinctive and uniquely recognizable covering that signifies an internal essence.

To understand why an essence needs an identifying covering, consider the state of happiness. Happiness, in and of itself, is an internal state, a feeling. It is an essence. But how does this essence make itself known? It does so by a sign. Often this sign is the smile of contentment. The smile of contentment is not happiness; it is only its sign. It is only a way of making itself known.

---

1. Job 31:35.
2. Ezekiel 9:4-6.

Likewise, for the energy intelligence of ת. אֱמֶת, *truth*, which is the expression of ת, is a sign of an inner essence that itself has no way of manifesting except as the expression of truth. Indeed, ת is the seal of truth.

> Resh Lakish said: "ת is the end of the seal of the Holy One, blessed be He." R. Hanina said: "The seal of the Holy One, blessed be He, is אֱמֶת, truth."[3]

Now why is it that the energy intelligence of ת is explained by אֱמֶת, whose last letter is ת, when all the other letters are explained by words that begin in that letter rather than end in that letter? The reason is that the power of truth lies in its *effects* or *manifestations*, תּוֹפָעָה. The energy intelligence of ת is an effect, not a cause. It is the end, not the beginning.

And this manifestation of truth *surrounds, encompasses, encircles, describes*, the root being תאר. It is like a *cell, room, compartment, cubicle, office* or *chamber*, which in Hebrew is תָּא, that *delimits* and *defines*, which in Hebrew is the root תאה, but in itself is not the essence.

In our inhabited *universe* or *world*, תֵּבֵל,[4] *intelligence, understanding, reason, wisdom*, and *knowledge*, תְּבוּנָה,[5] work with truth. And this truth is *regularly* and *frequently*, תָּדִיר, *again* and again, תּוּ, a *basis* and *foundation*, תּוֹשֶׁבֶת, of תּוֹרָה,[6] which is the True Law.

The gematria of תּוּ is 406. This is the gematria of תָאֵ, which means *the sign*.

> And it shall come to pass, if they will not believe thee, nor hearken to the voice of the first *sign*, that they will believe the voice of the latter *sign*.[7]

---

3. *The Babylonian Talmud, Seder Moed*, vol. 1, *Shabbat* (55a), trans. H. Freedman (London: Soncino Press, 1938), p. 254.

4. 1 Samuel 2:8; Psalms 9:9, 24:1, 33:8, 88:12, 90:2, 96:10, 96:13, 98:9; Jeremiah 51:15.

5. Exodus 31:3, 35:31, 36:1; Deuteronomy 32:28.

6. Genesis 26:5; Exodus 12:49, 13:9, 16:4, 16:28, 18:16, 18:20, 24:12; Leviticus 6:9, 6:14, 6:25, 7:1, 7:7, 7:11, 7:37, 11:46, 12:7, 13:59, 14:2, 14:32, 14:54, 14:57, 15:32, 26:46; Numbers 5:29, 5:30, 6:13, 6:21, 15:16, 15:29, 19:2, 19:14, 31:21; Deuteronomy 1:5, 4:8, 4:44, 17:11, 17:18, 17:19, 27:3, 27:8, 27:26, 28:58, 28:61, 29:20, 29:28, 30:10, 31:9, 31:11, 31:12, 31:24, 31:26, 32:46, 33:4, 33:10.

7. Exodus 4:8.

Let My people go, that they may serve Me. Else, if thou wilt
not let My people go, behold, I will send swarms of gnats
upon thee, and upon thy servants, and upon thy people,
and into thy houses. And the houses of Egypt shall be full
of swarms of gnats, and also the ground on which they are.
And I will separate in that day the land of Goshen, in which
My people dwell, that no swarms of gnats shall be there;
to the end that they mayst know that I am the Lord in the
midst of the earth. And I will put a division between My
people and thy people. Tomorrow shall this *sign* be.[8]

The gematria of the word בְּקֹדֶשׁ, which means *in holiness*, is also
406.

Who is like Thee, O Lord, among the gods? Who is like
Thee, glorious *in holiness*, fearful in praises, doing wonders?[9]

And the word בְּקֹדֶשׁ, which means *in the holy place*, has the gematria
of 406. There are two occurrences of it in the phrase בְּקֹדֶשׁ הַקֳּדָשִׁים,
which means *in the most holy place.*

And thou shalt put the covering upon the ark of the Testimony *in the most holy place.*[10]

In the most holy place shalt thou eat it.[11]

And the word לְשָׁלוֹם, which means *peace*, also has the gematria of
406.

When thou comest near to a city to fight against it, then
proclaim *peace* to it. And it shall be, if it make thee answer
of peace, and open to thee, then it shall be, that all the
people to be found in it shall be tributaries to thee, and they
shall serve thee. And if it will make no peace with thee, but
will make war against thee, then thou shalt besiege it: and

---

8. Exodus 8:17-19.
9. Exodus 15:11.
10. Exodus 26:34.
11. Numbers 18:10.

when the Lord thy God has delivered it into thy hands, thou
shalt smite every male of it with the edge of the sword. But
the women, and the little ones, and the cattle, and all that
is in the city, all the spoil of it, shalt thou take to thyself.[12]

This city, to whom we first proclaim peace, is the same city as in:

There was a little city, and few men within it. And there
came a great king against it, and besieged it, and built great
siegeworks against it. Now there was found in it a poor
wise man, and he by his wisdom saved the city; yet no man
remembered that same poor man. Then said I, Wisdom is
better than strength: nevertheless, the poor man's wisdom
is despised, and his words are not heard.[13]

And this city is the same city about which Rabbi Shneur Zalman
teaches.

The body is called a small city. Just as two kings wage war
over a town, which each wishes to capture and rule, that is
to say, to dominate its inhabitants according to his will, so
that they obey him in all that he decrees for them, so do
the two souls – the Divine and the vitalising animal soul
that comes from the *kelipah* – wage war against each other
over the body and all its limbs. It is the desire and will
of the Divine soul that she alone rule over the person and
direct him, and that all his limbs should obey her and surrender themselves completely to her and become a vehicle
for her as well as a robe [instrument] for her ten faculties
and three garments[14] mentioned above, all of which should
pervade the organs of the body, and the entire body should
be permeated with them alone, to the exclusion of any alien
influence, God forbid.[15]

---

12. Deuteronomy 20:10-14.
13. Ecclesiastes 9:14-16.
14. Thoughts, speech, and action.
15. Rabbi Shneur Zalman, *Likkutei Amarim – Tanya*, bilingual ed. (Brooklyn, NY:
Kehot Publication Society, 1993), p. 37.

From all this we learn that True Law makes a distinction. This is the sign. This is the mark. The distinction divides the holy from the unholy. And when we live in accordance with the True Law, our lives become a testimony of holiness. We live in the most holy place. And from this place, we will nevertheless encounter opposition, opposition from within ourselves. When we see this opposition we must meet it with peace. We tell it that there can be peace if it will be subservient to our Godly will. But if it does not desire peace, then we will make war against it. And God will deliver this opposition, whose roots are from the other side, to us. And we will smite its active dimensions and make its passive dimensions serve the holy as we serve the holy.

The full gematria of תָו is תָו וָיו, a total of 428. This is the gematria of the word בְּתוֹךְ, which means *in the midst*.

> And God said: "Let there be a firmament *in the midst* of the waters, and let it divide water from water."[16]
>
> And the Lord God planted a garden eastward in Eden. And there He put the man whom he had formed. And out of the ground the Lord God made to grow every tree that is pleasant to the sight, and good for food. *In the midst* of the garden was the tree of life and the tree of knowledge of good and evil.[17]

From this we learn that we are in the midst. We are a firmament in the midst of the waters that divides the upper waters from the lower waters. We exist in the midst of the garden. The tree of life is on our right and the tree of good and evil is on our left.

In the midst means that we connect the one to the other. We are the agents whose Godly service is the creating of the dynamic unity. Where do we do this? We do it in our consciousness by recognizing the mark. That which happens below is the mark. This is the appearance. That which happens above is the essence of the appearance.

We live our life in the physical. We think, say, and do in the physical. We feel in the physical. On another level, however, we live our life in the spiritual. For each thing that we initiate in the physical,

---

16. Genesis 1:6.
17. Genesis 2:9.

each thing we encounter in the physical is just the mark of its essence
in the spiritual. Our consciousness of the appearance (that which is
below) being attached to its essence (that which is above) is our life in
the spiritual. It is our Divine dance. This is the revealed meaning of
the True Law, ת.

The concealed meaning of ת reinforces the revealed meaning. Consider the letter ו, the letter whose energy intelligence is that of connection. What can the energy intelligence of ת help us connect with? It
helps us connect with the inner essence. We can learn this from words
like תם, which means *innocence, simplicity, wholeness, perfection,* and
purity, תֻּמָּה, which means *innocence, honesty, straightforwardness,* and
integrity, and תָּמִים, which means *innocent, whole, complete, full, whole-
hearted, naive, simple, upright, perfect,* and *without blemish.*

> Thou shalt be *whole-hearted* (תָּמִים) with the Lord your
> God.[18]
>
> I am God Almighty; walk before Me, and be thou *whole-
> hearted [perfect].*[19]

This means that we must live in a way that every second of our life
readily meets with God's approval.[20] The word תָּמִיד means *always,
constantly,* or *continually.* It is used frequently in Psalms in a context
telling us how God and the praise of God shall be constantly in our
consciousness.

> I have set the Lord *always* [תָּמִיד] before me.[21]
>
> My eyes are *ever* toward the Lord.[22]
>
> His praise shall *continually* be in my mouth.[23]
>
> Say *continually,* let God be magnified.[24]

18. Deuteronomy 18:13.
19. Genesis 17:1.
20. Joseph Breuer, *The Jewish Marriage* (Jerusalem: Feldheim, 1982), p. 7.
21. Psalms 16:8.
22. Psalms 15:15.
23. Psalms 34:1.
24. Psalms 70:4.

My praise is *continually* of Thee.[25]

I am *continually* with Thee.[26]

The word תַּמָּה means *wonder*, *surprise*, or *amazement*, *constancy*, or *continuity*, and the word תְּמִיהָה means *surprise*, *wonder*, *amazement*, and *astonishment*. These words remind us that we are constantly amazed at the miracle of existence that God gives to us. The inner essence, the concealed meaning of ת, is our feelings of amazement, wonder, and surprise for what it is that the truth expresses. It is because of this inner essence that we have *hope*, תִּקְוָה, a cord that keeps us connected to the essence, hope, and expectation.

For you are my *hope* my Lord, God.[27]

It is because of this inner essence that we have תּוֹחֶלֶת,[28] and תֹּקֶף,[29] which is *strength*, *power*, *force*, *vigor*, *validity*, or *might*. We understand how it is that our inner essence *completes* and *fulfills*, the root of which is תמם, and that our essence is a part of and a response to a greater essence that questions us. Our answer is given by our תְּשׁוּבָה, our *repentance*, our *return*, which is really a *changing of our ways* and a *turning toward perfection* and *turning toward completeness*. The Talmud tells us:

These are man's advocates: *repentance* and good deeds.[30]

Repentance and good deeds are as a shield against punishment.[31]

More beautiful is one hour spent in *repentance* and good deeds in this world, than all the life of the world to come.[32]

We understand about תַּכְלִית, the *end limit*. For man is the end and perfection of all creation. This is why we feel תּוֹדָה, which means

---

25. Psalms 71:6.
26. Psalms 73:23.
27. Psalms 71:5.
28. Psalms 39:8.
29. Esther 9:29, 10:2.
30. *The Babylonian Talmud, Seder Moed*, vol. 1, *Shabbat* (32a), p. 147.
31. *The Babylonian Talmud, Seder Nezikin*, vol. 4, *Aboth* (Mishnah 11), trans. J. Israelstam (London: Soncino Press, 1938), p. 50.
32. *The Babylonian Talmud, Seder Nezikin*, vol. 4, *Aboth* (Mishnah 17), p. 53.

thanks, *gratitude*, or *thanksgiving* and we engage in *prayer*, תְּפִלָּה. For our prayer is a prayer to God to hear us, to attend to our prayer, to help us change to become better and more perfect so that we can be closer to God.[33] And God does hear us.

> He heeds the *prayer* of the destitute, and does not despise their *prayer*.[34]

> The Lord has heard my supplication; the Lord receives my *prayer*.[35]

> Verily God has heard me; He has attended to the voice of my *prayer*. Blessed be God, who has not turned away my *prayer*, nor removed His steadfast love from me.[36]

And what does prayer do? Prayer, תְּפִלָּה, which is תפילה when spelled without the vowel signs, is פתילה, which means *thread*, *cord*, *wick*, or *interweaving*.

> Bid them that they make them fringes in the corners of their garments throughout their generations, and that they put upon the fringe of each corner a *thread* [פְּתִיל] of blue: and it shall be to you as a fringe, that you may look upon it and remember all the commandments of the Lord, and do them; and that you seek not after your own heart and your own eyes after which you go astray: that you may remember and do all my commandments and be holy to your God.[37]

Prayer is the thread that connects and interweaves us with God.

Other words that tell us something about the energy intelligence of ת include תֹּהוּ, which means *desolation*, *emptiness*, *waste*, *nothingness*, or *formless*.

> In the beginning, God created heaven and earth. The earth was formless and empty, with darkness on the face of the

---

33. Psalms 4:2, 39:13, 54:4, 55:2, 61:2, 84:9, 86:6, 102:2, 143:1.
34. Psalms 102:18.
35. Psalms 6:10.
36. Psalms 66:19.
37. Numbers 15:37-39.

depths, but God's spirit moved on the water's surface. God said: "There shall be light."[38]

The earth is that which is below. It is formless and empty, תֹהוּ וָבֹהוּ. Rashi translates the phrase תֹהוּ וָבֹהוּ as in an amazing state and empty. He says:

> The word תֹהוּ means "astonishment and amazement," because a person would be astonished and amazed at the emptiness of the earth.[39]

In and of itself the expression, that which happens below, is nothingness compared to the essence that causes the expression. It is the appearance that is the *boundary, limit,* or *realm,* תְּחוּם, of what can be known at the level of בִּינָה, Understanding. And yet the inner essence, which is at the level of חָכְמָה, Wisdom, is always beyond what can be known. That is why it is תְּמוּהַ, *mystifying, surprising, amazing,* and *enigmatic.* Indeed it is a *mystery* and *hidden thing,* תַּעֲלוּמָה. And we are *amazed,* תְּהוּ.

What we know of the *true law* is always in *oscillation,* תְּנוּדָה, and always in *movement* and *fluctuation,* תְּנוּעָה. For as we change, our knowledge of the true law changes, for the level of חָכְמָה enlightens the level of בִּינָה. As our knowledge of the true law changes, we change. Our heart becomes transformed. The ego knows that its own well-being is best served by subjugating itself to the rule of the Divine soul. Thus, from the seal of the energy intelligence ת, we gain a new perspective on the energy intelligence א, which leads us to reach higher and higher levels of unifying perfection and closeness to the Divine. We accomplish more and more מִצְווֹת with a joyful thrill and delight as we serve God. Whether it is day or night on earth below, we continue to dance our dance with the Divine in the heaven above. For in the dance above, our night is just a pause and our day is just an active step. The music is always playing. The celebration is continuous. The transcending of the dancing never stops. This is the *True Law.*

---

38. Genesis 1:1-3.
39. *The Mystery of Creation According to Rashi,* trans. and interp. Pinchas Doron (New York: Moznaim Publishing, 1982), p. 5.

Meditations

The Worlds

At my Crown in the world of Atzilut,
My spirit connects with the Divine Source
Pouring the Endless Light
Into my vessel for concealment or revealment.
With Wisdom I choose revealment.

Above me in the world of Briah,
My mental capacities connect to their source,
Providing the energy for Understanding and reasoning,
With the ten thousand myriad things
This world creates for me to receive.

Within me in the world of Yetzirah,
My emotional capacities draw their
Sustenance from the world of Briah.
Here with Mercy and Strength,
I create a balance in Beauty.
Then with Victory and Glory
I firmly determine to act.
I connect to the Foundation of the world,
And enthusiastically plan the fulfillment to be.

At my feet in the world of Assiah,
Is my home and Kingdom.
Here by sovereign acting and doing
I reveal the Endless Light,
Completing the Holy circuit
Making manifest the Divine.

Crown, Wisdom, and Understanding

Crown, Wisdom, and Understanding,
Light, Essence, and Appearance
Constitute one unified complete whole.
One reality without defect.
One energy.

Primal Intent is the source of life.
It is called will and the Crown.
It is the origin, the true earth.
It encloses everything.
In it there is nonaction.
Yin and Yang are harmoniously blended,
As one without distinction.

Wisdom is Essence.
Outwardly deep and inwardly bright.
Father is strong and vigorous.
Intuition taps this deep well,
Its water forever sharing and flowing downward.
Formless and not material,
It is not constrained.
It is Yang and true knowledge.

Conscious knowledge is Understanding.
Outwardly firm and inwardly flexible.
Mother of the ten thousand myriad things.
Reasoning orders its unfathomable changing Appearances.
As a burning fire, it is forever transforming.
Like fire, it ascends upward.
Formed and not material,
It is limited and constrained.
It is Yin and true intelligence.

Qualified by our choice of a limited state of being,
True Intent closes the channel to Essence.
Essence closes the channel to Appearance.
Appearance separates from Essence.

The One energy divides into three.
The ten thousand myriad things
Tug at one another.
Their essence becomes concealed.
The false is born.
Desire is king.
Emotional turmoil dominates.
The mind is stubborn and disturbed.
Primal Intent no longer maintains affinity with the Light.
The external forces control the Slave.

Qualified by our choice of an elevated state of being,
Primal Intent opens the channel to essence.
Essence opens the channel to Appearance.
Stabilized by will, the mind is free and still.
There is no lustful desire for results.
Multiple Appearances ascend into one Essence.
One Essence flows into the Crown.
The truth is revealed.
The play is spontaneous.
There are no external forces.
Yin and Yang cleave together.
The circuit becomes complete.
The light returns home.
And the Master delights.

Appearances

Nothing is what it appears to be,
Yet everything is its appearance.

As it is with appearance,
So it is with nothing,
And so it is with everything.

Each appearance always means more than itself
Since it is a symbol for something which
Transcends its own givenness.

Each appearance covers a deeper appearance;
The web of relationships between the cover and the covered
Develop the meaning of each of the involved appearances
And fulfills their essences.

Every action energizes a complex of appearances
And each energized appearance gives life to
Those appearances it covers.

When the energies of all activated appearances
Chain together and lovingly reinforce one another
In a way consistent with the highest good,
The highest good is experienced.

When the energies of all activated appearances
Do not chain together,
They tug against each other
In a way that prevents their fulfillment
And feeds external forces.
Disharmony and disruption are experienced.

Without the appearances in which I clothe
The unknowable nothing I am in material existence,
I cannot materially be.

Even though I choose, create, and am responsible for the
appearances,
I am not these appearances.

Hence, nothing is what it appears to be,
Yet everything is its appearance.

Appearance and Essence

1

Appearance is in unity.
Essence is in unity.

2

Everything has its appearance.
But its appearance is not its essence.

Everything has its essence.
But its essence is not its appearance.

3

Appearance is the manifestation of essence.
Essence is an idealization of appearance.

Appearance is instance.
Essence is meaning.

Appearance is thing or action.
Essence is symbol and relation.

4

Appearance conceals the essence.
Essence reveals through appearance.

Appearance gives existence to essence.
Essence gives unity to appearance.

Appearance is somewhere.
And being somewhere is separated.

Essence is nowhere.
And being nowhere is everywhere.

5

Appearance is garment.
Essence is body.

Appearance is body.
Essence is heart.

Appearance is heart.
Essence is mind.

Appearance is mind.
Essence is soul.

Appearance is soul.
Essence is God.

6

Appearance is in physical existence.
Essence is beyond physical existence.

Appearance has form.
Essence is formless.

Appearance has boundary.
Essence is without boundary.

Appearance has place.
Essence has no place.

Appearance is temporal.
Essence is eternal.

Appearance is in motion.
Essence is motionless.

7

Appearance is seen.
Essence is unseen.

Appearance is heard.
Essence is silent.

Appearance can be touched.
Essence is untouchable.

Appearance can be tasted.
Essence is not tastable.

Appearance can be smelled.
Essence is not smellable.

Appearance can be thought.
Essence is not thinkable.

Appearance is divided.
Essence is not dividable.

8

Appearance is transitory and changeable.
Essence is permanent and changeless.

Appearance is outer observed.
Essence is inner grasped.

Appearance is compound.
Essence is simple.

Appearance is descended essence.
Essence is ascended appearance.

Appearance is what receives.
Essence is what gives.

Appearance is physical.
Essence is spiritual.

Appearance is finite.
Essence is infinite.

Appearance is the Many.
Essence is the One.

Song of My Heart

Song of my heart,
Blessing of my soul,
Essence of my Being.
Gentle and Compassionate God.
The time has come.
I am here,
And I am ready to become
What I have promised to become.

On me there is the armor
I created to fight ancient battles.
Within me there are great sorrows
Old crystallized sadnesses,
Unwept tears,
And deep hurts.

All these which I in my ignorance,
Have held on to so dearly,
My spark of divinity no longer needs or wants.

Minister to me,
For my doors are open,
Knead the armor away,
I release it to you.
Touch the great sorrows,
The old sadnesses,
And the deep hurts.
I surrender them all through you.

Work on me,
And your hands of love,
Will I manifest in my life as love.
Talk to me,
And your words will I manifest as music.
Help me,
And your help will I multiply

Ten times over as I help others.
Touch me,
And I shall so expand the touch,
That it will hug, surround, and
Nurture Mother Earth herself.

O, Song of my heart,
Blessing of my soul,
Essence of my Being.
Gentle and Compassionate God,
I thank you,
For helping me become what I have wanted,
And what I have promised to become.

Related Reading

Berg, Phillip. *Power of Aleph Beth*, vols. 1. and 2. Jerusalem: Research Centre of Kabbalah Press, 1988.

Ginsburgh, Yitzchak. *The Hebrew Letters*. Jerusalem: Gal Einai Publications, 1992.

Glazerson, Matityahu. *Letters of Fire*. Trans. S. Fuchs. Jerusalem: Feldheim Publishers, 1991.

Glazerson, Matityahu. *Hebrew: The Source of Languages*. Jerusalem: Yerid HaSefarim, 1988.

Kushner, Lawrence. *Sefer Otiyot: The Book of Letters*. Woodstock, VT: Jewish Lights Publishing, 1990.

Munk, Michael. *The Wisdom in the Hebrew Alphabet*. Brooklyn, NY: Mesorah Publications, 1988.

Index of Translated Words

About the Author

Robert M. Haralick holds the Boeing Clairmont Egtvedt professorship of electrical engineering at the University of Washington, Seattle. He is a Fellow of the Institute of Electrical and Electronic Engineers, a Fellow of the International Association for Pattern Recognition, and is listed in *Who's Who in America*. He has published over 400 professional scientific papers in the area of computer vision and pattern recognition.

Professor Haralick has been a student of chasidic philosophy and Kabbalah since he was a graduate student at the University of Kansas, where he received a Ph.D. in 1969. He was introduced to Chabad Chasidut by Rabbi Aharon Goldstein and subsequently met the Lubavitcher Rebbe Menachem Schneerson, of blessed memory, who was acquainted with an early version of this book. He is a member of the Lubavitcher congregation Shaarei Tefillah.